Abraham 5/13/86

Children's Literature

Volume 14

Volume 14

Annual of
The Modern Language Association
Division on Children's Literature
and The Children's Literature
Association

Yale University Press
New Haven and London
1986

Children's Literature

Editor-in-chief: Francelia Butler
Coeditors, Volume 14: Margaret Higonnet, Barbara Rosen
Book Review Editor: John Cech
Editorial Assistant: Ian Andrews
Advisory Board: Robert Coles, M.D.; Lois Kuznets; Alison Lurie; William T. Moynihan; Sam Pickering, Jr.; Albert J. Solnit, M.D.
Consultants for Volume 14: Gillian Adams; Benjamin Brockman; Miguel Civil; Harris Fairbanks; Ann Fehn; Barbara Hardy; U. C. Knoepflmacher; Kathleen McCormick-Leighty; Perry Nodelman; Compton Rees; J. Craig Robertson; Denise Schmandt-Besserat; Mary Shaner; Richard Sherry; Åke Sjöberg; Piotr Steinkeller; Jack Zipes
Conference Representatives: Marilyn Apseloff; Richard Rotert

The editors gratefully acknowledge the support of the journal by the University of Connecticut.

Editorial correspondence should be addressed to:
The Editors, *Children's Literature*
Department of English, U-25
University of Connecticut
Storrs, Connecticut 06268

Manuscripts submitted should conform to the new *MLA* style. An original on non-erasable bond and two copies are requested. Manuscripts must be accompanied by a self-addressed envelope and return postage.

Volumes 1−7 of *Children's Literature* can be obtained directly from John C. Wandell, The Children's Literature Foundation, Box 370, Windham Center, Connecticut 06280. Volumes 8−14 can be obtained from Yale University Press, 92A Yale Station, New Haven, Connecticut 06520, or from Yale University Press, 13 Bedford Square, London WC1B 3JF, England.

Library of Congress catalog card number: 79-66588
ISBN: 0−300−03564−0 (cloth), 0−300−03565−9 (paper)

Set in Baskerville type by The Saybrook Press, Inc., Old Saybrook, Conn. Printed in the United States of America by Vail-Ballou Press, Binghamton, N.Y.

10   9   8   7   6   5   4   3   2   1

Contents

The First Children's Literature? The Case for Sumer

Gillian Adams

Children's literature, as the term is generally understood today, cannot be said to exist before the eighteenth century and the advent of printed books marketed to children for their enjoyment. Some scholars, however, believe that works from earlier periods routinely associated with children, even if their purpose is didactic or they were not written specifically for children, can also be classified as children's literature. Standard bibliographies of children's literature begin with texts from the medieval period; in addition, recent scholarship has focused on medieval and renaissance literature associated with children.[1] In fact, works just as closely associated with children are to be found at a much earlier period, in the oldest written literature so far recovered in any significant quantity, the Sumerian. This investigation of the Sumerian child's literary world will describe these works and attempt to demonstrate how they reflect certain values found in Sumerian culture as a whole and how they are an important means for transmitting those values to the more influential members of Sumerian society.

Extant Sumerian literature consists of more than thirty thousand lines of text found in over five thousand tablets and fragments. It was composed by a people who lived in Mesopotamia (now the southern half of Iraq), between the Tigris and Euphrates rivers. By the fourth century B.C., the Sumerians had developed an urban society organized into nine city-states headed by kings, who in turn were supported by a powerful priesthood and the scribal bureaucracy needed to administer an agricultural economy based on an elaborate, state-centered irrigation system. Although the earliest literary documents date from around 2400 B.C., before the conquest of Sumer and neighboring areas in 2334 B.C. by Sargon of Akkad, most of the texts discussed here come from the time of the Sumerian renaissance, which was ushered in by the founding of the Third Dynasty of Ur in 2112 B.C. The end of the Sumerian period and the

Illustrations reproduced by courtesy of the University Museum, University of Pennsylvania.

1

beginning of the Babylonian are marked by the accession of Hammurabi, King of Babylon, to the throne in 1792 B.C. Nevertheless, the culture of Mesopotamia, if not the language, remained predominantly Sumerian, and Sumerian language and literature continued to dominate the school curriculum until about 1000 B.C.[2]

I

Songs and lullabies provide the first literary experiences for many children. A "chant," purported to be created by the wife of Shulgi, a ruler of the Third Dynasty of Ur, is the first lullaby known, according to Samuel Noah Kramer (*History* 327).[3] Apparently troubled by the ill health of one of her sons, the Queen begins (trans. Kramer, *History* 329–31):

> *U-a a-u-a*
> In my *ururu*-chant may he grow big,
> In my *ururu*-chant may he grow large,
> Like the *irina*-tree may he grow stout of root,
> Like the *shakir*-plant may he grow broad of crown.

After several lines she continues:

> Come Sleep, come Sleep,
> Come to where my son is,
> Put to sleep his restless eyes,
> Put your hand on his painted eyes,
> And as for his babbling tongue,
> Let not the babbling tongue shut out his sleep.

She goes on to promise her son lettuce and cheeses to make him feel better and toward the end of the chant wishes he may have a family, food, happiness, and the good will of the gods:

> May the wife be your support,
> May the son be your lot,
> May the winnowed barley be your bride,
> May Ashnan, the *kusu*-goddess be your ally,
> May you have an eloquent guardian angel,
> May you achieve a reign of happy days,
> May the feasts make bright your forehead.

This lullaby fulfills the definition of the genre in the *Oxford Companion to Children's Literature*, "a song or chant designed to soothe babies or young children to sleep," and predates by at least a thousand years the Roman lullaby "Lalla, lalla, lalla" there referred to (326). The *Oxford Companion* adds that the beginning of the term is said to derive from "lu" and "la"; the Sumerian lullaby begins with the same vowel sounds, although the initial *l* is missing. The Sumerian lullaby in addition invokes sleep and wishes for a bright future for the child, two salient characteristics of the lullaby as it is known today. Similar conclusions wishing for future benefits are also to be found in Sumerian works associated with older children, as is the shift from third person to direct address. There is a difference between the Sumerian lullaby and current lullabies, however; the former is directed at a particular child, addressed as "son of the lord Shulgi," and not, as is usual, to an unspecified child. Still, it is not unreasonable to suppose the lullaby is a representative example of the lullabies Sumerian children heard from their elders.

The lullaby appears to be the only Mesopotamian text so far discovered that can be associated with preschool children. Although even very young children, to different degrees depending on their social status and location, would have come into contact with various types of oral literature, particularly of a religious nature, not enough is known about Mesopotamian oral culture to make valid generalizations about its content or audience.

There is much more substantive information about the literary world of those Mesopotamian children who went to school at the *edubba* or "tablet house." The edubba was a private, secular institution, a center of learning and literary creation, established to train scribes for the palace and temple; not only were the classics copied there, but new works were also composed. Most, if not all, of the students were male and came from wealthy families and, since it was traditional for at least one son to follow his father's profession, many were the children of scribes.[4] School exercises, like other Mesopotamian texts, were written on clay tablets, which, particularly when baked, form the most durable writing surface yet devised. This fact provides two special advantages to the investigator of the origins of children's literature. Not only have numerous baked tablets survived at sites of libraries, but unbaked clay tablets, discarded because clay was too cheap and readily available to bother erasing

"Schooldays: The Teacher's Blessing." Note the signature of the writer below the double line on the lefthand column of the tablet.

and reusing, have been found at school sites, providing a gold mine of ephemera for modern cultural historians.[5] Mesopotamians apparently learned to write by copying literary texts of progressive difficulty; on the premise that the skill of the calligraphy on a tablet provides an indicator of the educational level of the person who wrote it, the researcher is able to specify what texts formed a part of the student's literary universe at each level (Gordon, *Proverbs* 20).

The conquest of Sumer and neighboring areas by Sargon of

Obverse of the "Schooldays" tablet.

Akkad complicated the task of training the scribal bureaucracy, since the result was the gradual replacement of spoken Sumerian by Akkadian, a Semitic tongue. Because Sumerian continued to be the official state language, in spite of the fact it was fast becoming a dead literary language like Latin in the European Middle Ages, a scribal education centered on the difficult task of learning to read and write it, and this circumstance may be partly responsible for the large number of surviving practice exercises. Exactly how children learned the Sumerian language is not certain, but on the evidence of the lexical lists and grammatical texts that have survived, scholars once hypothesized that children first memorized vocabulary and the rules of grammar and then applied themselves to the texts (Kramer, *Sumerians* 235). Recently, however, H. L. J. Vanstiphout has demonstrated how the sixty-three line Lipit-eštar Hymn B, "Lipit-eštar, King of Justice, Wisdom and Learning," could have been used for the teaching of Sumerian at the elementary level and how, as a beginner's text, it covers the meaning of the signs used in Sumerian cuneiform, the basic features of the Sumerian verbal system, different sentence patterns, stylistic features, and phraseology. He bases his conclusion that the hymn served as an elementary text primarily on an analysis of its grammar and of the twenty tablets on which the text appears. Two tablets are obviously not first stage exercises; the remaining eighteen are large and clumsily written, and some contain vocabulary lists or short extracts of other works.

The simplicity of the hymn's lexical and grammatical construction is not the only feature that makes it peculiarly suitable for teaching Sumerian on the elementary level; the content is also important. Learning to read and write Sumerian is difficult and tedious because the system of writing is syllabic, not alphabetic; children need to be encouraged by a sense of the importance of the task they are undertaking. In his analysis of the contents of the hymn, Vanstiphout points out that about a third of the text glorifies scribal activity and equates that activity with the functions of royalty. This is not simply a matter of inculcating loyalty to the king as a patron of the arts in those destined to serve in his bureaucracy. Rather the young student working with the text is encouraged to believe that as a scribe he will be doing what the king does, and thus what the goddess of scribes Nisaba wishes done, since the king's hand is guided by hers ("How Did" 123–24). For example, the hymn addresses the king:

> Nisaba, the woman radiant with joy,
> The true woman scribe, the lady of all knowledge,
> Guided your fingers on the clay,
> Embellished the writing on the tablets,
> Made the hand resplendent with a golden stylus.
> The measuring rod, the gleaming surveyor's line,
> The cubit ruler which gives wisdom,
> Nisaba lavishly bestowed upon you.   (18–24a)

Later the hymn makes the identification of scribal and royal activity even more concrete:

> Lipit-eštar, king of Isin, king of Sumer and Akkad,
> To Nippur you are the Scribe;   (40−41).

The Lipit-eštar hymn posits an integral relationship between the goddess, the king as chief-scribe, and the scribes who serve as his instruments and act as his surrogates, literally as well as figuratively ruling his royal city of Nippur and the other city-states subject to it. The child is implicitly promised that if he learns to be a scribe, he will be second only to the king in power, in prestige, and in carrying out the will of the gods. The hymn to the king as the son of Enlil, the air-god, concludes:

> Your praise shall never disappear from the clay in the Edubba;
> May every scribe therefore sing of this bliss
> And glorify you greatly,
> So that your laudation in the Edubba shall not cease.
> O leading shepherd, youthful son of Enlil,
> Lipit-eštar, be praised!   (59−63) (trans. Vanstiphout,
>   "Lipit-eštar" 36−37)

In this passage the king's fame and the scribal art are inextricably entwined; the immortality of one depends on the immortality of the other, and the final wish is for the immortality of both by means of the clay tablets of the school. Both the king and the young student, then, participate in a shared immortality guaranteed by the survival of the king's persona in the literary work that embodies it and by the continuous copying of that work by beginning scholars.[6]

II

A type of literature which had much the same function as the Lipit-eštar hymn and which the Mesopotamians considered suitable for students at all stages of their education, but particularly at the first stage, was the proverb (Vanstiphout, "How Did" 126). Sumerian proverb collections contain not only the precepts, maxims, truisms, adages, and bywords generally classified as proverbs, but taunts, compliments, wishes, short fables, and anecdotes; it is often difficult to draw the line between one category and another (Gordon, *Proverbs* 17). The proverbs are found on seven hundred tablets and fragments; some of these contain whole collections, while the most primitive are large, often clumsily written, school practice exercises containing one proverb or a line or two from one of the longer proverbs.[7] Although there is evidence that scribes collected some of the proverbs, particularly those relating to household and family and those in dialect, from the oral tradition, they composed many of them themselves, presumably for the edubba (Gordon 19). Indeed the simplicity, brevity, and moral point of proverbs make them particularly attractive to educators working with beginners, especially if some of the proverbs are already well known to them. In addition, the proverbs and fables cover a wide range of subjects, enabling the student to master a large vocabulary in a number of fields.[8] Whatever the source of the proverbs may have been, it was the scribal teachers who selected them and arranged them in the order in which they are to be found in the collections.

Not all of the twenty-seven or so proverbs found on the most primitive tablets, those used at the elementary teaching level, correspond to present-day American conceptions of what is suitable for young children. In fact, due to lack of concrete information, at present there appears to be no scholarly consensus on the age at which Mesopotamians began their studies at the edubba or how long they remained there. Kramer and Gadd routinely use the terms "boys," "lads," and "schoolboys"; Kramer, in his translation of the text "School-Days" discussed in detail below, calls the protagonist "young fellow" and "little fellow." The student portrayed in this text is clearly quite young, as the opening question, "Where did you go from earliest days?" as well as the nature of his activities at school and of his infractions of the rules indicates (Kramer, *Sumerians* 237). On the other hand, one Sumerologist who read an earlier version of this essay suggests that students began about age nine to thirteen; yet another feels that the nature of the edubba curriculum makes an age before the early teens unlikely. But studies in child development and language acquisition indicate that it is far easier to teach computation, reading, writing, and foreign languages, even difficult languages such as Greek, to children than to adolescents, and that the mechanisms in the brain that facilitate learning of this type actually become moribund at puberty.[9] Given the much shorter lifespan of the average person prior to the twentieth century (and thus the brevity of childhood), any culture that delayed educating its members until almost half their lives were over would be highly inefficient.

If Sumerologists are correct in believing that texts were chosen primarily for their grammatical and lexical features and that their primary purpose was pragmatic—to teach writing—with content a secondary concern, the appropriateness or inappropriateness of certain texts to certain ages according to present standards is not a reliable indicator of the approximate age of the Sumerian student. Thus two proverbs that occur on more than one tablet, for example, have to do with the necessity for making a will; their purpose must have been to introduce pupils to the legal vocabulary (Gordon 1.67, 2.10).[10] Other proverbs do seem to be more appropriate in content for young people: 1.79 (trans. Gordon 79), "Like a clod thrown into the water, he will be destroyed in his own splash," is a warning against ostentation and presumption reiterated by 2.65 (trans. Kramer, *Sumerians* 226), "The fox trod upon the hoof of a wild ox, saying, 'Didn't it hurt?'" and 2.67 (trans. Gordon 222–223), "The fox, having urinated into the sea, [said,] 'The whole[?] of the sea is my urine.'" But three more tablets of the same type contain proverbs from Collection Two about the evils of poverty, reflecting the Sumerian preoccupation with money and status: a variation on this theme is 2.137 (trans. Gordon 270):

> Build like a [lord], go about like a slave!
> Build like a [slave], go about like a lord!

Eight proverbs concern the scribal art as did the Hymn to Lipit-eštar: for example 2.49 (trans. Gordon 208), "A scribe who does not know Sumerian, where will he obtain[?], a translation[?]?"

When the proverbs that occur on tablets of the next higher level of skill are added to the twenty-seven on the most elementary tablets, practically every proverb in the two main collections is represented, since a number of proverbs occur on different tablets. Taken as a whole, the proverbs translated by Gordon in Collections One and Two, as well as those from the other five collections translated into English by Gordon, Kramer, and others, advocate good conduct, hard work, common sense, right-speaking, humility, and prudence, and condemn haste, greed, and selfishness (Kramer, *History* 123).

Proverbs are considered to be a valuable index to the cultural preoccupations of a society; although Sumerian proverbs are diverse and cover a wide range of experience, it seems significant that a relatively high proportion of proverbs concern the scribal profession and promote effective communication between men and animals in direct or fable form.[11] A number of the animal proverbs and fables found in the Proverb Collections make fun of ineffective communication like boasting, thus promoting effective communication by reverse example. Animals loom large in Sumerian culture; they are, for example, a major source of imagery for Sumerian poets (Kramer, *History* 294). Sumerian literary animals are, for the most part, characterized in ways familiar to us from Aesop's fables: we meet the enormous elephant, the insignificant insect or bird, the sly fox, the greedy wolf, the foolishly stubborn donkey, the helpless sheep or goat, and the predatory lion, the strongest of the beasts, who can also be friendly. Only the dog is portrayed unconventionally: it is often faithless and greedy instead of faithful and true.[12]

Most Sumerian fables are of the Aesopic type: they begin with a short narrative passage and conclude with a speech by one of the characters demonstrating how his opponent is a boaster or a fool lacking contact with reality (Alster 211). This is true of the two proverbs about the fox quoted above; in the story about the elephant and the wren below, the theme is reversed and it is the larger animal who has an exaggerated idea of himself and receives his comeuppance (trans. Kramer, *History* 128).

> The elephant boasted[?] about himself, saying: "There is nothing like me in existence! Do not [compare yourself to me?]." The wren answered him saying: "But I, too, in my own small way, was created just as you were!"

This fable has a second theme which is reiterated not only in proverbs and other fables, but in the debate literature discussed below: an insistence that the small and the humble are in some way equal in worth to the mighty and powerful. One way in which the weak and the hunted could defend themselves and prove their equality was by effective communication. Thus a number of fables, like the one which follows, instead of making fun of poor speaking, celebrate the witty speech, prudence, and quick thinking of the weaker animal (trans. Alster 214).

> The lion had caught a helpless she-goat:
> "Let me go! I will give you an ewe, a companion of mine, in the bargain!"
> "If I am to let you go, tell me your name!"
> The she-goat gave the lion the following answer: "You do not know my name?
> 'I cheated you' is my name."
> When the lion came to the fold,
> "I have released you!" he shouted.
> She answered from the other side:
> "You have released me, 'You were clever': as far as sheep are concerned, there are none of them here!"

Not only has the goat gotten away from the lion by playing on his greed (that is, by promising him better eating and then not keeping her promise), but she has also twisted the knife in the wound by the play on her name: "I cheated you" sounds almost identical to "you were clever" in Sumerian (Alster 214).

The most complex and fully characterized of the animals of proverb and fable is the fox, perhaps because, as both hunted and hunter, he is the most like man. On the one hand, he is a coward: "The fox gnashes its teeth, but its head is trembling" (trans. Kramer, *History* 125). On the other hand, he is always on the make, reflecting the self-aggrandizing spirit also to be found in the literature about scribes discussed below and raising the possibility that the juxtaposition of proverbs about scribes and foxes in Collection Two may be design and not accident:

> The fox could not build his [own] house, [and so] he came to the house of his friend as a conqueror[?]   (trans. Gordon 218).

> The fox had a stick with him [and said]: "Whom shall I hit?"
> He carried a legal document with him [and said]: "What can I challenge?"   (trans. Kramer, *History* 125)

As a result of his aggressiveness, the fox is always on the run:

The fox with . . . heart was seeking the "way of the lion,"
For the "way of the wolf" he was exploring the meadow land.
As he approached the city gates, the dogs drove him away:
To save his life he departed like an arrow   (trans. Lambert 217).

But the fox runs effectively; like his heir Reynard, he epitomizes the
quick-wittedness and self-reliance of the born survivor. "The man
who seized the tail of the Lion sank in the river. He who seized the
tail of the fox escaped" (trans. Lambert 281).[13] Perhaps of all the
animals the fox most clearly mirrors what Kramer calls "the conten-
tious and aggressive behavioral pattern which characterized [Sumer-
ian] culture" (*Sumerians* 267).

   Thus as elementary students copied and recopied proverbs and
fables like these, learning from them the rudiments of the literary
language, they also learned the importance of understanding the
nature of their place in a hierarchical society mirrored by the structure of animal society. As the weakest and smallest of humans, they
would be led to identify with the weaker and smaller animals and
reassured by their survival skills. Although Sumerian religion portrayed the world as a difficult and fearful place, yet these fables and
proverbs confirm that it is not strength that wins in the end but
intelligence, and that the tongue (and by extension the stylus) can be
mightier than the sword.[14]

III

The nature of the tablets on which the Hymn to Lipit-eštar and the
material used from the Proverb Collections appear make it clear that
they pertain to the most elementary level of education. This literature is not, moreover, mentioned in the "Ur Curriculum," the desig-
nation given the list of works found in three literary catalogues from
Ur.[15] Vanstiphout believes that this is because as first-year exercise
texts, they may not have been considered worthy of inclusion in the
official literary curriculum ("How Did" 123). The Ur curriculum
does list, however, the works that Vanstiphout surmises were used at
the second educational stage; most of the literary debates and all of
the "school compositions" ("How Did" 126). The greater length, the
more sophisticated language, and the higher quality of the tablets
support Vanstiphout's hypothesis; it is further supported by the

nature of the works themselves, which seem singularly appropriate for pupils at the middle level, given the aims of a Sumerian scribal education.

Literary debates of the mythological type, in a sense longer and more complex fables, form one category of the literature studied at the next educational level.[16] Unlike some of the proverbs and short fables, the mythological debates were apparently not originally intended for use in the schools; in several cases the evidence indicates that they were composed as court entertainment for the kings of the Third Dynasty of Ur (Lambert 150). They were no doubt chosen by the scribes as educational material because, like many of the proverbs and fables, they emphasize the value of hard work, intelligence, and verbal ability. The debates consist of a confrontation between two entities in which one has the final say. The winner, however, is not revealed until the very end of the composition, the verdict being delivered by a third party, usually the air-god Enlil. Most of the debates begin with a mythological introduction which sets the scene, explains the creation of the participants and their place in the scheme of things, and sets up the terms of the argument. This always centers on the question of which contestant is most useful to man.

Seven Sumerian literary debates have survived, and five of them appear in the Ur curriculum: the best preserved are the disputes between Summer and Winter, Cattle and Grain, and the Pickax and the Plow. The debate between the Pickax and the Plow is a representative example, although it lacks the mythological introduction. It begins with a description of the Pickax as a "poor fellow, always losing his loincloth."[17] Nevertheless, the Pickax challenges the more aristocratic Plow on the basis of the greater number and range of tasks that the Pickax accomplishes. The Plow responds to the challenge by trying to pull rank, calling himself "the noble field-registrar of Father Enlil," and claiming that the king pours out beer and sacrifices sheep and oxen to him at his feasts, even taking hold of his handles while the great nobles walk beside; the Pickax, on the other hand, is used by slaves. The Pickax responds by calling the Plow an incompetent bungler who is always breaking and only works part of the year at that; then he emphasizes how helpful he is to the working classes: "I make it possible for the worker to support his wife and children." His final argument is:

I in the waterless steppe,
Have dug up its sweet water,
He who is thirsty is revived by the side of my trenches   (trans.
    Kramer, *History* 346).

Enlil then gives the verdict in the Pickax's favor.

This debate is interesting not only because it considers water and
its management the crucial element in the maintenance of Sumerian
civilization, but because it affirms that the lowly Pickax, on the basis
of his greater productivity and range of achievement, is of greater
worth in the god Enlil's eyes than the aristocratic Plow, in spite of his
royal connections.[18] All of the debates, in fact, stress the value of
hard work for gods and men, no matter in what area it may be
carried out or by whom, and emphasize the rewards to be gained by
such work. Since the loser of the debate has also worked hard, he is
not punished; but he does have to accept that he is in some sense
inferior to the winner, at least in the eyes of the gods. This idea is also
found in a number of the proverbs. It is not only the actions of the
contestants, however, that enable them to win their disputes, but
their eloquence in describing those actions: an eloquence which is
above all aggressive and self-aggrandizing. The literary debates,
then, on the one hand, place an emphasis on the rewards to be
gained by hard work and, on the other hand, serve to reinforce a
major implied lesson of the literature already copied by children on
the elementary level: that verbal skills are of prime importance in
achieving success.

Unlike the mythological debates, the "school compositions," the
other category of texts used at the second educational stage, may
well have been created expressly for teaching purposes. Six of these
compositions, all of which appear on the Ur curriculum list, have
survived: two works, usually referred to as "essays," which involve a
student and his father, and four debates between two students or
recent graduates of the school. In these texts, the term *ummia* ("ex-
pert" or "school-father") is used for the head of the school, while the
pupil is known as the "school-son." There is also a "big-brother" or
assistant, perhaps an older student, something like a graduate student, and there are monitors and proctors who take care of attendance and discipline (Kramer, *Sumerians* ch. 6).

Of the four surviving school debates, the one most often ex-
cerpted is "School Rowdies." This recounts a quarrel between a
student, Enkimansi, and his "big-brother" Girnishag. The "big-
brother" begins the dialogue (trans. Gadd 32–33):

"Son of the tablet-house, what shall we write today after the tablet?"

Enkimansi replies:

"Today in grammar[?] we will not write out individual dialects.
We will say anything that the master knows,
We will answer just so-and-so.
I'm resolved to write something of my own; I'll give the orders."

This burst of independence appears to irritate Girnishag, who responds:

"If you're giving the orders, I'm not your 'big-brother.'
How, pray, does my 'big-brotherhood' come in?
In being a scribe, a name too great [i.e., conceit]
    destroys 'big-brotherhood.'"

Girnishag then begins the series of insults which comprise much
of the text. Not only is the student Enkimansi quite able to defend
himself, but he is also able to respond with insults of his own,
charging that his "big-brother" is stupid, uncreative, unlearned in
both sacred and secular matters, and mathematically and linguistically incompetent, with a "broad tongue, an evil tongue." Girnishag
defends himself in turn, concluding (trans. Kramer, *Sumerians*
241–42):

"Me, I was raised on Sumerian, I am the son of a scribe. But you
are a bungler, a windbag. When you try to shape a tablet, you
can't even smooth[?] the clay[?] tablet. . . . You 'wise-fool,' cover
your ears! Cover your ears! [Yet] you [claim to know] Sumerian
like me!"[19]

The debate continues, but the text at this point is fragmentary.
Finally someone appears, perhaps a monitor, and upbraids the
student Enkimansi, threatening to beat him and to put him in
chains.

"Why do you raise a commotion in the school!—Why were you insolent[?], inattentive[?], [why do you] curse and hurl insults against him who is your 'big-brother' and has taught you the scribal art to your own advantage[?]! Even the headmaster who knows everything shook his head violently[?] [saying]: 'Do to him what you please.' If I did to you what I pleased—to a fellow who behaved like you [and] was inattentive[?] to his 'big-brother'—I would [first] beat you with a mace—what's a wooden board?—[and] having put copper chains on your feet, would lock you up in the house [and] for two months would not let you out of the school."

After four unintelligible lines, the piece ends, "In the dispute between Girnishag and Enkimansi, the headmaster gave the verdict."

It is a verdict delivered by man, not a god as in the mythological debates, and what that verdict was has not survived. Nevertheless, it is possible to guess what it might be. In his initial response to his "big-brother's" polite request for a suggestion about the next writing assignment, Enkimansi gets more and more outrageous, ending up with the statement, "I'll give the orders." Girnishag recognizes right away that this is a violation of the chain of command at the school and that Enkimansi, like the proverbial fox in relation to the ox and the sea, does not understand or choose to recognize his proper place. Girnishag is not only superior to Enkimansi because he is his "big-brother," but because, according to him, he is the son of a scribe and raised on Sumerian. The monitor's speech toward the end of the debate affirms that Enkimansi is out of place, commenting as it does on his insolence and his rudeness to a "big-brother" to whom he should be grateful. Perhaps the monitor's threat of beating and chains is an exaggerated one, meant to be humorous, but that he believes that some punishment is due such upstart behavior is clear; the monitor's status is being threatened, too.[20]

Although it is not always clear in the body of the debate who is speaking, the insults traded demonstrate what the attainments of a scribe should be: good handwriting, a knowledge of Sumerian and the ability to speak it as well as write it elegantly, creative literary skill, and mathematical ability, particularly as it applies to surveying. Moreover, like the mythological debates, the school debates serve as a further illustration of the aggressive, competitive nature of Sumerian culture. The same emphasis on what the competent scribe should be able to do, the same self-praise, and the same disparagement of the opponent are evident in the other three school debates.

Gadd speculates about the purpose of the debates, noting that they "have decidedly an air of burlesque, though of no very agreeable kind." He concludes that "it was pure interest in contemporary life (naturally, with a bias to their own profession) which inspired the writers of these scenes" (36–38). It does not appear to have occurred to Gadd, nor to other commentators on this material, that it was composed expressly for an audience of would-be scribes and was designed to teach them what young scholars should be striving for in school and out. There is an age at which schoolchildren particularly enjoy exchanging insults; it is possible that the scribes who created these dialogues were deliberately trading on this propensity in order to promote good behavior and scholarship in school.

The promotion of good behavior and scholarship also appears to be at least part of the purpose behind the two other school compositions, usually referred to as "essays," although the one called "School Days," the narrative of a boy's two days at school and their aftermath, is arguably a story. "School Days" begins with a dialogue between a student and his father (trans. Kramer, *Sumerians* 237–39):[21]

> "Schoolboy, where did you go from earliest days?"
> "I went to school."
> "What did you do in school?"

The student's account of one day's activities takes up the first part of the narrative. They do not sound unfamiliar: he recites his tablet, eats lunch, prepares a new tablet, writes it, finishes it, gets his oral and written assignments, and finally goes home to tell his father about his work and recite his lessons. His father is delighted with his son's progress. The student's next day does not go as well. He asks the servants to wake him on time and gets two rolls for lunch from his mother on his way out, but somehow he gets to school late and is reprimanded by the monitor. Then he is caned by various members of the school staff for not completing his homework, for loitering in the street, for sloppy clothing, for talking without permission, for going out of the gate without permission, and for not speaking Sumerian. Finally the headmaster canes him for poor handwriting. It is because of all this punishment, presumably, that the student loses interest in learning and his teacher loses interest in teaching him.

> I [began to] hate the scribal art, [began to] neglect the scribal art. My teacher took no delight in me; [even stopped teaching?] me his skill in the scribal art; in no way prepared me in the matters [essential] to the art [of being] a "young scribe," [or] the art [of being] a "big-brother."

The student then suggests to his father that he soften up the headmaster.

> Give him a bit [sic] extra salary, [and] let him become more kindly[?]; let him be free [for a time] from arithmetic; [when] he counts up all the school affairs of the students, let him count me [i.e., not neglect me any longer].

The father agrees to invite the headmaster to dinner.

At this point the narrator takes over and describes the ensuing events as if he were an eyewitness. The father seats the headmaster in the seat of honor and flatters him:

> My little fellow has opened [wide] his hand, [and] you made wisdom enter there; you showed him all the fine points of the scribal art; you made him see the solutions of the mathematical and arithmetical [problems], you [taught him how] to make deep[?] the cuneiform script[?].

After this, the father orders the servants to pour out fragrant oil and announces his intentions of bestowing clothes, a ring, and an extra salary on the fortunate headmaster. As a result of these attentions, the headmaster's attitude toward his pupil changes radically. His final speech reads:

> Young fellow, [because] you hated not my words, neglected them not, [may you] complete the scribal art from beginning to end. Because you gave me everything without stint, paid me a salary larger than my efforts [deserve], [and] have honored me,

may Nidaba, the queen of guardian angels, be your guardian angel; may your pointed stylus write well for you; may your exercises contain no faults. Of your brothers, may you be their leader; of your friends, may you be their chief; may you rank the highest among the schoolboys, satisfy[?] all who walk[?] to and fro in[?] the palaces. Little fellow, you "know" [your] father, I am second to him; that homage be paid to you, that you be blessed—may the god of your father bring this about with firm hand; he will bring prayer and supplication to Nidaba, your queen, as if it were a matter for your god. Thus, when you put a kindly hand on the . . . of the teacher, [and] on the forehead of the "big-brother," then[?] your young comrades will show you favor. You have carried out well the school's activities, you are a man of learning. You have exalted Nidaba, the queen of learning; O Nidaba, praise!"

If this schoolboy is as young as his activities and the epithets used in Kramer's translation indicate, and if it can be assumed that the Sumerians believed a story about a young schoolboy was appropriate for use by students of the same age, much as primers today have first- and second-graders as major characters, then it seems likely that this story was written for the use of elementary students and that those students were young. The student's misadventures would be amusing to young children; even more so, perhaps, to children who viewed corporal punishment as a matter of course. Finally, the immediate goal emphasized by the headmaster's final speech, scholastic success, would be easy for children to understand.

The headmaster not only wishes for perfect work from his student, but he also wishes that perfect work will lead to tangible social rewards for him: top-rank among his fellow-students and their recognition of him as a leader. In addition, the headmaster wishes that the student, as a result of his achievement in school, will eventually receive the same kind of homage now paid to his father who is clearly, on the internal evidence in the story, a man of wealth and status; the headmaster places himself second to him even though the scribal class was a privileged one. As a final guarantee of success, the headmaster hopes that the father's personal god will intervene on the student's behalf with Nidaba, the goddess in charge of writing

and literature, much as the father had intervened with her representative, the headmaster.[22] There is no mention in the headmaster's
words of learning for learning's sake; rather it is assumed that the
rewards of learning are material, not spiritual.

There is a further materialistic slant to "School Days" that, viewed
from a modern perspective, makes the story appear to be ironic. The
radical change of attitude on the part of the headmaster toward his
pupil takes place only after the receipt of flattery and tokens of
respect, as well as considerable material benefits. Indeed, the headmaster admits as much: "Because you gave me everything without
stint, . . . may Nidaba . . . be your guardian angel." While the headmaster is not exactly bribed, since he only wishes for the future
success of his pupil but does not guarantee it, the implication is that
the student will be viewed more favorably from this point on. Is the
story advocating that a student encourage his father to treat his
teacher handsomely in order to promote his son's success? That the
Sumerian culture may have been one that viewed such pay-offs
positively is not only probable on the evidence of current practices in
many places, but on the evidence of the text as well. The headmaster has already made an equation between the relationship of the
father to himself and the relationship of the father's personal god to
the scribal goddess Nidaba. The Sumerians believed that you must
do something for your god in order for him to do something for
you: that there was a reciprocal relationship between man and deity
(Jacobsen 154, 160). "School Days" implies that the same kind of
reciprocal relationship applies between the student and those in
authority in the school, indeed, perhaps applies in all social relationships.

Since it was the scribal teachers who decided which compositions
were to be copied by their students, the message that it pays to be
good to your teacher may partially account for the popularity of
"School Days": twenty-one copies exist, some with translations into
Akkadian, the demotic language, to help the student (Kramer, *History* 12). Moreover, the piece may contain a warning directed at its
adult audience: excessive punishment results in poor performance,
since the schoolboy's inability to apply himself in school appears to
stem from his continuous chastisement by school personnel. On the
other hand, it is possible that "School Days" is to be read by its adult

audience as a satire on the materialism and limited goals of certain headmasters and parents. That the Sumerians were quite capable of such satire has been the conclusion of several recent studies; Alster, for example, speaks of the "constant play on ambivalent possibilities" to be found in Sumerian literature. If this is indeed the case, teachers must have enjoyed the irony of the work while correcting their students' exercises.

A text even more popular than "School Days," judging by the fifty-seven extant copies and fragments, is "A Scribe and His Perverse Son."[23] This is an amusing diatribe by an angry father who complains that his son is not living up to parental expectations. The piece opens with a typical father-and-son dialogue.

"Where are you going?"
"I'm not going anywhere."
"If you aren't going anywhere, why are you wasting your time?
Go to your school, be ready for school!
Read your lesson, open [your] . . .
Write your tablet,
let your big [brother] write [your] new tablet for you.
When you have finished [your] lesson
and have recited it [before] your monitor, then come here
    to me.
Say . . .
Don't wander around [on the street].
Give me [quickly your answer?]
. . . Do you know what I have said to you?"
"I know it and I'll say it to you!"
"Now then, repeat it to me!"
"I know it and I'll say it to you!"
"Now then, repeat it to me!"
"I'll repeat it to you."   (1–16)

After similar exchanges, the son does repeat what the father has said to him. Then the father embarks on a long and not unfamiliar monologue containing advice mixed with complaints about his son's grumbling, his imperiousness, his laziness, and his love for pleasure. The father remarks that he never asks his son to work in the fields as other fathers do, that he has worked harder than anyone for his

Copy of the popular text "A Scribe and His Perverse Son," sometimes called "Juvenile Delinquency."

son, and yet all he gets is ingratitude. He urges his son to imitate his older and younger brothers. He follows this with some remarks about the scribal profession.

> "Under the expert masters who dwell in the land,
> who are named with names, has Enki [the god of wisdom
>   and the arts]

no profession which is as difficult as scribal work—now then
    he has named it!
He names with names, with the exception of the art of song:
like the sea-shores which are far away from each other,
so far away is the 'heart' of the art of song.
You do not direct your understanding to my . . .
You do not say: 'I will attend to . . . of my father!'
That which Enlil has established for men is
    that the son follow his father's profession." (107–16)

There are fifty-eight more lines, many of them fragmentary, of complaints and advice. Then the father concludes, as did the headmaster in "School Days," with good wishes for his son's future.

"May you find favor before your god!
May your humanity 'exalt your neck and your breast!'
May you become the best among your city's scholars,
so that your city, that beautiful place, calls your name
    glorious!
May your god name you with a good name, an enduring word;
May you find favor before [the moon-god] Nanna, your god;
May you be well-regarded by Ningal [his consort]!
Nidaba be praised!" (176–83)

The son in this work appears to be somewhat older than the schoolboy of "School Days," but he is still young enough to be under the supervision of a "big-brother." The father's complaint that he has never asked his son to work for him and support him is no indication of maturity, given the age at which young children are still sent out to work in certain cultures.[24] Thus there is no conclusive evidence on the age of the son addressed here; perhaps he is approaching adolescence, the age when, in our culture, boys are prone to "stand around in the market place and wander about in the street" (29–30).

A son older than the one in "School Days," however, as well as an older audience for the work, is indicated by the father's sophisticated perception of the nature of the scribal arts and of the future benefits to his son he wishes to result from the mastery of those arts. Sjöberg's translation makes clear the distance of the art of song from the scribal art, which is only the most difficult of the professions which Enki has named.[25] The art of song is the exception (*Aus-*

nahme) to the naming process, and song's "heart," presumably its essence, is as far away from what can be named as the sea-shores are from each other. To name, for the Sumerians, is to make what is at the heart of a thing manifest, to make it known to the consciousness (Kramer, *Inanna* 138–39). Thus these lines emphasize the ultimate ineffability at the heart of song, while seeing the scribal art which transmits it as the most difficult of those things which can be named. The father's recognition that there is something in the creative act that cannot be "named" is evidence of a philosophical stance that moves beyond the materialism of "School Days."[26]

The type of ultimate success that the father wishes for his son also transcends the material. In line 177 the father uses the term *nam-lú-ulù*, usually translated as "humanity." According to J. J. A. Van Dijk (23), *nam-lú-ulù* corresponds to the Latin *humanitas* and has the same two senses: it refers both to men collectively and to that through which man is what he is, the complete blossoming of human values, or, as Kramer puts it, "all conduct and behavior characteristic of humanity and worthy of it" (*Sumerians* 264).[27] The student must not rely solely on his technical ability as a scribe to gain glory and status, but on the humanity, the inner worth as evidenced by outer conduct, which is the fruit of a scribal education. Humanity will lead to an even greater benefit, the favor of the personal god, who was not only a kind of sublime parent but the "personification of the power that causes luck and success in an individual" and the source of all pride in accomplishment (Jacobsen 161). The father wishes, then, not simply that his personal god intervene with the goddess of scribes, Nidaba, on behalf of his son as did the father in "School Days," but that the student will win his own favor before his personal god Nanna, such favor that his god will give him an "enduring" name and perhaps the kind of immortality an enduring name guarantees.[28] In the hymn to Lipit-eštar, the scribe's immortality was only to be gained through his association with the king and was dependent on the survival of the king's name; here the scribe may win immortality through his own deeds and in his own right.

This work, given its more sophisticated content and its concern with goals that are not only material, may serve as a transition to the literature which was included in the third stage of a scribe's education, that "song" whose essence is so unapproachable. The last years at school were spent in the copying and perhaps memorization of the longer wisdom tests and the hymns, myths, and epics of the Sumerians. At this stage, however, the student should probably no longer be considered a child, but a young adult who is well-embarked on his scribal career.

IV

Such a survey of the literature to which Mesopotamian children were exposed from about 2500 B.C. to the end of the Sumerian period, about 1800 B.C., is necessarily limited by the fragmentary nature of the surviving evidence. The oral component of the child's literary universe can never be reconstructed; in addition, the children that are known to have come into contact with written literature formed only a small segment of the population and for the most part belonged to the wealthier and more powerful stratum of society. In spite of these limitations, however, the presence of certain texts on the Ur curriculum lists, the nature of the tablets on which those texts are found, and the location of the tablets at school excavation sites render certain the association of a small number of school-age children with a significant group of literary works.

Can this literature be called "children's literature"? Certainly not using definitions such as the Opies' "books intended to be read by children in their leisure hours for enjoyment."[29] This is because, with the exception of the "lullaby," which is arguably not a real lullaby since it is directed at a particular child, the proverbs, fables, debates, and school compositions either were not written specifically for children, or, when they were, seem to have been composed primarily in order to educate them and only secondarily to amuse them.

What can be said with certainty is that the Mesopotamians had a literature which they considered peculiarly suited for children at the elementary and intermediate levels of their education. Even if the primary consideration for choosing a given text was based on lexical and grammatical grounds, its content was also significant. Thus while some of the literature used at the earliest educational stages was not composed for children but came out of oral tradition, with the exception of the mythological debates, the material used at the second educational stage, centered as it was on the school and its graduates, was probably written specifically for students by teachers. Moreover, these are imaginative literary works, not designed to impart specific information, and are not as overtly didactic as Aelfric's *Colloquy*, St. Anselm's *Elucidarium*, or Comenius' *Orbis Sensualium Pictus*, which are sometimes cited as early children's books. In addition, the Sumerian animal fables and "school compositions" belong to two of the most common categories of children's literature, the school story and the animal story.

A definition of children's literature, then, that would prove serviceable for the eras before the invention of printing and that would include the works with which Mesopotamian children came into contact could be: "an imaginative literature which may or may not have been originally composed for younger children or directed at them, but which was considered particularly suitable for them and to which they were regularly exposed." Given a definition as inclusive as this, children's literature is as ancient as the adult literature to which it is so intimately related.

The literature which the Sumerians thought "particularly suitable" for children, the proverbs, fables, debates, and school compositions, is considered by most scholars to belong to the category of wisdom literature, and it does transmit an identifiable ethical stance. The fact that a given ethic is pervasive in the literature to which children are deliberately and regularly exposed is a good indicator that such an ethic is considered of major importance. Indeed the ethical stance (perhaps a better term would be agenda) to be found in Sumerian children's literature reflects the characteristics of a philosophy of life that Kramer and Jacobsen see in Sumerian culture as a whole. The highest good appears to be the favor of the personal god and then of the king, in those texts which mention them, but chiefly because their favor, implicitly or explicitly, is a guarantee of fame, status, and material prosperity in this life.[30] Even the literature to which younger children were exposed, the lullaby and the hymn to the king Lipit-eštar, reflect this point of view. The proverbs, fables, and the literary debates portray in addition a competitive society in which hard work, perseverance, prudence, initiative, a certain aggressive, self-aggrandizing foxiness, and, above all, verbal skills were prerequisites for gaining the rewards of this life. In the school debates and compositions, as in the hymn to Lipit-eštar, it is clear that a total mastery of the scribal arts is the key to ultimate success. On the other hand, "A Scribe and His Perverse Son," directed at older children, posits the limits to self-aggrandizement: know one's place and act for the benefit of other men and of the gods in order to receive the divine favor essential for continued success. Thus for enduring fame in one's own right, it was necessary to cultivate nam-lú-ulù, humanity, a concept which included the practice of truth, goodness, justice, mercy, courage, loyalty, and other virtues.

The Sumerians achieved at a remarkably early date, and with unusual rapidity, a high civilization in every sense: artistic, intellectual, legal, political, and even scientific and technological. They are responsible, as far as is known, for a great number of "firsts" in the cultural history of man. The impetus behind the Sumerians' rapid cultural development was provided by the scribal bureaucrats who were exposed from early childhood to a literature, created largely by themselves, which not only promoted the primacy of their profession, but which emphasized hard work, intellectual achievement, and humanity as the prerequisites for every kind of success including an enduring name.[31] Even at the beginning of history, then, children's literature played an important and well-recognized role in shaping the minds of the future leaders of a society and thus the direction in which that society would move.

Notes

1. For example, see Brockman, the McMunns, and Smith; volume 1 of the recent series *Masterworks of Children's Literature* begins at 1550.

2. Kramer, *Inanna* 115–19; Brinkman 335–37; Hallo and Simpson 27–29.

3. Kramer (329) remarks of the lullaby that its "translation and interpretation are difficult and to a considerable degree uncertain."

4. There was at least one female scribe, and it is worthy of note that the deity of scribes, Nidaba, is female. Kramer surmises that women who were literate were privately educated (*History* 351).

5. Olivier (49) notes that a private house excavated at Ur contained a bench for pupils, a podium for the teacher, and nearly two thousand tablets.

6. This is only one of a number of texts that promote the scribal arts; see Sjöberg ("In Praise") and the works discussed below. Vanstiphout ("How Did" 124) notes that "the closing passage may well be intended as a self-fulfilling prophecy: of course his

fame will endure when this text will remain in use for many centuries (with some interruption, just about forty by now) as a school text."

7. For a detailed description of the types of tablets on which the proverbs occur and the arrangement of their contents, see Gordon, *Proverbs* 6–10. All further citations in the text and notes, except n. 8 below, refer to this work. It is possible, thanks to Gordon's careful scholarship, to pinpoint which proverbs from Collections One and Two are found on the tablets of the four general types that he describes. Type A and B tablets are composed by professional scribes, perhaps as library copies; type C are rough, badly written, often consisting of only one line accompanied by vocabulary lists and mathematical exercises; type D contain short excerpts and represent a higher level of writing skills; and type E are fairly well-written and contain longer excerpts.

8. Gordon in "Sumerian Animal Proverbs and Fables" lists allusions to the following: geography, weather, wild fauna and flora, minerals, agriculture, domestic animals, animal anatomy, crafts and industry, commerce and transport, hunting, property rights and inheritance, social status, political and legal institutions, family, household, religion, education, art, recreations, human physiological and pyschological traits, interpersonal relationships, and abstract ideas about time, quantity, truth, and pleasure.

9. See, for example, Lenneberg, particularly ch. 8, sec. 5, "Growth Characteristics of the Human Brain and Their Possible Relationship to Language Acquisition."

10. A more extreme example is provided by the fragmentary proverbs 1.41–43 also found on elementary tablets; Gordon (61) thinks they may refer to "sexual acts frowned upon by the Sumerians," although he admits that the text is problematical and the translation uncertain.

11. Gordon gives valuable cultural analyses of the proverbs; he discusses proverbs about children on 304 and proverbs about education on 311–12.

12. Gordon (287) does not think that the fox of Sumerian proverbs is the clever, sly beast he later becomes.

13. Both these texts are Neo-Assyrian, but the first is similar in theme to the longer Sumerian fable, 2.69, in Gordon. Of the second, Lambert says, "If this is really a proverb, its point eludes us." The point is that when one is in trouble, it is more effective to act like a fox than like a lion.

14. The Sumerians saw the world as a place in which man was put only to serve gods who were unpredictable and whose favor was difficult to win. Life after death was merely a dusty, grim reflection of life on earth; see Kramer, *Sumerians*, vii.

15. A collation of the three catalogues is provided by a table in Hallo (90–91).

16. Lambert (150) classifies the later Babylonian and Assyrian debates as "fables, not of the Aesopic type." The key to the difficulty in classifying this material may lie in Alster's observation (210) that a proverb, a fable, and a debate contain the same "traditionally coined statement" but in a more or less expanded form.

17. Kramer (*History* 133–36) translates part of the debate and summarizes the rest.

18. Sumerian civilization was not only based on a complex irrigation system, but flooding was a constant threat. The Sumerians had a flood story remarkably similar to that found in Genesis.

19. "Wise-fool" (*galam-hu-ru*), according to Gadd (34), is the literal equivalent of the Greek *sophos-moros*, from which we get the term "sophomore."

20. For Mesopotamian brutality to children, see DeMause (33–34).

21. The work was first edited and translated by Kramer in 1949, who gave it then the title "School Days." Kramer's translation in *Sumerians* uses "Old Grad" in the first line. All other translations, including Kramer's excerpt in *History* 10, use the term "schoolboy." Saggs (346) claims that "the boy is in his second year."

22. Every Sumerian had his own personal god, among the many deities of the Sumerian pantheon, with whom he had a close personal relationship. A father passed on his personal god and goddess to his sons. For a recent discussion, see Jacobsen ch. 5, "Second Millennium Metaphors. The Gods as Parents: Rise of Personal Religion."

23. Until recently the only relatively complete translation has been that of Kramer in *Sumerians* 63ff. Kramer adds some more lines in *History* 15−17. I have translated into English the German translation of Sjöberg, which is based on forty more tablets and fragments than Kramer's and which adds about sixty lines.

24. Kramer translates lines 124ff. as "You have accumulated much wealth, have expanded far and wide, have become fat, big, broad, powerful, and puffed," giving the impression that a young man is being addressed. On the other hand, Sjöberg has "You with your exploits! You are bloated, you make yourself big, you make yourself broad, you are imperious[?]" "Du mit deinen Grosstaten! Du bist aufgedunsen, / Du . . ., du machst dich gross, / Du machst dich breit, du bist gebieterisch[?], du . . .'", and the context supports the meaning "You have become too big for your breeches."

25. A comparison of Sjöberg's translation of lines 107−14 with Kramer's (*History* 17) underlines the complexity of the father's approach to his profession. Kramer's rendering is, "Among all mankind's craftsmen who dwell in the land, as many as Enki called by name, no work as difficult as the scribal art did he call by name. For if not for song [poetry]—like the banks of the sea, the banks of the distant canals is the heart of the song distant—you wouldn't be listening to my counsel and I wouldn't be repeating to you the wisdom of my father." Kramer's translation implies that there is an equation between song (poetry) and the scribal art and that it is the transmission of the former by the latter which enables the father to carry on the wisdom tradition by transmitting that tradition to his son.

26. Alster (212) sees the text as "a satire on the art of the singers, from the viewpoint of the scribes." His reading is very different from mine.

27. Van Dijk (24) sees the development of the concept in certain edubba compositions, particularly this one, as an illustration of the evolution that the Sumerian intellectual milieu has undergone in the direction of rational humanism, that is, the idea that man's humanity is the result of his formation by men, not by the gods.

28. Van Dijk's (26) translation of line 180, "que ton dieu t'appelle d'un nom doux 'dans une parole inchangeable! " underlines the enduring quality of the name. Sjöberg has "ein festes Wort."

29. As quoted in Bator (4). His discussion of modern authors who claim that they leave it up to their publishers to decide whether a work is juvenilia or adult fiction demonstrates that intention is probably not a reliable component of a definition of children's literature.

30. Buccellati (37) notes that "the gods are considered as procurers, they are intermediaries to something else which is in reality the main reason for the relationship." Buccellati finds "no trace of a unified doctrine, system, or intellectual program" among the Mesopotamians.

31. For the influential status of bureaucrat-scribes and their importance for the development of Mesopotamian civilization, see Oppenheim.

Works Cited

Alster, Bendt. "Paradoxical Proverbs and Satire in Sumerian Literature." *Journal of Cuneiform Studies* 27 (1975): 201−27.

Bator, Robert. "Definition: Perpetual Exception." In *Signposts to Criticism of Children's Literature*. Ed. Robert Bator. Chicago: ALA, 1983.

Brinkman, J. A. "Appendix: Mesopotamian Chronology of the Historical Period."
    In A. Leo Oppenheim. *Ancient Mesopotamia: Portrait of a Dead Civilization.* Chi-
    cago: U of Chicago P, 1964. 335–37.
Brockman, Bennett A. "Robin Hood and the Invention of Children's Literature."
    Children's Literature 10 (1982): 1–17.
Buccellati, Giorgio. "Wisdom and Not: The Case of Mesopotamia." *Journal of the
    American Oriental Society* 101 (1981): 35–47.
Butler, Francelia, ed. *Masterworks of Children's Literature.* Vol. 1 of 8 vols. Gen. ed.
    Jonathan Cott. Bryn Mawr: Chelsea, 1983.
Carpenter, Humphrey, and Mari Prichard. *The Oxford Companion to Children's Litera-
    ture.* Oxford: Oxford UP, 1984.
DeMause, Lloyd. "The Evolution of Childhood." In *The History of Childhood.* Ed. Lloyd
    DeMause. New York: Psychohistory Press, 1974. 1–65.
Gadd, C. J. *Teachers and Students in the Oldest Schools: An Inaugural Lecture Delivered on 6
    March, 1956.* London: School of Oriental and African Studies, U of London, 1956.
Gordon, Edmund I. "Sumerian Animal Proverbs and Fables: 'Collection Five.' " *Jour-
    nal of Cuneiform Studies* 12 (1958): 1–6.
———. *Sumerian Proverbs: Glimpses of Everyday Life in Ancient Mesopotamia.* Philadel-
    phia, 1959; rpt. New York: Greenwood, 1968.
Hallo, William W. Rev. of *Literary and Religious Texts, First Part* by C. J. Gadd and
    Samuel Noah Kramer. *Journal of Cuneiform Studies* 20 (1966): 89–93.
———, and William Kelly Simpson. *The Ancient Near East: A History.* New York:
    Harcourt, 1971.
Jacobsen, Thorkild. *The Treasures of Darkness.* New Haven: Yale UP, 1976.
Kramer, Samuel Noah. *History Begins at Sumer: Thirty-Nine Firsts in Man's Recorded
    History.* Philadelphia: U of Pennsylvania P, 1981.
———. "Sumerian History, Culture and Literature." In Diane Wolkstein and Samuel
    Noah Kramer. *Inanna, Queen of Heaven and Earth.* New York: Harper, 1983.
———. *The Sumerians: Their History, Culture, and Character.* Chicago: U of Chicago P,
    1963.
Lambert, W. G. *Babylonian Wisdom Literature.* Oxford: Clarendon, 1960.
Lenneberg, Eric H. *Biological Foundations of Language.* New York: Wiley, 1967.
McMunn, Meradith Tilbury, and William Robert. "Children's Literature in the
    Middle Ages." *Children's Literature* 1 (1972): 21–29.
Olivier, J. P. J. "Schools and Wisdom Literature." *Journal of Northwest Semitic Lang-
    uages* 4 (1975): 49–60.
Oppenheim, A. Leo. "The Intellectual in Mesopotamian Society." *Daedalus* 104.2
    (Spring 1975): 37–46.
Saggs, H. W. F. *The Greatness That Was Babylon.* New York: Hawthorn, 1962.
Sjöberg, Åke W. "Der Vater und Sein Missratener Sohn." *Journal of Cuneiform Studies*
    25.3 (July 1973): 105–69.
———. "In Praise of the Scribal Art." *Journal of Cuneiform Studies* 24 (1972): 126–29.
Smith, Elva S. *The History of Children's Literature.* Chicago: ALA, 1937; rev. 1980.
Van Dijk, J. J. A. *La sagesse suméro-accadienne: recherches sur les genres littéraires des
    textes sapientiaux.* Leiden: Brill, 1953.
Vanstiphout, H. L. J. "How Did They Learn Sumerian?" *Journal of Cuneiform Studies*
    31.2 (April 1979): 118–26.
———. "Lipit-eštar's Praise in the Edubba." *Journal of Cuneiform Studies* 30.1 (Jan.
    1978): 33–39.

Impeccable Governesses, Rational Dames, and Moral Mothers: Mary Wollstonecraft and the Female Tradition in Georgian Children's Books

Mitzi Myers

If exploring storybooks is no longer the literary slumming expedition it once was, Georgian writing for the young still suffers something like the critical equivalent of urban blight. Hopelessly defaced by injunctions to improvement, commentators on children's literature imply, the moral tale excites a merely antiquarian interest, is necessarily devoid of imaginative force. Only recently was its didactic "yoke" shaken off, one critic asserts: "We do actually believe now that children's books need to be fun and nothing else" (Lively 18). With a similarly Whiggish view of children's literary history as a progress toward pure amusement and imaginative fantasy, historians typically gesture toward John Newbery as a quaint signpost to freer territories and hurry through the Georgian scene in a single chapter. And that section is mostly devoted to the Perfect Tutor, à la *Émile* (1762) or Thomas Day's *Sandford and Merton* (1783, 1786, 1789).

Even when scholars seriously examine this key period which marked the establishment of children's books as a distinctive genre, they focus on fathers, begetters, progenitors. Sylvia W. Patterson, for example, analyzes Rousseau's influence; Samuel F. Pickering, Jr., makes Locke central. Locke, Newbery, Rousseau, Day, Richard Lovell Edgeworth—these are the ritually invoked parents of late eighteenth- and early nineteenth-century juvenilia, and the women who quickly appropriated the emergent genre are hardly more than daddy's girls. Thirty years ago, Percy Muir noted the so-called "monstrous regiment" of women who made children's stories a female specialty from 1780 on, remarking that "there is woefully

Illustrations reproduced by courtesy of the Department of Special Collections, University Research Library, University of California at Los Angeles.

This typically educative Georgian mother is wearing the more formal style of the 1780s. (Frontispiece to Wollstonecraft's adaptation of C. G. Salzmann, *Elements of Morality* [London: J. Johnson, 1791].)

little on the women writers for children who were active at the turn of the eighteenth-nineteenth centuries," and his observation still stands (93). Reviewing recent studies of nineteenth-century children's literary and cultural history, Elaine Showalter finds that "parents" still means fathers, "children" means sons, and even when documenting a decline in patriarchal authority, critics fail to connect their topic to the "increased authority of mothers" she rightly insists on as characteristic of the time (237–38). This authority emerges clearly in the many didactic children's books written for children at the turn of the eighteenth century.

The recognition of such a change is far more important for an understanding of the period than may at first appear. Because children's tales perform a variety of cultural functions, they are crammed with clues to changes in attitudes, values, and behavior. Above all, these key agents of socialization diagram what cultures want of their young and expect of those who tend them. Addressed as much to mothers as to children—"*by the* Public *the writer means* Mothers," affirms the *Female Guardian* (1784) in its dedication— juvenile texts are thus an invaluable resource for students of women's cultural status and literary production. For with the late eighteenth-century expansion of the reading public (much of it more leisured middle-class women), female writers crowded into the juvenile market. Sharing their era's appetite for educational reform, this early generation of professional women found in children's books not just an outlet available to their sex, but a genuine vocation. In their capacity as surrogate mothers, these writing women testify to maternal and pedagogical power. Reflecting the concrete social changes that "greatly expanded and specialized the maternal role," their narrative constructs enact in fictional form the new primacy of the mother, what social historians term a "cultural redefinition of motherhood" (Bloch 114). The characteristic flavor of their didacticism and moral tone, the way they define power, heroism, and social good, all bear the impress of that active and benevolent materialism which was a key component in the period's female self-image. As Muir and Showalter suggest, late eighteenth-century children's literature is in many ways a genre shaped by gender; a matrilineage of nursery novels exists. It comprehends an undervalued and almost unrecognized female literary tradition, the more revelatory precisely because it *is* didactic, because it accepts and emphasizes the instructive and intellectual potential of narrative.

Most critics of historical children's books try to look through the youthful reader's eyes (a gaze filmed by modern psychological notions of what children like and read, and by contemporary critical separation of the educational and the entertaining). This essay observes these texts from a different angle—that of the mother-teacher, both outside and inside the tales. It reads her moralizing discourse seriously as a distinctive literary genre with distinctive literary features. Over the fictional structures and topoi that make up Georgian juvenilia presides a maternal persona, controlling and dominating the tale in virtue's name. Maternal mentors write from within a female frame of reference, emphasizing, as the title of Wollstonecraft's first book indicates, *Thoughts on the Education of Daughters: with Reflections on Female Conduct in the More Important Duties of Life* (1787) and typically working—as in her *Female Reader— for the Improvement of Young Women* (1789). And—with its stress on real event, familiar style, the cultivation of heart and under-standing—the title of Wollstonecraft's *Original Stories from Real Life: with Conversations Calculated to Regulate the Affections, and Form the Mind to Truth and Goodness* (1788) illustrates the purposeful aesthetic of the female tradition to which her tales belong. Women's special anxieties and moral perspective hallmark her characters and plots, which resonate with the themes dear to other bourgeois female writers, from the progressive humanitarian advocacy of animals, slaves, and the downtrodden or victimized of every description to the cultural reform of morals and manners through self-govern-ance, self-respect, and everyday female heroism.

For, however tirelessly didactic and ostensibly down-to-earth, women writers' moral and domestic tales smuggle in their own symptomatic fantasies, dramatizing female authority figures, co-vertly thematizing female power. The educating heroine (and her educable pupils) signals a shifting female cultural ideal, a bourgeois reinvention of womanhood in the stylish new mode of enlightened domesticity. Advocating new pedagogical techniques and goals, women's tracts and tales show how girls should be educated in a new mode of female heroism—in rationality, self-command, and moral autonomy. And the absolute assurance and moral self-confidence which never fail their authors bespeak the female writer's freshly authoritative public voice. Women writers used stories for mothers and children and childrearing advice manuals for parents to address broader educational and social issues with a sense of confidence in their power to effect change. Innocent-looking stories about talking animals, heroic girls, authoritative mothers, and worthy peasants served the well-born Georgian woman as a fiction of ideas. Indeed, for the writing woman, instructive genres like the storybook are not peripheral to the Georgian literary canon, but central; teaching shapes her persona and her stance, grants her a mode in which to have her social say.

To be sure, Rousseau directs *Émile* to the "tender, anxious mother" and pronounces "the earliest education" the "most important and it undoubtedly is woman's work . . . . Address your treatises on education to the women," he urges, for their influence is "always predominant in education" (5), and he was warmly seconded by such later male theorists as C. G. Salzmann, R. L. Edgeworth, and Pestalozzi, and by such pediatric specialists as Dr. Hugh Smith and Dr. William Buchan. "The more I reflect on the situation of a mother, the more I am struck with the extent of her powers," which approach "our ideas of the Deity," Buchan reflects: her "instructions and example will have a lasting influence, and of course, will go farther to form the morals, than all the eloquence of the pulpit, the efforts of school-masters, or the corrective power of the civil magistrate" (107, 3, 107).

Responding with surprising enthusiasm to the evolving notions of child nurture, maternal duty, and familial structure that these male contemporaries exemplify and that Lawrence Stone and other recent social historians document, women writers for the young displace male instructors with maternal guides.[1] Rousseau's "real teacher" is the father and the mother he celebrates is only a nurse (6); but from Sarah Fielding's Mrs. Teachum in *The Governess; or, Little Female Academy* (1749, the pioneer junior novel written specifically for the young) on through the mother-pedagogues of Madame de Genlis, women writers transform Mentor to *Mentoria*, as Ann Murry's 1778 title has it. Elizabeth Helme's *Maternal Instruction; or, Family Conversations* (1802) sums up this female version of the pedagogic tradition: "As I regard an informed mother the most proper and attractive of all teachers, I have chosen that character as the principal, in the following sheets" (iii). Women writers fished in a common pool of educational ideas, but they appropriated the period's maternal myths in their own distinctive ways, reading motherhood as social opportunity and valorizing heroines as rational educators.

Few characters more vividly typify the new educating heroine
than Wollstonecraft's Mrs. Mason, the maternal surrogate of *Original Stories*, and few careers more thoroughly work out the implications of female pedagogical power than Wollstonecraft's. From first
to last, she was reformist through education. Her *Rights of Woman*
(1792) was correctly placed by its initial reviewers as an educational
treatise (Janes), and her progress from Mason to the heroic citizen-
mother of the later tract develops issues latent in the women educators' moral tradition. Wollstonecraft herself ran the gamut of the
female mentor's activities. She kept a school; she worked as a
governess; like most of her sister authors for the young—Genlis,
Anna Laetitia Barbauld, Ellenor Fenn, Sarah Trimmer, Dorothy
Kilner, Hannah More, Mary Pilkington, Mary Hughes, Maria Edgeworth, to name but a few—she wrote from long contact with youth.
Not only an early writer and translator of juvenile moral tales (she
adapted Salzmann's *Elements of Morality* to English taste in 1791),
Wollstonecraft was also a pioneer reviewer of children's literature,
who added wide reading and earnest theorizing to her practical
experience. Like Trimmer's rating service for harried mothers in
the *Guardian of Education* a few years later (1802–06), Wollstonecraft's many notices for the *Analytical Review* have much to say about
the aesthetics and cultural implications of children's literature as a
genre. Warmly praising Day's *Sandford and Merton* or Maria Edgeworth's *Parent's Assistant* (1796), she emphasizes how "the many
ingenious works of this class, produced within the last twenty or
thirty years, will have a sure, though, perhaps, slow effect on the
understanding of the succeding generations" (428). Conservatives
like Trimmer and Wollstonecraftean progressives alike could agree
with Priscilla Wakefield that the age's "spirit of improvement . . .
shines in nothing more conspicuously than in education" (*Mental
Improvement* 2: 61). Georgian children were the locus of a revolution-
ary generation's hopes and fears. No wonder improving books were
constantly thrust into their hands, and no wonder women writers
directed so much energy to formulating exemplary mothers and
governesses.

The preface to *Original Stories* is charged with female writers' new
sense of educational mission, which demands education of mothers
as well as children. Much as Wollstonecraft's full title highlights their

predilection for moral nurture and domestic realism, so her foreword offers a deliberate rationale for their meliorism and paragon-matriarch characters. Revealing a rather more sophisticated attitude toward didacticism than Georgians are usually credited with, it suggests how pedagogic theory functions as cultural criticism. Healthy habits, Wollstonecraft recognizes, "are far preferable to the precepts of reason." But her dialogues and tales must be "accommodated to the present state of society." If parents neglect their natural duties for artificial pleasures (a recurrent theme in reformist educational rhetoric), then stories must be "written to illustrate the moral," correctives in lieu of the good parental example so central to the period's psychology of learning. With an eye to sales, Joseph Johnson, Wollstonecraft's publisher, objected to her criticism of parental neglect, but she refused to compromise: "The few judicious parents who may peruse my book, will not feel themselves hurt—and the weak are too vain to mind what is said in a book intended for children . . . . If parents attended to their children, I would not have written the stories; for, what are books—compared to conversations which affection inforces!—" (*Collected Letters* 167). When real-life matriarchs fail, fictional ones may fill the gap; but the aim is always to empower the living mother as teacher.

With its dual attitude of blame and idealization toward the parent-figure, Wollstonecraft's preface implies what recent students of mothering call "the Fantasy of the Perfect Mother" (Chodorow and Contratto). Born in the eighteenth century (and still influential), this cultural myth assumes an all-powerful mother, totally responsible for her children's fate and much else besides, for Georgian maternal pedagogy, linking private and public spheres, insists on the communal consequences of domestic instruction. Recognizing this energizing fantasy goes some way toward explaining the peculiar flavor of the surrogate-mother's texts, now chastising the maternal audience for neglect and mismanagement, for spoiled children and cultural decay; now valorizing motherhood, whose power rightly used can transform the nation (a presumption as potent in Wollstonecraft's *Rights of Woman* as in the works of her evangelical contemporary Hannah More). "Under the inspection of a judicious mother . . . what might—what might *not* be done?" Fenn's *Rational Dame* (1786) asks (vii, ix).

Knowledge, Wollstonecraft progressively argues, should be "gradually imparted" and individualized to fit each child. Ideally, children should learn not from direct teaching but from living examples apprehended through the senses, "the first inlets to the heart; and the improvement of those instruments of the understanding is the object education should have constantly in view, and over which we have most power." Her fictional "Conversations," then, "are intended to assist the teacher as well as the pupil." They posit model educational programs to be transformed or superseded by the maternal instructors they instruct. Hence pedagogic theory directs fictional technique, shaping plots to approximate the learning process as closely as possible. Hence Wollstonecraft's narrative frame interweaves "histories" that comment on and foster the main characters' maturation, the kind of "little detached stories" that Sarah Fielding pioneered and that Madame de Genlis refined into a woman's specialty (*Adelaide and Theodore* 1:63). Hence, too, bourgeois educators like Wollstonecraft strive to infuse their reformist concern with usefulness and sincerity into "perspicuity and simplicity of style," the aesthetic equivalent of the hostility toward aristocratic manners that informs so much of the period's literature for children. Wollstonecraft's concern "to fix principles of truth and humanity on a solid and simple foundation" thus fashions her characters, format, and style (*Original Stories* iii–xi). Other female-authored children's books, like *Original Stories*, typically reinforce content through their formal conventions: colloquial dialogues and conversations, homely natural and household detail, anecdotes of meaningful moral choice drawn from the everyday world—a taste for "truth" and middling life that blends domestic realism and portraits of domestic heroism into what might be called exemplary realism.

Original Stories is a book about growing up female in Georgian England. It is about the options available to the mature woman, and the means by which she can gain some sense of control over her life (and perhaps also the lives of others). It is a how-to-do-it manual of the latest educational techniques, dramatized by its mentoria: punish only by withholding affection, incarnate the virtues you would teach, draw upon your own experience and the neighborhood annals for entertaining instructional material. It records the period's

emergent narrative strategies, full of evocative natural details, plots
that link character and consequences, and an organic awareness that
the girl is the mother of the woman, as in the contrasted tales of how
Lady Sly and Mrs. Trueman earn their patronymics. Its miscellany
of moral tales is painfully astir with the era's humanitarian sympathies: here is crazy Robin, the victim of debtor's prison and the death
of all his family; here is the Bastille prisoner who befriends a spider
and sees it crushed by his tyrannical keeper; here is honest Jack the
sailor, wounded by war's horrors but saved by his sagacious dog;
here are a picturesque Welsh harper ruined by a despotic landlord, a
shopwoman ruined by rich customers who won't pay their bills,
starving workers ruined by fickle consumer taste. With its debts to
such female predecessors as Barbauld, Trimmer, and Genlis and its
prefigurings of the *Rights of Woman*, the book at once traces representative patterns in Georgian women's juvenilia and forecasts reformist themes in Wollstonecraft's later work.

These motifs fuse in the person of Mason, the book's vital center;
Original Stories is, above all, her story. She embodies the teaching
heroine, the maternal persona, in her most rigorous and revealing
guise. Like such mother-governesses as the Baroness d'Almane and
the Marquise de Clémire in Genlis's *Adelaide and Theodore* (1782) and
Tales of the Castle (1784), Mason forms the text with her explanations, anecdotes, and histories, and she stars within it. She steers her
wards through carefully selected tales and experiences; she guides
the reader through the book. As heroic exemplar, she is herself a
text, whose message adolescent Mary and Caroline must decipher
and internalize. Her background is only gradually revealed, so the
girls spend some time speculating—as must more mature readers—
on how her character and actions are to be interpreted. She and
mother-teacher figures like her generate complex pedagogical relationships. The teacher in the tale educates her pupils—and often
serves as moral guide to adults in her community as well. At the same
time, the fictional instructor readies her audience of child and
parent readers to export Georgian faith in moral regeneration
through education into the real world.

Sometimes, too, creating a fictional pedagogue may teach the
writer herself lessons serviceable later in her career, as the *Stories*
hint was the case with Wollstonecraft. The book meant much more

to its author than the immature potboiler soon forgotten for more radical projects that some critics see. No one seems to have noticed that Wollstonecraft was meticulously revising the 1788 first edition—word by word, line by line—while *Rights of Woman* was gestating in her head. Her changes do not repudiate her earlier conception; rather, they emphasize that educational reform moves along a continuum from the child to the family and thence to its environing culture. Educated children presuppose educated mothers; cultural change depends on improved instruction. If Mason echoes the religiosity, "Moral Discipline," and redemptive faith in education that inform the *Education of Daughters*, she also anticipates Wollstonecraft's set piece on female "virtue and dignity" in the *Rights of Woman*, the widow whose "affection gives a sacred heroic cast to her maternal duties." "Raised to heroism by misfortunes," this good mother updates and feminizes the parable of the talents, employing her "independent principles" to "see her children attain a strength of character sufficient to enable them to endure adversity without forgetting their mother's example." Like the widow of Wollstonecraft's paean, like the wise matrons in other women's tales, Mason exemplifies that "enlightened maternal affection" so central to Wollstonecraft's feminist agenda in the *Rights*. "It is time to effect a revolution in female manners—time to restore to them their lost dignity—and make them, as a part of the human species, labour by reforming themselves to reform the world" (90–91, 226, 84). In measurable ways, Mason serves as dress rehearsal for her creator's later educational reformism.[2]

Apparently, however, she is a heroine whom no one but a Georgian audience will much like. The *Monthly Review* praised the *Stories'* "excellent principles and morals" and their "judicious and engaging manner" (271–72). The *Analytical Review* found them "the production of a mind that can think and feel . . . calculated to convey instruction in the most pleasing form" (478–79). Perhaps Wollstonecraft's most popular book, the work was reprinted for generations, but Mason has received a bad press in the twentieth century. The terms of the modern disapproval are revelatory—and relevant to historical children's literature other than Wollstonecraft's. Mason is criticized for the content of the stories that she tells and for the attitude toward children (and also, one suspects, toward women) that she typifies. A Blake critic who prefers *Songs of Innocence* faults her "bleak view of existence" (Welch 5); she "leads the children to dark and eerie places and there recounts to them unwholesome stories of death and insanity as the result of wrongdoing" (Meigs et al. 82). Florence V. Barry equates "hard grip of Reason" and "monstrous creation" (116); sixty years later, the most recent critic echoes her assessment (Summerfield 229). "Let us flee," Paul Hazard cries. "There is a whole battalion of these fearsome women: Hannah More, Mary Wollstonecraft, who undertook to transform young girls into essentially reasonable creatures." Moreover, "to instruct and amuse at the same time" is "hopeless" (37). According to E. V. Lucas, whose introduction to the 1906 reprint of *Original Stories* laid down an interpretive line uncannily echoed for eighty years (even by many Wollstonecraft biographers), "The great fault of Mrs. Mason is that she had none." And he pays a backhanded compliment to her mythic resonance: "A new kind of nightmare has come into my slumbers . . . The greatness and goodness of Mrs. Mason surround me, dominate me, suffocate me . . . She knows not only everything, but herself too: she has no doubts . . . The awful reality of Mrs. Mason proves that Mary Wollstonecraft . . . might have been a great novelist." Revealingly, Lucas pictures himself as a small boy on the losing end of a power relationship, his "neatly-gloved hand" firmly clasped by an authoritative mother-figure: "Mrs. Mason was the first and strongest British Matron" (xii–xiii). Even F. J. Harvey Darton cannot resist accusing Mason (and Rosamond's mother in Edgeworth's tales) of glass eyes and a wooden tail, like the new mother in Mrs. W. K. Clifford's *Anyhow Stories* of a century later. "You hate the mother" because "you know she is right" (196, 141).

All amusement and mock awe, these patronizing commentaries betray a nostalgia for postromantic childhood, especially girlhood, as a golden world free of trouble—and reason. Refusing to face the issues the genre raises, they lump "didactic" stories together and dismiss them as literary curiosities. Most recently, the moral tale such as Wollstonecraft's has been portrayed even more dismissively as transparent sociocultural record: crass propaganda for a purely materialistic bourgeois ideology or for stereotyped sex-role repression (I. Kramnick; Agress). Only Ellen Moers, recognizing motherhood as a historical locus of power and attending to the nuances of women's writing, offers a sentence of praise for *Original Stories*: "one of the best of all 'courtesy books,' " a demonstration of "the firm grasp that educating heroism requires" (228, quoting Hemlow; 217). If historians of children's literature misidentify their discomfort with the tales, they are, Moer's remarks suggest, nevertheless responding to a real dimension of these works, the subtext of the educational enterprise: maternal aggression, seduction, domination, power.

Wollstonecraft's book illustrates what happens when serious pedagogic theory is filtered through "educating heroinism," when *girls* learn "principles of truth and humanity" (vi). *Original Stories* is a "female *Sandford and Merton*," pronounces one; Mrs. Mason, a "Mr. Barlow in petticoats" or "a female super-Barlow," others agree. Alternatively, she is the "female counterpart" to Rousseau's pedagogue or even "a kind of female Sir Charles Grandison."[3] But Wollstonecraft, like most sister contemporaries, develops her moral success tale differently from these male authors. Émile's is the world of the isolated natural *man*; Day's is a saga of British manliness, full of yeomanly courage and Crusoelike survival strategies gleaned from adventurous travels. The most memorable mother in his book is the archetypally silly Mrs. Merton, who has so spoiled her son that Mr. Barlow needs three volumes to straighten him out. For Rousseau and for Day, boys are the models of human development; Sophie's training in feminine passivity and Day's few pages on Selene's schooling in rationality—by her father—are authorial afterthoughts.[4] But, as in the typical woman's nursery novel, girls are the focus of Wollstonecraft's tale, and the way the book construes the world is conditioned by female experience and values.

Bereft of their mother, "shamefully ignorant" and chock-full of prejudices, Caroline, twelve, and Mary, fourteen, are placed "under the tuition of a woman of tenderness and discernment," Mrs. Mason. Following the ripened "suggestions of her own reason," Mason inducts her charges into the world of experience, and she inculcates women's ways of coping with this hard world: rational reflection and religion, self-command and charity, "strength of mind" and a humanitarian maternal ethic. Shadowed by poverty and death, populated by tormented animals, severed families, and social victims gone mad from grief, the world of *Orginal Stories from Real Life* assumes a symbolic dimension (vii–viii, 157); Mason's girl-centered lessons in moral autonomy and cultural responsibility not only envision social melioration, but actually bring it about in miniature. Even while she is converting pupils with classic feminine flaws—vanity, "a turn for ridicule"—into mirrors of the enlightened female ideal she so tirelessly enacts, she interprets, controls, and heals the microcosmic world of the *Stories* (xii). The portrayal of Mason is tied to the actual facts of Wollstonecraft's governessing (like Genlis, she even used the pupils' very names and faults), but Mason also embodies female fantasies of heroism. She is a dream of strength and power. Barred from participation in Georgian sociopolitical life, the tales suggest, women can redefine power as the realization of internal capacities, as spiritual aspiration, as pedagogic and philanthropic power. Oriented toward woman's roles and opportunities, Wollstonecraft's maternal pedagogy both shows and tells how girl and parent readers can reform themselves to help reform the world. In glorifying female moral agency, the book demonstrates how qualities culturally associated with women—nurturing, empathy, the habit of thinking in terms of human relationships—are vitally needed in the larger community.

Under Mason's guidance, Mary and Caroline serve a carefully structured apprenticeship that eventuates in their rational and affective awakening: "I hope you have learned to think," Mason comments as they near the end of tuition, "and that your hearts have felt the emotions of compassion" (168). As Mason is a model for maternal readers, so her protégées eventually become patterns for girlish emulation. Like the heroines of *Little Women*, these sisters are a bit older than the presumed audience, the better to serve this function. But first the girls have to be cured of squashing snails, throwing temper tantrums, lying, ridiculing cripples, dawdling, primping, stuffing until they are sick, or spending all their money on frippery. Wollstonecraft does not set up a good child versus a bad one, as Day does, for example. (Her characters, like Edgeworth's Rosamond, are refreshingly prone to lapses right up to the penultimate chapter.) Each sister has her own differentiated pattern of flaws, the same follies that get taken down by other women writers such as Genlis.[5] Indolent Mary procrastinates and fancies herself a wit, for example. Prettier Caroline affects airs to display her fine features and has trouble foreseeing consequences and controlling her appetite. When a poor family needs help, she can only wish the "paltry ornaments she had thoughtlessly bought, in the bottom of the sea," and when the trio's morning walk strategically brings them upon breakfasting pigs, she "blushed, she saw this sight was meant for her, and she felt ashamed of her gluttony" (172, 78).

Wollstonecraft's pedagogic fictions trace the girls' advance toward a revitalized ideal of women as reasonable, responsible—and hence virtuous—beings, away from the eighteenth-century stereotype of females as erratic creatures of feeling, in Chesterfield's phrase, only "children of a larger growth"—passive, weak in mind and body, charming, frivolous, fixated on beauty (Chesterfield 66). The conduct books' list of feminine traits, newly sentimentalized by Rousseau, adds up to thoughtless immaturity: "Most women, and men too, have no character at all," as Wollstonecraft sardonically rephrases Pope in *The Education of Daughters* (111). When mother-teachers praise grownupness—enlightened reflection and disciplined action—their intention is not to shortchange girlhood. Quite otherwise. They believe that young heroines like Wollstonecraft's sisters and Edgeworth's Rosamond, culturally disposed toward puerility, need special help in forming "a taste for truth and realities" (*Early Lessons* 121). Contemporary maternal readers alive to the background of dispiriting commonplaces would appreciate why the new rational pedagogy acquires a special resonance and urgency in women writers.

Countering the equation of femininity with arrested development, Wollstonecraft's Mary and Caroline learn to take themselves seriously as accountable beings. Their opportunities may lie close to home, but the book insists these are not trivial. Fulfilling "apparently insignificant duties," the girls must "do all the good you can the present day, nay hour" (41, 94). The sisters move beyond girlish egocentrism toward the "accomplished and dignified mind that relies on itself" and the "tender, social heart" that characterize the book's mature role models (46, 139). Not only in Mason, but in other central characters, the *Stories* offer affirming images of womanly experience and achievement, patterns of selfhood for mimetic pupils and readers to follow. A benchmark of virtue throughout the book, Mrs. Trueman, the curate's wife, plays the bourgeois matron in the kind of domestic idyll Wollstonecraft was fond of throughout her career (such idylls punctuate her letters as well as the *Rights*). Exemplary in her companionate marriage, she turns "a most excellent understanding, and a feeling heart; sagacity and tenderness, the result of both" toward "her children, whom she teaches in the most persuasive manner, important truths and elegant accomplishments" (59, 47). Because she has "received the most liberal education" in youth, her whole life contrasts with that of her cousin, Lady Sly, whose poor childhood training is now augmented by "the want of rational employments" (48, 43), a second edition insertion that not only heightens the contrast with Mrs. Trueman, but also marks Wollstonecraft's progress toward the *Right of Woman's* central contrast: the idle fine lady versus the civic-minded mother who forms citizens.

Anna Lofty, the spinster schoolmarm whom Mason has assisted toward earning "her own subsistence," offers yet another paradigm of educating heroinism. When her weak father kills himself in remorse following a duel of honor, she rejects life as a "humble companion" to her fashionable relatives: "When I am my own mistress, the crust I earn will be sweet" (136, 138). Like Mason herself, Anna now "seems above the world and its trifling commotions." Since the teacher's "spirit of independence," her "elevated" character, her heart "regulated by her understanding," and her painful awareness of women's limited work options suggest those of her creator, it is not surprising that hers is the only label name in the first edition (139, 137, 132; Mrs. Trueman, Lady Sly, Jane Fretful, Mrs. Dowdy, and Mrs Goodwin all bore initials alone). Having heard the histories of how these women have created themselves morally and intellectually, and achieved (in the words of one chapter title) "True Dignity of Character," the girls must begin to approximate the ideals they have learned before they are rewarded by visits to the exemplars themselves.

Like Fielding's or Genlis's or Edgeworth's heroines, Mason's charges thus demonstrate the formation of moral identity, a progress toward principled intelligence that gradually moves them from symbiosis with the mother-mentor toward earned autonomy. Because the girls have been "left entirely to the management of servants, or people equally ignorant," Mason at first keeps a firm rein and "never suffered them to be out of her sight" (vii–viii). With good reason. If she takes them out for a morning's walk, they rush to destroy insects. Omnipresent as the God she likes to say she emulates, she "silently observed their cruel sports, without appearing to do it" (2). Unerringly, she structures the girls' reformation, working symbolically from revering bugs and birds to relieving the dreadful poverty of a London slum family, whose children "come into the world only to crawl half formed,—to suffer, and to die" (172). The pattern, the book eventually reveals, is her own. Rescuing a mother bird from a bad boy, the girls' "hearts now first felt the emotions of humanity," and Mason discloses that tending animals also "humanized my heart, while, like wax, it took every impression; and Providence has since made me an instrument of good—I have been useful to my fellow creatures"; in return, she feels "the greatest pleasure life affords,—that of resembling God, by doing good" (9–11, 17, 6). Mason rewards her pupils with Sarah Trimmer's *Fabulous Histories* (1786; the robin family's story was a nursery staple for over a century): "Give me your hands, my little girls, you have done good this morning, you have acted like rational creatures" (10).

As this introductory episode suggests, Mason is everywhere in the *Stories*—as instructor, raconteur, and behavioral model. She talks up and acts out the mental training that women writers favor over ornamental accomplishments. To teach her lessons of rational thought and moral discrimination, she employs a diversity of techniques. She converts everyday situations into her instructional medium—a bad habit, a passerby, a visit, a natural scene, a holiday festivity. As Madame d'Epinay observes, "une mère vigilante" always turns to account "les heures perdues" (1822 [xv]). Mason also makes rich use of her own experience, recounting histories of people she has known or lives she has touched. "I will tell you a story, that will take stronger hold on your memory than mere remarks," or "I will describe two characters, that will . . . very strongly enforce what I have been saying," or "I every day set you an example," she will start (31, 42, 40). To focus the girls' self-esteem and "virtuous emulation," she points to the book's network of strong, wise women or tells them of a vain beauty who learned good sense from her bout with smallpox (99). To warn them away from their besetting vices, she describes Jane Fretful (another casualty of a "fond weak mother"), whose unrestrained temper broke her mother's heart and laid her own life waste, and Charles Townley, whose continual delays demonstrate that men too can be ruled by "present emotion" and lack "any strength or consistency of character" (31, 85). Finally, to rouse their social conscience and humanitarian aspiration, Mason takes her pupils to view poverty and social injustice, and she rechannels their selfish feelings with stories like crazy Robin's. The histories and visits that educate the girls' imaginations are acutely observed (the natural settings are especially good), and they are indeed often grim—that is what the world looks like through women's eyes, empathically alert to disadvantage and injustice. But Caroline and Mary also learn how women can make a difference in their world, as in the story of the Welsh harper, where Mason's maternal benevolence defeats a landlord's patriarchal oppression. Significantly, all the philanthropic interludes return to focus on Mason herself (just one of the many ways in which the book's very structure reflects its theme): "I might now have been begging about the streets, but for the Madame," sailor Jack typically exclaims (74). When Wollstonecraft wants to mark the girls' progress to resocialization, Mason sends them out alone on a charitable errand "to represent her, and act like women . . . to exercise their own judgment" (108).

As Mason shapes the girls' minds and experiences, the values she stands for and her own character gradually clarify. At first, she seems scary, an enigmatic figure with decided views. Always composed, benevolent, efficient, she will not harm a snail or a spider but can dispatch a suffering lark with an unflinching twist. She crisply defines goodness and virtue; she despises irresolution, gluttony, idleness, lying, and anger. For her, to be human is to be "capable of improvement" (5, 14). Though she only punishes with "quiet steady displeasure," Mary's and Caroline's wrongdoings make them "feel so little in their own eyes, they wished her to smile that they might be something; for all their consequence seemed to arise from her approbation" (52). ("Filial esteem always has a dash of fear mixed with it," Wollstonecraft observes in the *Rights* [237].) Gradually, as the girls progress from prerational childhood toward rational adolescence, Mason reveals a gentler side. She is a widow who lost both husband and daughter in one harsh winter. Through religion, exercise of her understanding, and philanthropic endeavor, she has achieved strength and self-possession. Now she experiences herself as a powerful maternal nurturer; she adopted a poor girl on the death of her own, she presides over something like a female support network, and she busies herself with benevolent projects: perhaps the longest 1791 addition describes her activities among the local poor (77). (Men are curiously peripheral in the work; they are bad, weak, absent—as is Mr. Trueman—or lower-class charitable objects rescued by Mason.)

"To attain any thing great, a model must be held up to our understanding" (126), Mason observes, and as she calmly models herself on God, she redefines the exemplary for female readers. Mason's values are austere but also bracing; her talkiness and ubiquity testify to the urgency of Wollstonecraft's concern. Point by point, Mason discredits the stereotype of femininity as arrested development to offer an alternative model of enlightened womanhood. Within the stereotyped tale of moral success, her maternal rhetoric converts standard moral lessons into heroic female endeavor. By the time she sums up the book's message—"Avoid anger; exercise compassion, and love truth" (176)—the seeming platitudes have been endowed with reformist resonance and autobiographic bite. Take the usual cautions about controlling one's temper, for example. Mason interprets self-mastery not as submission, but as heroism, a woman's way toward autonomy: "It is easy to conquer another; but noble to subdue oneself . . . a proof of superiour sense" (30–31). "Did you," Caroline asks Mary of Mason, "ever see her in a passion? No, said Mary, I do believe that she was never angry in her life" (52; Wollstonecraft strengthened the wording in the second edition to emphasize her exemplar's self-command). Everything to Mason "affords an exercise for virtue" (11)—but her moral object lessons always imply intellectual content; cultivating the mind and enlarging the heart travel together in her lectures, as they do in her creator's letters: "Intellectual and moral improvement seem to me so connected I cannot, even in thought separate them" Wollstonecraft remarks about this time (*Collected Letters* 149).

Mother-teachers, devaluing beauty, insist that women's power derives not from passive charm, but from inner spiritual strength. "Mental acquirements only, give a just superiority," says Mason, and she defines beauty itself as a form of psychic strength: "virtue, internal beauty" as opposed to mere "*bodily* beauty" (66, 61, 54). "It is the proper exercise of our reason that makes us in any degree independent," she advises Mary, and she marks the girl's progress in characteristic terms: "Coming home I called her my friend, and she deserved the name, for she was no longer a child; a reasonable affection had conquered an appetite; her understanding took the lead, and she had practised a virtue" (103, 81). When Mason shows the girls that "Honour consists in respecting yourself," that it is a matter of internal "Truth," that "sincerity" is the "chief strength" of a woman's mind, she counters the weakness and dissimulation urged by male preceptors such as Rousseau and Dr. John Gregory with values drawn from eighteenth-century literature on the sublime (39–41). Wollstonecraft uses natural scenes to allegorize Mason's state of mind—moonlit, wintry landscapes or sublime storms in which Mason walks undaunted, for the "great mind fear[s] not death" (68). To convey her message for female readers that achievement comes from within, Wollstonecraft substitutes the strength, force, and mental expansion associated with the heroic sublime for the littleness, delicacy, and beauty that Rousseau and aestheticians such as Burke equate with womanhood, a strategy she also employs in *A Vindication of the Rights of Men* (1790) and in the *Rights of Woman*.[6] Mason may be "no feminist" in twentieth-century terms, but she richly exemplifies the energy of matronly virtue, and she demonstrates the cultural and literary forms that Georgian women's self-assertion might legitimately take (M. Kramnick vii).

Each of Wollstonecraft's tales mimics the learning process, and the linked stories stop when the child characters have "visibly improved" (161) and learned to "think and act for themselves," as she describes her goal for women in both the *Education of Daughters* and the *Rights* (22; 86). "It is your interest to obey me till you can judge for yourself," the ideal parent in the latter work declares, "but when your mind arrives at maturity, you must only obey me, or rather respect my opinions, so far as they coincide with the light that is breaking in on your own mind" (232). And so "I tremble for you," Mason worries as the book ends, for her pupils must now practice alone what she has preached. She literally inscribes herself on their lives, for maternal pedagogy's parting gift is *Original Stories* itself: "I have written the subjects we have discussed; recur frequently to it

... and you will not feel in such a great degree the want of my personal advice" (176—77). Much as she had earlier incorporated Trimmer's *Fabulous Histories* as a teaching tool within her own text, she makes her object-lessons into a textual object, one that is also a gift to maternal pedagogues outside the tale. And here Wollstonecraft borrows again from the book she thought "wonderfully clever," Genlis's *Adelaide and Theodore*, which similarly concludes when the mother-teacher presents their completed lessons to her students (*Collected Letters* 132; *Adelaide and Theodore* 3: 282—83). Initiates groomed for the mature woman's world of virtuous action, Mary and Caroline are "now candidates for my friendship, and on your advancement in virtue my regard will in future depend" (177). Not surprisingly, Blake images Mason as protective cruciform in his frontispiece to the second edition; under Mason's extended arms, each pupil's hat forms a halo as the girls gaze up at their teacher. Through her own forceful example and through that of other strong women, through her instructive conversations, and through the stories that test the girls' spiritual and moral progress, Mason has demonstrated a favorite theme of the period's women writers: the heroic potential available in ordinary female life, in everyday female roles.

Analyzing eighteenth-century uses of typology, Paul Korshin recently remarked on the *Christianus perfectus* and *imitatio Christi* themes in children's literature (260—65), but he failed to notice the feminization and domestication of these patterns in women's juvenilia. Heroic, even Christlike, matrons structure the female mentorial tradition. Sarah Fielding's Mrs. Teachum has "a lively and commanding Eye, insomuch that she naturally created an Awe in all her little Scholars" (102). "I declare I cannot go to sleep," says Wollstonecraft's Mary in her capacity as aspirant to virtue: "I am afraid of Mrs. Mason's eyes . . . I wish I was as wise and as good as she is. The poor woman with the six children . . . said she was an angel, and that she had saved her's and her children's lives . . . Nobody [before] told me what it was to be good. I wish to be a woman . . . and to be like Mrs. Mason" (53—54).[7] In Ellenor Fenn's *Fairy Spectator; or, the Invisible Monitor* (1789), Miss Sprightly similarly begs Mrs. Teachwell for a Fairy Guardian "because she would teach me to be good" and duly receives "a Dialogue in which the Fairy shall converse, and I will give you a Moral for your Dream" (8—9). Fenn also

Frontispiece.

Look what a fine morning it is.—Insects,
Birds, & Animals, are all enjoying existence.

Published by J. Johnson. Sept: 1st 1791.

William Blake's cross and halo shapes make Wollstonecraft's theme of female heroism visually explicit. Notice too the narrower, more functional women's styles at the
close of the eighteenth century. (Frontispiece, *Original Stories* [rev. ed., London: J.
Johnson, 1791].)

regales the readers of her *Female Guardian* (1784) with Genlis's paean to maternal power, and then she translates the French from *The Good Mother* (1779) to be sure no one misses it. In return for her heroic self-command, Genlis's play makes clear, such a mother enjoys total command over her family. Nor does she sacrifice the strong "sense, and that independence of mind" which Wollstonecraft requires "to be a good mother" in the *Rights* (227).

"Health, Learning, Morals, Salvation, depend upon *maternal* Instruction: our Happiness in *this* Life, and the *next*, is the Result of our Mothers' Care:—How highly, then, ought we to revere the name of a Mother!" exults Mrs. Lovechild (alias Fenn), in her tribute to "the most engaging object on earth—a judiciously fond Mother" (*Friend of Mothers* 2). Fenn's *Fables* (1783) again eulogize the force of the "*perfect Mother*. How important the office! how valuable the character!—To such Mothers we look up to form the manners of the rising generation;—to such women, to save a nation from impending ruin, by training its youth to virtue—these are MOTHERS!" (84–85). Likewise, Ann Taylor's popular verses testify to the influence of "My Mother" (1804), and the *Evangelical Magazine* (1809) avers that "mothers can do great things!" Aikin and Barbauld's *Evenings at Home* (1792–96) teach "Presence of Mind" with tales of resolute mothers who face down bulls and tigers or who coach queasy daughters in womanly courage by undergoing bloodletting without turning a hair.[8] Shamefaced Rosamond in Maria Edgeworth's series of early lessons (1801–21) discovers that a disfigured woman who offends her taste was maimed by the fire from which she saved her granddaughter ("The Black Bonnet"). In the key chapter of *Original Stories*, "Fortitude the Basis of Virtue," Mason lectures Caroline for weeping over a wasp sting and sternly informs her that a "great" mind "knows how to endure," that she requires "proper pride," "firmness," and "strength of mind"—the "just pride" and "noble ambition" that her older sister begins to evince. To "hold fast virtue as the only substantial good," the girls must eschew self-indulgence for the *Rights'* heroic "power . . . over themselves," for the very "term virtue," Mason significantly observes, "comes from a word signifying strength" (155–60; *Rights* 107).[9]

Wollstonecraft thus makes explicit the equation that informs women's juvenilia. These women's imaginations conjoin forti-

P. 94

Be calm, my child, remember that you must do all the good you can the present day.

Published by J. Johnson, Sept.ʳ 1. 1791.

Firmly but protectively, Mrs. Mason urges her charges to face the melancholy setting of an instructive story. Blake's engraving captures the poetic quality of Wollstonecraft's natural description. (*Original Stories* [rev. ed., London: J. Johnson, 1791].)

tude and fostering; their construct of mothering unites self-respect and responsibility with an active and resistant virtue which is neither self-indulgent nor unaware. Reflective and competent, always alert to consequences, the Mentorias of makebelieve possess the rationality to choose the good and the self-command to follow it. Theirs is an energetic vocabulary full of moral exercise and shaping up; their womanly virtues, sturdier than the usual conduct book ascriptions, run to self-control, endurance, usefulness, and an unsentimental compassion with a decided social reference. They specialize in moral management, of the self and of others. They both embody and love to talk about the power of being good and doing good. Mentorias never speak of women's rights, but they make large strategic claims for female nature and capacities and for woman's ability to make a difference in her social world. Because they think in terms of moral solutions, of personal philanthropy or pedagogy, for example, we may slight their reformism, but not their family likeness, their grave, intelligent look. The very fashions caught in the period's illustrations—slender, crisp, erect—echo their moral posture, their unexpected powers of action and self-control. Busily benevolent, morally ambitious, the upright matrons who people the world of Georgian children's fiction strive to revise that world in accordance with their female construct of values. We need not deny the importance of Locke, Rousseau, or R. L. Edgeworth to recognize Mrs. Mason's kinship with Mrs. Benson and Mama Redbreast in Trimmer's history of the robins or with Rosamond's mother in "The Purple Jar" and others of Maria Edgeworth's lessons for girls. Mutatis mutandis, Wollstonecraft's earnest Mrs. Mason typifies a whole body of female authority figures: the Mrs. Lovechilds, Teachums, and Teachwells, the Mentorias and Arabella Arguses, the Rational Dames, the Moral Mothers, the Female Guardians, Preceptors, and Instructors, as women writers of juvenilia like to imagine themselves.

These paradigms of benign and powerful maternal governance and good girlhood reflect both female fantasies and real cultural change. On the one hand, they read nurture as power, showing a decided preference for maturity over the childishness male preceptors recommend to women and perhaps also evincing a longing to have been nurtured themselves, for a surprisingly large number of the period's women writers record unhelpful or absent mothers. On the other hand, the little books of the "lady writers," as one historian of juvenilia summarily brands them, encode more complex social messages than the belittling epithet suggests (Townsend). They capture emergent notions of the family, women, children, and pedagogy, and they clearly outline an evolving concept of motherhood, that "substantive redefinition of the maternal role" that current social historians situate in this key transitional period (Bloch 113). With their homely plots where small actions have large moral implications and where women, children, and the lowly are taken seriously as moral agents, the little books tidily demonstrate women writers' resourceful exploitation of the available literary and cultural conventions to suit their own ends. To analyze the content and implications of the tiny tales domestic heroines inhabit is to gain fresh insight into the ways in which women writers both shape and are shaped by their historical milieu. And it is to recognize in their self-conscious didacticism a resilient and purposeful maternal discourse, a female mode of cultural reform directed toward improvement of both self and community.

Notes

Research for this project was facilitated by grants from the Children's Literature Association and the American Philosophical Society and by the courteous assistance of the Children's Book Collection, UCLA.

1. Scholarship in this period's family history is a growth industry. For representative examples, see Stone, Lorence, Plumb, Bloch, and Cott. The American patterns of maternal instruction that Bloch and Cott describe follow eighteenth-century English patterns.

2. Wollstonecraft's revisions show her in the process of working out a feminist position, for instance, when she expands a sentence on neat dress to make it "an essential part of a man's as well as a woman's duty" (97). Chapter 10 of the *Rights*, "Parental Affection" (which is filled with parallels to the *Stories*), shows how the thinking mother is central to Wollstonecraft's feminism, a point further developed in my "Reform or Ruin: 'A Revolution in Female Manners.' "

3. *Saturday Review* 294; Repplier 159; Darton 196; Thwaite 73; Korshin 265.

4. Sophie emerges only in Book 5 of *Émile*, when the hero's education is complete and he needs a mate; Day devotes but two pages in the third volume to female education. Wollstonecraft's argument in the *Rights* is in large part a refutation of Rousseau's ideal of womanhood. She quotes Day approvingly, not knowing that his real-life views were less liberal than his story (*Rights* 77–78, quoting Day 3: 205–07). Maria Edgeworth satirized the retrograde notions of Day that postponed her own literary career in *Letters for Literary Ladies* (1795).

5. The first of Genlis's *Tales of the Castle*, "Delphine: or, the Fortunate Cure," similarly rehabilitates a girl whose mother "wanted fortitude and strength of mind to give her daughter a proper education" (1:15).

6. See, for example, *Rights of Men* 2, 6, 111. Wollstonecraft's use of Burke's sublime is documented in Myers on *Rights of Men* and Paulson.

7. As McAleer's biography of Wollstonecraft's eldest pupil makes clear, Wollstonecraft herself inspired similar enthusiasm. In later years Margaret King, the original for Mary, adopted "Mrs. Mason" in the place of her own name, wrote about children, and testified to her "unbounded admiration" (5).

8. Mrs. Barbauld is usually credited with most of *Evenings at Home*, and even such recent scholarship as I. Kramnick's essay perpetuates the misimpression. According to the family editors, however, she wrote only 15 of 101 pieces. "Presence of Mind" is her brother's.

9. Wollstonecraft typically turns the equation that Émile's tutor uses to control his pupil's sexuality (408) toward endorsing women's moral power.

Works Cited

Agress, Lynne. "Mothers and Children: The Relegated Roles." *The Feminine Irony: Women on Women in Early-Nineteenth-Century English Literature.* Rutherford: Fairleigh Dickinson UP; London: Associated U Presses, 1978. 78−86.

Aikin, Dr. [John], and Mrs. [Anna Laetitia] Barbauld. *Evenings at Home, or, the Juvenile Budget Opened.* 1792−96. Ed. Arthur Aikin and Miss [Lucy] Aikin. Rev. 15th ed. London: Baldwin and Cradock, et al., 1836.

Rev. of *Original Stories. Analytical Review* 2 (1788): 478−80.

"Argus, Arabella." *The Juvenile Spectator; being Observations on the Tempers, Manners, and Foibles of Various Young Persons, Interspersed with such Lively Matter, as It Is Presumed Will Amuse as Well as Instruct.* London: Darton, 1810.

Barry, Florence V. *A Century of Children's Books.* 1922. New York: Doran, 1924.

Bloch, Ruth H. "American Feminine Ideals in Transition: The Rise of the Moral Mother, 1785−1815." *Feminist Studies* 4 (1978): 101−26.

Buchan, William. *Advice to Mothers* [1803]. In *The Physician and Child-Rearing: Two Guides, 1809−1894.* Medicine and Society in America. New York: Arno Press; New York Times, 1972.

Burke, Edmund. *A Philosophical Inquiry into the Origin of our Ideas of the Sublime and Beautiful.* 1757. Ed. J. T. Boulton. London: Routeldge and Keagan Paul, 1958.

Chesterfield, Philip Dormer Stanhope. To his son. 5 September 1748. *Lord Chesterfield's Letters to his Son and Others.* Introd. R. K. Root. Everyman's Library. 1929. London: Dent; New York: Dutton, 1963. 63−67.

Chodorow, Nancy, and Susan Contratto. "The Fantasy of the Perfect Mother." *Rethinking the Family: Some Feminist Questions.* Ed. Barrie Thorne with Marilyn Yalom. New York and London: Longman, 1982. 54−75.

Clifford, Mrs. W. K. [Lucy]. "The New Mother." *Anyhow Stories, Moral and Otherwise.* London: Macmillan, 1882, 8−47.

Cott, Nancy F. "Notes toward an Interpretation of Antebellum Childrearing." *Psychohistory Review* 6 (1978): 4−20.

Darton, F. J. Harvey. *Children's Books in England: Five Centuries of Social Life.* 1932. 3rd ed. rev. by Brian Alderson. Cambridge: Cambridge UP, 1982.

Day, Thomas. *The History of Sandford and Merton.* 1783−89. 3 vols. Classics of Children's Literature, 1621−1932. New York: Garland, 1977.

Edgeworth, Maria. "The Black Bonnet." *Continuation of Early Lessons.* 2 vols. London: J. Johnson, 1814. 1:204−13.

————. *Letters for Literary Ladies*. 1795. The Feminist Controversy in England, 1788–1810. New York: Garland, 1974.

————. *The Parent's Assistant*. 1796. 1800 ed. 6 vols. in 2. Classics of Children's Literature, 1621–1932. New York: Garland, 1976.

Edgeworth, Richard Lovell. "Address to Mothers." *Continuation of Early Lessons. By Maria Edgeworth*. 2 vols. London: J. Johnson, 1814. 1:vii–xxxvi.

[d'Epinay, Louise Florence Pétronille Tardieu d'Eslavelles, marquise]. *Les Conversations d'Émilie*. 1781. Nouvelle éd. Paris: Alexis Eymery, 1822.

"Juvenile Department." *Evangelical Magazine* 17 (1809): 331.

[Fenn, Ellenor]. *Fables by Mrs. Teachwell: in Which the Morals are Drawn Incidentally in Various Ways*. London: John Marshall [1783].

Teachwell, Mrs.[————]. *The Fairy Spectator; or, The Invisible Monitor*. London: J. Marshall, 1789.

[————]. *The Female Guardian. Designed to Correct Some of the Foibles Incident to Girls, and Supply Them with Innocent Amusement for their Hours of Leisure*. London: John Marshall, 1784.

Lovechild, Mrs. [————]. *The Friend of Mothers: Designed to Assist Them in their Attempts to Instil the Rudiments of Language and Arithmetic, at an Early Age, and in a Manner Agreeable to their Children*. London: E. Newbery, 1799.

[————]. *The Rational Dame; or Hints Towards Supplying Prattle for Children*. London: John Marshall [1786].

Fielding, Sarah. *The Governess, or, Little Female Academy*. 1749. Ed. Jill E. Grey. London: Oxford UP, 1968.

Genlis, Madame la Comtesse de [Stéphanie Félicité Ducrest]. *Adelaide and Theodore: or, Letters on Education: Containing All the Principles Relative to Three Different Plans of Education*. 1782. Trans. "some ladies." 3rd ed. 3 vols. London: T. Cadell, 1788.

————.*Tales of the Castle: or Stories of Instruction and Delight, Being Les Veillées du Château*. 1784. Trans. Thomas Holcroft. 2nd ed. 5 vols. London: Robinson, 1785.

————.*The Good Mother*, in *Theatre of Education*. 1779–80. Trans. anon. 4 vols. London: T. Cadell, P. Elmsly, and T. Durham, 1781. 2:241–374.

Gregory, Dr. [John]. *A Father's Legacy to His Daughters*. New ed. London: W. Strahan, 1774.

Hazard, Paul. *Books, Children, and Men*. 1944. Trans. Marguerite Mitchell. 5th ed. Boston: Horn Book, 1983.

Helme, Elizabeth. *Maternal Instruction; or, Family Conversations, on Moral and Entertaining Subjects, Interspersed with History, Biography, and Original Stories*. 1802. 3rd ed. London: Longman, Hurst, Rees, and Orme, 1810.

Hemlow, Joyce. "Fanny Burney and the Courtesy Books." *PMLA* 65 (1950): 732–61.

Janes, R. M. "On the Reception of Mary Wollstonecraft's *A Vindication of the Rights of Woman*." *Journal of the History of Ideas* 39 (1978): 293–302.

Korshin, Paul J. *Typologies in England, 1650–1820*. Princeton: Princeton UP, 1982.

Kramnick, Isaac. "Children's Literature and Bourgeois Ideology: Observations on Culture and Industrial Capitalism in the Later Eighteenth Century." *Culture and Politics from Puritanism to the Enlightenment*. Ed. Perez Zagorin. Berkeley: U of California P, 1980. 203–40.

Kramnick, Miriam Brody. Preface. *Original Stories from Real Life*. By Mary Wollstonecraft. Classics of Children's Literature, 1621–1932. New York: Garland, 1977. [A reprint of the 1788 1st ed.] iii–xi.

Lively, Penelope. "Children and the Art of Memory: Part I." *Horn Book* 54 (1978): 17–23.

Lorence, Bogna W. "Parents and Children in Eighteenth-Century Europe." *History of Childhood Quarterly* 2 (1974): 1–30.

Lovechild, Mrs., *see* Fenn, Ellenor.

Lucas, E. V. Editor's introduction. *Mary Wollstonecraft's Original Stories.* London: Henry Frowde, 1906. [A reprint of the 1791 rev. ed.] iii—xiii.

McAleer, Edward C. *The Sensitive Plant: A Life of Lady Mount Cashell.* Chapel Hill: U of North Carolina P, 1958.

Meigs, Cornelia, et al. *A Critical History of Children's Literature.* New York: Macmillan, 1953.

Moers, Ellen. "Educating Heroinism: Governess to Governor." *Literary Women.* Garden City: Doubleday, 1976. 211—42.

Rev. of *Original Stories. Monthly Review* 79 (1788): 271—72.

Muir, Percy. "A Monstrous Regiment." *English Children's Books, 1600 to 1900.* New York: Praeger, 1954. 82—99.

Murry, Ann. *Mentoria: or, The Young Ladies Instructor, in Familiar Conversations on Moral and Entertaining Subjects.* London: Edward and Charles Dilly, 1778.

Myers, Mitzi. "Politics from the Outside: Mary Wollstonecraft's First *Vindication.*" *Studies in Eighteenth-Century Culture.* Vol. 6, ed. Ronald C. Rosbottom. Madison: U of Wisconsin P, 1977. 113—32.

————. "Reform or Ruin: 'A Revolution in Female Manners.'" *Studies in Eighteenth-Century Culture.* Vol. 11, ed. Harry C. Payne. Madison: U of Wisconsin P, 1982. 199—216.

Patterson, Sylvia W. *Rousseau's Émile and Early Children's Literature.* Metuchen, NJ: Scarecrow, 1971.

Paulson, Ronald. *Representations of Revolution (1789—1820).* New Haven: Yale UP, 1983. 79—87.

Pestalozzi, Johann Heinrich. *Pestalozzi's Leonard and Gertrude.* 1781. Trans. and abr. Eva Channing. Boston: Ginn, Heath, 1895.

Pickering, Samuel F., Jr. *John Locke and Children's Books in Eighteenth-Century England.* Knoxville: U of Tennessee P, 1981.

Plumb, J. H. "The New World of Children in Eighteenth-Century England." *Past and Present* 67 (1975): 64—93.

Repplier, Agnes. *A Happy Half-Century and Other Essays.* Boston: Houghton Mifflin; Cambridge: Riverside Press, 1908.

Rousseau, Jean Jacques. *Émile.* 1762. Trans. Barbara Foxley. Everyman's Library. London: Dent; New York: Dutton, 1911.

"A Female Sandford and Merton." *Saturday Review* 102 (1906): 294.

Showalter, Elaine. Rev. of *The Child Figure in English Literature*, by Robert Pattison, and *Guardians and Angels: Parents and Children in Nineteenth-Century Literature*, by David Grylls. *Nineteenth-Century Fiction* 34 (1979): 234—38.

Smith, Hugh. *Letters to Married Women, on Nursing and the Management of Children.* 1767. 1st Amer. ed. from 6th London ed. Philadelphia: Matthew Carey, 1792.

Stone, Lawrence. *The Family, Sex and Marriage in England 1500—1800.* New York: Harper and Row, 1977.

Summerfield, Geoffrey. *Fantasy and Reason: Children's Literature in the Eighteenth Century.* Athens: U Georgia P, 1985.

Taylor, Ann. "My Mother." 1804. *The Oxford Book of Children's Verse.* Ed. Iona and Peter Opie. London: Oxford UP, 1973. 114—15.

Teachwell, Mrs., *See* Fenn, Ellenor.

Thwaite, Mary F. *From Primer to Pleasure in Reading.* Rev. ed. Boston: Horn Book, 1972.

Townsend, John Rowe. "Rousseau and the Lady Writers." *Written for Children: an Outline of English-language Children's Literature.* Rev. ed. Boston: Horn Book, 1974. 36—46.

Trimmer, Sarah. *Fabulous Histories*. 1786. Classics of Children's Literature, 1621–1931. New York: Garland, 1977.

———. *The Guardian of Education, A Periodical Work . . . conducted by Mrs. Trimmer*. London: Hatchard, 1802–06.

Wakefield, Priscilla. *Mental Improvement: or, the Beauties and Wonders of Nature and Art. In a Series of Instructive Conversations*. 1794. 3rd ed. 3 vols. London: Darton and Harvey, 1797.

Welch, Dennis M. "Blake's Response to Wollstonecraft's *Original Stories*." *Blake: An Illustrated Quarterly* 13 (1979): 4–15.

[Wollstonecraft, Mary]. Rev. of *The Parent's Assistant. Analytical Review* 24 (1796): 426–28.

———. *Collected Letters of Mary Wollstonecraft*. Ed. Ralph M. Wardle. Ithaca: Cornell UP, 1979.

———. *Elements of Morality, for the Use of Children, with an Introductory Address to Parents*. Trans. and rev. from C. G. Salzmann. 3 vols. London: J. Johnson, 1791.

———. *The Female Reader; or Miscellaneous Pieces in Prose and Verse; Selected from the Best Writers, and Disposed under Proper Heads; for the Improvement of Young Women*. 1789. Introd. Moira Ferguson. Del Mar, NY: Scholars' Facsimiles and Reprints, 1980.

———. *Original Stories from Real Life; with Conversations, Calculated to Regulate the Affections, and Form the Mind to Truth and Goodness*. 1788. 2nd ed. London: J. Johnson, 1791.

———. *Thoughts on the Education of Daughters: with Reflections on Female Conduct in the More Important Duties of Life*. 1787. Reprints of Economic Classics. Clifton, NJ: Augustus M. Kelley, 1972.

———. *A Vindication of the Rights of Men (1790)*. Introd. Eleanor Louise Nicholes. Gainsville, FL: Scholars' Facsimiles and Reprints, 1960.

———. *A Vindication of the Rights of Woman, with Strictures on Political and Moral Subjects*. 1792. Ed. Charles W. Hagelman, Jr. Norton Library. New York: W. W. Norton, 1967.

Schooling through Fiction

Joanna Gillespie

> *It has been my design, in this little book, to direct the minds of children to subjects of higher importance than those which generally occupy the pages of books put into their hands . . . the silly stories which their fathers read in their childhood will soon be, perhaps in a double sense, "tales of other times."*
>
> —William M'Gavin, 1849

Frontispiece to *The Week; or the Practical Duties of the Fourth Commandment* (New York: Emory and Waugh for the Methodist Episcopal Church, 1829).

Illustrations reproduced by permission of the Drew University Library, Madison, New Jersey.

Nearly all early nineteenth-century children's literature was instructive, but the authors of Sunday school library books were completely forthright about "schooling" the reader. Imagery and illustration were selected, consciously and unconsciously, to promote an (as they saw it) achievable model of living. In the late eighteenth and early nineteenth centuries zealous English and American writers were impelled to new literary outpourings by their global mandate to evangelize, and American Protestant publishing houses produced thousands of hardbound, pocket-size (4" × 6") volumes aimed at a specific end—schooling through the schoolbook. Fed by British imports as well as the products of American evangelicals, Sunday school fiction was the nineteenth-century equivalent of today's educational film: prescription was cloaked in a form usually associated with pleasure.[1]

Writing morally improving fiction that would shape the rising generation of American children seemed like an opportunity sent literally from heaven for the ambitious, if often anonymous, Sunday school writer. And print-starved readers in burgeoning cities and new frontier settlements consumed masses of it, to judge from contemporary reports of itinerant Methodist preachers and journal-keeping mothers. By the mid-nineteenth century the popularity of didactic religious stories had helped to both create and supply a new market in children's literature.[2]

This essay approaches such unabashedly ideological nineteenth-century children's literature from the author's point of view because the Sunday school library was in effect a writer's market; Sunday school commissions or superintendents, not the individual consumers, were the buyers of these little books, and one way we can perceive the writers' intentions is by reimmersing ourselves in the "school" of the stories in their own times. That in turn requires a reawakened sympathy for the emotions which shaped these children's stories, as well as for their readers.

Often evangelical writers appear to have adopted wholesale the literary conventions of a genre firmly established in the English tract stories of Hannah More (1745–1833) and later Mrs. Mary Butts Sherwood (1775–1851), a widely reprinted writer. Their stories, imitating older hagiographic works, generally centered on the conversion of a child or young adolescent. The beneficent influence of that child on family or friends was traced, leading to a crisis (often consumption) and a Christian apotheosis. Christian dying was the educational core of the tale for fictional witnesses and the actual readers, because such final triumphs could happen to ordinary people like the readers—to Mary Sherwood's Little Henry and the dairyman's daughter immortalized by the Rev. Legh Richmond—not just to nobles or sages. Storytellers were determined to shape their childish readers through writing about a world filled with recognizable Christians whose lives were not unlike those of their readers. The children's literature that followed in the wake of More's *Cheap Repository Tracts* (1795) was one expression of the expanded literary realism emerging in the late eighteenth and early nineteenth centuries.

The link with real life was crucial to this story world. Children's fiction promoted both the emotional individualism and the sense of being caught up in a vast modernizing movement that characterized nineteenth-century religion, according to historian Perry Miller. America's leading revivalist of the period, Charles Grandison Finney, proclaimed that "religion without excitement" was boring, absurd, and finally unavailing (Miller 3). Doctrine and traditional authority were subordinated to "the heart" and a new activist energy. To achieve a jubilant sense of empowerment Methodists and other revivalist groups followed a method of self-examination, prayer, scripture study, public worship, and "social religion" gatherings. Even early American Episcopalians were not immune to the contagion of religious excitement; their Sunday school stories, however, treated conversion as a gradual rather than a cataclysmic event, and their treatment of "enthusiasm" was discreet.[3] The new focus on *self* which was encouraged among ordinary folk by these evangelistic tactics contributed to the tone of excitement; as G. Elsie Harrison found in studying the Brontë children, "to *methodize* was to infuse with passion" (135).[4]

Evangelical passion was formative in boys' and girls' own internal psychic development and self-management; it also spilled out visibly into the convert's community, in new charitable activities. The second great wave of evangelical excitement in America, culminating in the 1830s and 1840s, drew upon ideas going back to Locke and Rousseau, ideas about childhood as a time of malleability. Eager evangelicals reaching out to accomplish something in their own neighborhoods seized the then-new idea of free instruction in literacy as a reason to initiate Sabbath day schools. Concomitantly evangelicals grasped at modern technological advances (steam-powered printing presses and inexpensive bindings) to disseminate salvation through a cheap children's literature, hoping it would crowd out the hornbooks and replace the vulgar broadsides then dominating the market in literature written specifically for children. "The words of the preacher vanish with the breath that utters them," one Sunday School Union report acknowledged in 1849, "[but] the words of the printed book will live and speak to generations yet unborn" (102). Practical Methodists recognized the new miracle of inexpensive print as the teacher that never retired.[5]

In general, Sunday school books, whether published interdenominationally to attract a wider readership or consciously promoting a distinctive church doctrine, had two major messages for their readers. They taught that any problem, secular or spiritual, could be broken into manageable components and thereby mastered; and they encouraged the hope that under the sponsorship of God and within the value system of Protestant Christianity, effort would equal success. Those views were peddled in varying degrees by most children's literature of the period, for example the Peter Parley books, but Sunday school fiction gave "success" a scriptural authority that made it accessible to every reader from an Illinois frontier child to a New England shop-girl.[6]

The very ease with which characters in Sunday school stories achieve their goals makes them offensive to us, like heavy-footed fairy tales. Yet their incessant trumpeting of the new possibilities of self-management and "success" undoubtedly encouraged many thousands of naive readers. "Self elevation" (Meyers 176) was becoming the grand American principle and Sunday school how-to stories brought the means right to the farmhouse door, conveyed through "such pictures of life as carry the internal evidence of reality" (Temple 36).

Not many of the Sunday school writers took the time to craft a story that had complexity and finesse; indeed, they seemed to distrust literary skills. Their style, which often started out in a tone of typical authorial detachment, constantly slipped into special pleading and was more like primitive barn-painting than china-painting.

They justified this urgency because they were sure the effect of unstructured, direct storytelling in children's stories was "highly pleasing to the young . . . distorted views and extravagant notions . . . are not relished unless [one's] taste has been perverted. The child craves the simple truth" (Temple 98). Reality was thus the watchword to a representative American Sunday school writer, Abigail Bent (1782–1841). "Narratives of real life, varied from actual occurrence only by fictitious names . . . have the attraction which reality always gives to depicted scenes" (Temple 9). This could be your story, Sunday school authors asserted. In the case of beautiful-death "memoirs," the stories were indeed of Eliza Barker of Brandon, Vermont, dead at eleven (Rose), or Lucy Kent who died in her eighth year in Brookfield, Massachusetts, in 1785 (Kent)—literally girls next door. These "print memorials," which were genuine, constituted the bereaved parents' attempt to prolong a child's memory and thus make such early tragedies accomplish something "useful." The success of their method accounts for fictional imitations adopting the testimonial format. Telling the tale of a life has always been the best "school" for a listener; Sunday school storytellers simply reclaimed that ancient form for the people of the everyday nineteenth-century Anglo-American religious world.

If they lacked construction skills, enthusiasm about their instructional task gave evangelical writers a vivid style which emphasized emotion rather than doctrine. In typical hyperbole, the Methodists described their Sunday school library books as "an arrow directed at the heart" (*Minutes* 69). The thrill of religiously inspired possibilities for change extended itself into a connection with progress in the world at large. Methodist stories were frankly exuberant about new scientific accomplishments; the railroad was "a flying monster," the steamship "a beautiful aquatic palace." New ideas such as those of universal education or unrestricted access to God's grace were rushing through nineteenth-century minds "with the force and grandeur of a majestic river" and would surely "cut a wide, deep, tortuous bed through the social strata," rearranging the whole horizon of human aspiration and opportunity ("Sunday School Literature" 284). In this grand design, Sunday schools were the incarnation of civilization at the local level, bringing education, social respectabilty, and dignity to the citizens of a frontier town—as earlier they had transformed English child factory-workers in the 1780s from "the shape of wolves and tigers into that of man" ("Memoir" 294). "To live forever in the world of example" was the enlarged goal of these Christian writers (Hibbens title page).

Much of the writers' word-play is recognizable as sheer joy in literacy and authorship among people hitherto excluded from publishing their writings. The stories they recorded often instructed their characters, and thus the readers, through the literary device of a school. "School" seems to have been a deeply satisfying "summarizing symbol" for both writers and readers of evangelical children's stories, even if the late twentieth-century reader has difficulty imagining it (Ortner). The controlling metaphor of school permitted Sunday school fiction to achieve its fictionality. Educational need, evangelical imperative, and the new literary realism met felicitously in the medium and message of Sunday school stories.

Two anonymous stories distributed by denominational presses in America in the 1840s, both probably written earlier in the century by English women, exemplify the "school fiction" that so curiously internalized the didacticism of evangelical literature. Each of them idealizes a "school" in which children—and thus the readers—are the focus of a self-dramatizing and empowering story. Even a contemporary reader can be drawn into that process through the emotion evoked by the father-teacher in the first story or the true-to-life pupils in the second.

In *Learning to Feel* (1845),[7] the unknown author pursues a dual agenda. She idealizes a prosperous, warm family school while simultaneously providing rules for those emotions appropriate for a mid-nineteenth century Protestant child. Each chapter deals with a profound abstraction such as sympathy, meekness, or "liberality" in both pedantic and illustrative ways, as the writer's attempt "to aid the cultivation of moral feelings in young children" (5). But here is an unusual family drama in which the father, rather than the mother, is the teacher.[8]

At father's initiative the Railton family gathers each Wednesday after noon-dinner for a "school" session of religious instruction. Mrs. Railton is an assistant to her husband, commissioned to report to him "little incidents occurring in his absence, that he might avail himself of her support in observing the dispositions of the young

This romantic family scene—opposite the title page of *Learning to Feel* (1845)—is undoubtedly an addition for the American edition; it was an unusual editorial decision to include more than one illustration.

people" (22) as they assimilate the moral program. These story parents are firmly and satisfyingly united in their nurturing plans.

Though the characterization is sketchy, the reader warms to the image of family closeness, especiallly the all-knowing and all-protecting father-teacher. Fanny, age three, supplies what comic relief is allowed, as children new to language often do. William, age twelve, is brash and his sister Mary impulsive. The infant on mother's lap isn't named, and there are two other siblings who remain shadowy.

Sunday school writers quite often collapsed both theological and psychological complexities into a system of one-dimensional symbols or literary conventions: the authoritative father, the dutiful child, the "resistless authority" of the mother (Kiefer 77), the contrast between good and naughty sisters, and that holds true here. But in *Learning to Feel*, didacticism and conventionalized portrayals meld into a romance of the family. "There is no more pleasant sight in the world than that of a happy family," the author beams. "Perhaps a more happy family than that of Mr. Railton is not to be found." Of course the writer knew that no family was perfect; "[Mr. Railton] had his crosses and losses; Mrs. Railton had her domestic cares and anxieties . . . yet they feared God, brought up their children to do the same, and they all dwelt together in affection and peace" (45). This religious version of "living happily ever after" could easily translate into an image of God as lovingly in charge of the outside world as father Railton was of his own family world.

For it was within the family that evangelical heroes and heroines were supposed to define their ideals and goals. Secular boys' adventure stories might escape domestic confinement, and the typical stories for women ended at marriage or early death, before the formation of the family; but event and development in Sunday school stories were set almost exclusively within the domestic world. The evangelical writer was articulating a view of Christianity that was "not so much a theology as a cluster of anxieties, values, perceptions and aspirations" (Mathews 58), and stories with school settings, even within a family, constituted a shorthand message to the reader that a carefully designed lesson was underway. The form the "romance quest" for identity—moving from darkness to light—took in such schooling stories was always that of enablement. Whether they were about a prosperous city child in England or an ambitious working-class farm boy in America, evangelical children's stories were not just about socially improving one's position, "though that was certainly part of it, but rather [about] converting children through education from illiteracy, ignorance and powerlessness to learning, power, self-respect, self-discipline, and moral accountability" (Mathews 14).

Within the romance-of-the-family device, the writer of *Learning to Feel* has set the primary enabling device, school. The narrative is in effect a series of lessons. At one level brothers and sisters "play school" with a teacher as important in their lives as dear Papa. At another level, Mr. Railton embodies enlightened pedagogy, instructing the reader how to instruct, for example, by encouraging his children to speak up in an open "holy-day conversation" with him (10). The author's idealization of free exchange between parent and child is part of the story's persuasiveness. Another is the way she affirms the story-pupil's possibilities. Can children really be taught how to feel? "I have learned to read and to write, to sew and to net, because these things have been taught me," muses Mary, "but can I really learn to feel as I ought?" (14). Mary's cry from the heart, articulated by the author, is answered encouragingly by Mr. Railton; of course feelings can be shaped because "they are called forth by our knowledge. A man passing by whom you don't know calls forth little feeling" (13). "To make quick progress in any attainment or study, it is necessary first to fall in love with it," he reasons, and so with right feelings. He often sweetens his instruction with anecdotes though in his rhetoric he firmly opposes fiction. Feeling must be acknowledged and used, but it must also be shaped and directed.

Neither Mr. Railton nor his wife is concerned with pushing children toward the emotional crisis of conversion as their Calvinist predecessors would have been. "Mr. Railton's is one of the many Christian families which set forth how much trouble [innate since the Fall of man] may be mingled with peace, cheerfulness and joy" (103–104). The writer's moderate view of original sin reflected the mid-nineteenth century emancipation from a more severe understanding of damnation, as well as hinting that within a well-schooled family it might somehow be avoided altogether. Set in a cozy fictional family where the Railton children were being schooled to their own self-management, the reader might be led to assent to goodness, rather than be frightened into it.

One of the hallmarks of school fiction was the writer's liberty to voice her views directly through the teacher-character, as well as to deal with contradictory feelings by dramatizing them in the characters of the children. In the third session, Mr. Railton mentions "having seen a mastiff-dog chained to his kennel" and a peacock "standing on the wall spreading his tail at full liberty. These two creatures put me directly in mind of our meeting together to learn to

feel," he states in a leading manner (56). Mary asks how that might
be, and saucy William conjectures that if the mastiff should bite,
they'd feel very quickly indeed! Mrs. Railton disallows such frivolous
meaning, but Mr. Railton draws out the grain of truth in William's
joke. "My meaning is this: when I saw the mastiff chained that might
do a good deal of mischief if allowed to run loose, and the peacock
which gives pleasure to all permitted to wander as he pleased, I
thought to myself . . . [that] when my children have learned to feel
properly they will act as the honest farmer does. I hope they will
keep all bad feelings that would do mischief fast-bound and chained,
and allow all kindly feelings that give pleasure to others free liberty"
(56). A loving father, using vivid analogues for right and wrong
feelings, was a schooling voice with deep appeal for his children and
for willing readers.

In contrast to this enclosed family-school for privileged children
with educated parents, the second story shows us a village school
for girls who would be domestic servants. *My Station and Its Duties* (1830[?] reprinted 1845)[9] offers a visible goal—upward social
mobility—to the pupils who learn the "right feelings" for daily
proximity to the upper classes, through Christian self-management.
For both the Railton children and the village children, "school" is the
vehicle of their romantic quest. The second author, however, is far
more novelistic in detail and skilled in creating believable characters.
The same relations of authority prevail between teacher and pupils
in both the family school and the village servant-school: a child
reader is given a verbal and emotional map by which to shape his or
her life, and the map-giver is seen as a benefactor, not, as we might
assume, a dictator or an oppressor.

The Teacher (who is never named), like Mr. Railton, instructs
through a hidden curriculum—the organization and social-psychological message implicit in the structure of the school itself—as well
as through an overt curriculum of "learning how to feel." Interestingly there is no instruction in specific tasks such as cleaning or
cooking. It is Teacher's thesis that each girl will learn those skills
quickly in a specific household, once her attitudes have been properly schooled. This practical education for the lower classes has the
same general rationale as schooling for the privileged: "It would be a
sad loss to you and to society" (15) if the instructors, father and

Illustration facing the title page of *My Station and Its Duties* (1849). In a different, edited copy (1849) at Drew University Library, this lively scene has been pasted over a picture of a tranquil English village with church, rose-covered cottage, and two bonneted country girls strolling together. Note the hands of the kneeling girl, the drooping shoulders of her companion, and the frayed brushes.

Teacher, were unwilling to do the good work of shaping children according to their enabling world-view.

Two organizational groups are described. The younger girls, probably from six to ten years of age, attend school to learn to read and sew. They are supervised by a group of older girls, probably between the ages of twelve and fifteen, who act as assistant teachers. All in turn are supervised by Teacher. As each group does its assigned work, "some occupied in reading, others in needlework, others in spelling," Teacher circulates among them, "reminding [them] of the stations they were filling at that moment" (16). Here the word "station" is given an existential context along with its occupational and religious content; the present stations of the children are not, as we might assume, the socioeconomic position of their fathers' "employments"—day laboring, shoemaking, tailoring, shopkeeping—which locate the school in the artisan or upper working class where John Wesley's Methodist reforms were most successful.[10] The title phrase and the hierarchical structure of the school reproduce the prevailing mid-nineteenth century British culture and the religious legitimation it enjoyed.

"My station and its duties" was a theme from the 1662 Church of England catechism, still in use by English Methodists in the mid-nineteenth century.

> *Question:* What dost thou chiefly learn by these [the Ten] Commandments?
> *Answer:* Two things, my duty toward God and my duty toward my neighbor.

An extended paragraph then details the latter, ending "to do my duty in that state of life unto which it shall please God to call me" (Shepard 580), that is, in my station. Station was clearly a dimension of one's identity but the girls' stations could not be those of their parents; theirs must be those of child, sister, pupil and school-fellow. Whom does it offend, Teacher asks, if the girls neglect the duties that flow from these stations? Their parents, then each other, then Teacher, and above all God. Teacher concludes this somewhat circular lesson with an evangelical note of self-interest: "Paying these duties will be to your own *advantage*; you will improve; you will attract the regard of those to whom you would render them" (16). Already the reader is eager to see who improves and for what reward.

The identified characters are older girls except for Little Mary. Lucy Fenton is very pretty but vain. Fanny Crocker manages her supervising stint poorly. Some characters are "outsiders"—servant girls who have not had the benefit of Teacher and schooling. Jane Henley, for example, represents the undisciplined and therefore irresponsible worker; Sarah Ingles commits an actual "crime" against her mistress by attempting to read a note sent in confidence, her perfidy implicating two of the schoolgirls. Pretty but immodest Margaret Lonsdale, a school alumna gone wrong, has sunk into prostitution (the word itself is never used). Lucy Fenton's gossipy mother and the over-indulgent father of Maria Goodwin are negative parental types.

On the positive side, Esther Emmet[11] is the author's nominee for model Christian servant girl; she cares for nothing so much as Teacher's approval. Elizabeth Norris is also pleasing to Teacher. But the most interesting character, and the one who gives the reader most scope, is Maria. She is the high-spirited, impulsive, open-hearted model of improvement. Maria makes the greatest change; her visible struggle to harness her emotions, to modify them from being only responses to external authority to being a solid inner-directedness, constitutes the romantic quest of this story.

Focusing the plot on achievable goals, Teacher announces four apprentice-level positions friends have asked her to fill: assistant cook, assistant nursery maid, assistant housekeeper, and assistant lady's maid. "Many eyes sparkled with hope as these various situations were named," (47) because actual jobs "gave rise to desires and hopes among the scholars" (28). And then a test is devised for Esther and Maria. They are to deliver a sealed note to a lady next morning before coming to school and wait to bring back an answer. (Only later is it revealed that the note asks the lady receiving it to designate which of them, Maria or Esther, she chooses to replace Sarah Ingles, the bad maid already given her notice.) Teacher of course explains nothing about the commission, and the girls dare not presume to ask. Winning the approval of Teacher and the future employer, without knowing all the clues and explanations, is the task of self-management set for Maria and the reader.

Next morning Maria's "forwardness" betrays her into rushing off without remembering to wait for Esther. The maids at the lady's house treat her with hostility and contempt; unknown to her, before they deliver the note to their mistress, they "tumble" it in order to discern its contents. (Poor Sarah Ingles, already fired, is illiterate—never having had the privilege of schooling—but she colludes with the parlor maid who reads the note to her.) Generally shaken by the maids' disrespect for their mistress's summons—an overly leisurely response to her bell—and by their rudeness to her, Maria slips out and runs on to school without waiting for an answer, and without realizing the terrible suspicion that is about to fall on her. She is further mortified when Esther reproves her for not obeying Teacher explicitly: they were to do the errand *together* and come back with a reply.

As always, Esther was absolutely right. School convenes and Teacher confronts the girls with the horrid news that somehow the note to the potential employer was received with the seal cracked, as if someone had tried to pry it open. Unravelling this "crime," bringing the culprit to justice, and conquering the unschooled emotions that precipitated this crisis constitute the romantic denouement of the story. In line with the approved reward structure, Maria and Esther each earn one of the coveted jobs. In addition to teaching the schoolgirls what is acceptable and unacceptable behavior, the author confirms the right and wrong kinds of ambition. The good parents of Esther "stood prepared for her going out to service . . . as that they would most desire for their child" (182), while the bad mother of Lucy Fenton was accused of the worst possible designs—of "knowing how to make tea-drinkings and invite people, and set [her daughter] off, thinking to get a gentleman and make her face [Lucy's] a lady's face" (122).

Conflict between the schoolgirls and the unschooled maids illustrates the important teaching that would-be maids must rise above their origins. The working maids envy the schooled maids for their ability to read, for having a mentor in Teacher, and for manners and attitudes which make the unschooled maids feel inferior. The move from working-class homes to noble houses is more than just an occupational step, the reader begins to realize; it involves reshaping the schooled maids into a new view of themselves. They are learning an entirely new set of "feeling rules" through the evangelical principles honored in their school. A revised sense of *self* and *place* is the purpose of their curriculum and the message for their eager readers.

An illustrative moment early in the story lets the reader participate in Maria's learning. After announcing the four jobs she must fill, Teacher invited the older girls to name those they viewed as

"ready to go out." Forthright Maria promptly said, "I could do it."
Esther and another student demurred. They stated, self-effacingly,
that they were sure they hadn't learned nearly enough and would
gladly wait until Teacher, "who would know better than they, should
pronounce them ready" (36–37). Gradually Maria and the others
begin to see that waiting to be nominated was the correct stance;
Teacher had tricked them into learning that. The lesson was "maids
don't presume"; the inner attitudinal adjustment was to make one's
self believe that one *wanted* to wait to be chosen—authority knows
best. Maria's gradual schooling in "learning how to feel" would
probably win her one of the jobs, the reader could see. But Maria is
so real a character that it is never a foregone conclusion. This
Sunday school author knew how to maintain the reader's suspense.

Maria and Esther also have a conversation about their present
value to an employer which contrasts their differing personalities.

> *Esther:* I have heard from others who have gone out that it's a
> long time before one can get to know what will please . . .
> *Maria:* I see nothing so very difficult, when I think of it. I
> suppose we can any of us dandle a baby, or tie a frock, or
> scour a floor, or clean a grate.
> *Esther:* Ah Maria, I suppose we shall do none of those things
> as *they* would have them done till we have been a long
> time learning. Things that we fancy are right, they will
> perhaps think all wrong. (57–58).

Maria's presumption was then skillfully undercut and redirected
through a long recital of a nightmarish exposure in the alien world
of employers. The unmistakable terror in Hannah Porter's one
appearance in this story highlights the dark side of ambition—the
fear of being revealed as an imposter—and reinforces the reader's
willingness to be schooled. "When my sister fell ill at Mrs. Marsden's," Hannah began, "she sent for me to help for a few days. . . . I
was told to answer the drawing room bell. . . . And while Mrs. Marsden was telling me what she wanted, I stood holding the door and
twirling the handle of the lock." Her nervousness drew sharp re-
proof from Mrs. Marsden: "What do you do that for? I did not send
for you to rattle the lock; bring some coals and sweep up the hearth."
This brings Hannah to the next disaster. "I brought the coals, and in

coming in, I hit the coal pan against the fine painted wall. . . . There's a mark to this day!" Mrs. Marsden scolded again. "You awkward girl! Come in clear and shut the door after you." But in hastening to obey, Hannah's grimy hands "left all the spots of my fingers' ends" on the door. Now thoroughly panicked, Hannah tried to wipe the finger spots off with her apron, but it made them "a deal worse, for I smeared it all over." Meanwhile Mrs. Marsden was still working on the first blemish she had created.

" 'What do you cry for?' the mistress asked crossly; 'make haste and sweep the hearth.' " But in throwing on the coals, poor Hannah "knocked the edge of the chimney-stone with the pan. 'Mind what you are about,' said Mrs. Marsden sharply, and snatched the brush and shovel away from Hannah. 'Do you see what clouds of dust you are raising? Look . . . the chimney ornaments are covered! Go away . . . send somebody else!' "

Hannah's humiliation was transformed, however, into self-knowledge and realism.

> You can't think how one gets puzzled at seeing everything new about them. I'd never carried such a coal-pan before, nor swept with such a brush; and if I'd made dirt in our house, I should only have wiped it off again . . . our house is a dark colour, and when I came to touch a white door, I didn't think of the difference. If I go to a place, I wish it may be in a kitchen, and then I shall get broken in by degrees. (58)

Combining the fear of an unknown environment and the need for schooling in Hannah's vignette is an effective stratagem on the part of this evangelical author.

Maria's indomitable buoyancy must have seemed both marvelous and audacious to the mid-nineteenth century reader. Her lack of guile would have endeared her to the emerging "modern American girl." Too honest to simper about her ambition, she frankly delighted in leadership: "I don't like school so well this week; last week I had chief superintendence, and this week I have to be looked at and examined and directed. It is very disagreeable and I don't want it. I can do all right without it!" (34).

By contrast Esther's humility may have been a little hard to bear, even if American readers could recognize it as the cultural ideal their mothers were supposed to promote. Esther's self-effacement led her to tell Maria that *she* would want to start as a kitchen girl or a shoeblack, "just as one must learn A, B, C before reading or numeration before summing." "Not me," retorts Maria, "I'd rather start at the top" (34). The author who created such a lively character as Maria and refused to impose narrative control on her makes this schooling of a reader's feelings a pleasant engagement.

Though the school metaphor endorsed a curriculum and authority structure that seemed, on one level, to devalue initiative and encourage subservience, the other side of the pupils' learning was exactly the opposite. They and their readers were to develop a strong sense of self direction—to try to fill their "stations," whatever they might be, to the very top of their abilities. Finding the balance between too much self-confidence (a metaphor for irreligion, the reader understood) and too little self-management was the crux of their schooling. Being able to manage one's self in the employer's world while carrying out one's religious obligation to self and God required a new social-psychological framework, a new independence of mind. Teacher's instruction was two-pronged: the would-be maids must be responsible for themselves, taking charge of their own inner lives with the method and spiritual discipline supplied by evangelical Christianity. But they must do it within the existing external social structure, balancing the demands of God and man, self and station.

In such schooling stories we can begin to sense the creative energy unleashed in their readers by these early nineteenth-century Protestant writers, as well as the "methods" they instilled which encouraged readers to manage rather than submit to given circumstances. If we allow ourselves to "fall in love with" such a story system, to use Mr. Railton's percipient phrase, we can understand how a mid-nineteenth century American Sunday school reader might have become intensely involved with an English family school or an English village school for girls. She would have absorbed the lessons from these faraway schools—the right feelings that would help her cope in her own life—which were meant for her in her own "station," as well as for the story characters.

Fiction intended to school children in religion is clearly not susceptible to the usual liberal-humanist traditions of analysis. But it may well be that the schooling provided in mid-nineteenth century Sunday school books helped foster in American boys the strong desire for individual autonomy which was a factor in the burst of professionalization in America following the Civil War (Bledstein). Girl readers also internalized the view that they were intelligent, had a need for accomplishment, and could manage their own lives. For them in particular, Sunday school fiction may have fulfilled the limited but necessary function identified by George Eliot, of a friend at your elbow to whisper, "you really are not a confounded noodle" (3:31). Through the metaphor of school, salvation and social skills could be learned together.

Notes

1. Sunday School library books had their critics from the 1860s on. Bernard J. Steiner, librarian at the Enoch Pratt Free Library in Baltimore, put the case for such reading material succinctly: "Their influence was and still is very great. I do not think I exaggerate when I say that the great majority of the people in the United States live in localities where they can have no access to free public libraries but a Sunday school one. . . . This being the case, the Sunday school library looms before us as a vital matter in the culture of the people" ("The Sunday School Library Question," *Library Journal* 23 [July 1898]: 276–77.)

2. Wardle quotes an 1857 Methodist statistic boasting that "639,120 children— one tenth of the children of this nation between age 5 and 15—are, at this moment, in the Sunday schools of our church." (69).

3. *Dingle Parish*, 1856. In this story, the rector of an Episcopal church defends his nonparticipation in a town revival and his use of "set" (instead of spontaneous) prayers as providing no proof that the Episcopal church is less spiritually fervent than more evangelical churches.

4. MacLeod provides an analysis of children's books that specifically excludes Sunday school stories, but stresses the view that a child is "not a completed product," rather "a being in process" (90).

5. I have examined aspects of Methodist Sunday school literature (see Gillespie "Sun," "Enginery," and "Modesty") and Episcopal Sunday School stories ("Carrie"). See Boylan for ASSU publications. Bratton (1981) provides a more sympathetic evaluation of this type of children's literature than her predecessors Grylls and Avery. Cutts emphasizes evangelical children's books as "ennobling the doer" and portraying the child as the major bearer of the evangelizing impulse (71). British writers make a distinction between evangelical books directed toward the working-class child and the child of gentry or the urban educated family, as well as between the Evangelical (Church of England) faction and the broader evangelical movement involving people from many churches. Kiefer includes religious books but not Sunday school library books as a genre.

6. The relationship of Sunday school stories to the wider humanistic tradition of domestic conduct books is undoubtedly more complex than evangelical writers acknowledged. Caroline Matilda Thayer (1837) repents her early fascination with

godless European writers such as Rousseau and Wollstonecraft, and an American clergyman in this same period "deplored publicly that Maria Edgeworth made light of religious truth" (Meigs et al. 125). Nevertheless the pattern for religious fiction was not so different from the line of prescriptive children's stories begun by Sarah Fielding (1710–68) and Mrs. Sarah Kirby Trimmer (1741–1810). Hannah More's *Cheap Repository Tracts*, issued three per month from 1795 to 1798, set the model, although (as evangelical writers viewed it) the godless moral tradition of Maria Edgeworth's *Harry and Lucy* (1801) and *Frank* (1801, 1820) also used "a stock literary character who knew everything, who could answer all questions" and provided the model for what these critics call "the Age of Admonition" (Meigs et al. 89).

7. *Learning to Feel*, vol. 1. A reader must rely on internal evidence for speculation about the author's gender. In this story the idealization of the father and the identification of the mother's anxieties lead me to think the author was a woman. Each chapter may have been envisioned as a chapter-by-chapter "curriculum" for successive Sundays in an actual Sabbath day school.

8. Gillespie, "Sun" 51. Father was most often on the sidelines as far as religious instruction was concerned, by the 1830s—dead or in India, if the stories were English, dead or away at business if they were American.

9. *My Station and Its Duties* was first published in England (I have not been able to establish the original date) and then was republished in New York by Methodists and Episcopalians, its Britishisms intact.

10. The contribution of the evangelical religious reform movement in England— the largest and most successful sect of which was that led by John Wesley (1703–91) and known as Methodist (although it remained part of the Church of England until after Wesley's death)—has been evaluated by Thompson as negative because it interfered with the formation of labor unions, though he granted its psyche-organizing gift to the poor. Halevy is more positive. His student Bernard Semmel quotes Thomas Taylor, an itinerant minister who wrote *Britannia's Mercies, and Her Duties* (1799): "The poor in general are profligate . . . but the Methodists . . . are squaring their lives by reason and grace" (128). Osborne's study of the Industrial Revolution talks about working-class self-improvement programs in England without acknowledging their origins in the Sunday school movement. Laquer links the wildfire growth of Sunday schools in England with the bursting desire for self-improvement, education, and leadership among ordinary people—the Sunday school movement being largely lay-founded and lay-led.

11. I am grateful to an anonymous reviewer for pointing out that "Emmet" is a dialect word for "ant," an insect rated highly by evangelicals for its industry (Proverbs 6:6–8).

Works Cited

Avery, Gillian. *Childhood's Pattern: A Study of the Heroes and Heroines of Children's Fiction*. London: Hodder & Stoughton, 1975.

Bledstein, Burton J. *The Culture of Professionalism*. New York: W. W. Norton, 1976.

Boylan, Anne M. "Sunday Schools and the Changing Evangelical View of Children in the 1820s." *Church History* 48 (September 1979): 320–33.

Bratton, J. S. *The Impact of Victorian Children's Fiction*. London: Croom Helm, 1981.

Connor, Martha. *Outline of the History of the Development of the American Public Library*.

Chicago: American Library Association, 1931.

Cutts, Margaret Nancy. *Ministering Angels*. Wormley, England: Five Owls P, 1979.

Dingle Parish. By a Presbyter of Western New York. New York: General Protestant Episcopal Sunday School Union, 1856.

Eliot, George. *Letters*, ed. Gordon Haight, 9 vols. New Haven: Yale UP, 1954–78.

Gillespie, Joanna B. " 'The Sun in Their Domestic System': The Mother in Early 19th Century Methodist Sunday School Lore." In *Women in New Worlds: Historical Perspectives on the Wesleyan Tradition*. 2 vols. Ed. Rosemary S. Keller, Louise L. Queen, and Hilah F. Thomas. Nashville: Abingdon, 1982. 2: 45–69.

———. " 'An Almost Irresistible Enginery': Five Decades of 19th Century Methodist Sunday School Library Books." *Phaedrus* 2 (1980): 5–12.

———. "Modesty Canonized: Female Saints in Antebellum Sunday School Literature." *Historical Reflections* 10 (1981): 159–220.

———. "Carrie; or The Child in the Rectory: 19th Century Sunday School Prototype." *Historical Magazine of the Episcopal Church* 51 (1982): 359–71.

Grylls, David. *Guardians and Angels*. London: Faber & Faber, 1978.

Halevy, Eric. *The Birth of Methodism in England*. Chicago: U of Chicago P, 1971.

Harrison, G. Elsie. *The Clue to the Brontës*. London: Methuen, 1948.

Harrison, J. F. C. *The Common People: A History from the Norman Conquest to the Present*. London: Fontana Paperbacks, 1984.

Hibbens, the Rev. W. W. *The Rev. James C. Havens, One of the Heroes of Indiana Methodism*. Indianapolis: Sentinel, 1872.

Kent, the Rev. Asa. *A Sketch of the Life of Lucy Kent (1777–1785)*. New York: Sunday School Union of the Methodist Episcopal Church, 1855.

Kiefer, Monica. *American Children through Their Books 1700–1835*. Philadelphia: U of Pennsylvania P, 1948.

Laquer, Thomas. *Religion and Respectabililty: Sunday Schools and Working Class Culture, 1780–1850*. New Haven: Yale UP, 1978.

Learning to Feel. Vol. 1, revised by the editor, D. P. Kidder. New York: Sunday School Union of the Methodist Episcopal Church, 1845. Vol. II (a second series of lessons, same title), 1854.

M'Gavin, William. *Maternal Instructions. Or The History of Mrs. Murray and Her Children*. New York: Sunday School Union of the Methodist Episcopal Church, 1849.

MacLeod, Anne Scott. *A Moral Tale: Children's Fiction and American Culture 1820–60*. Hamden, Connecticut: Archon Books, 1975.

Mathews, Donald G. *Religion in the Old South*. Chicago: U of Chicago P, 1977.

Meigs, Cornelia, Elizabeth Nesbitt, Anne Thaxter Eaton, and Ruth Hill Vigeurs, eds. *A Critical History of Children's Literature*. London: MacMillan, 1969.

"Memoir of Robert Raikes," *American Methodist Magazine* (1828): 293–302.

Meyers, Marvin. *The Jacksonian Persuasion*. Stanford: Stanford UP, 1951.

Miller, Perry. *The Life of the Mind in America: From the Revolution to the Civil War*. New York: Harcourt Brace and World, 1965.

Minutes, Annual Meeting of the Sunday School Union of the Methodist Episcopal Church. New York: Methodist Publishing House, 1849.

My Station and Its Duties. By the author of *The Last Day of the Week*. New York: Sunday School Union of the Methodist Episcopal Church, 1849.

Osborne, John. *The Silent Revolution*. New York: Charles Scribner's Sons, 1970.

Ortner, Sherry B. "On Key Symbols." *American Anthropologist* 75 (1973): 1338–46.

Rice, Wilbur. *The Sunday School Movement and the ASSU 1780–1917*. Philadelphia: American Sunday School Union, 1917.

Rose, A. C. *Memoir of Eliza M. Barker (1829—40)*. New York: Sunday School Union of the Methodist Episcopal Church, 1851.

Semmel, Bernard. *The Methodist Revolution*. Chicago: U of Chicago P, 1973.

Shepherd, Massey. *Oxford American Prayer Book Commentary*. New York: Oxford UP, 1950.

Steiner, Bernard. "The Sunday School Library Question." *The Library Journal* 23 (1898): 276—77.

"Sunday School Literature." *Methodist Quarterly Review* 32 (1850) 238—91.

Temple, J. H. *History of the First Sabbath School in Framingham, Massachusetts, 1816—1868*. Boston: Wright & Potter, 1868.

Thayer, Caroline Matilda. *Religion Recommended to Youth in a Series of Letters*. New York: Sunday School Union of the Methodist Episcopal Church, 1837.

Thompson, E. P. *The Making of the British Working Class*. New York: A. A. Knopf, 1966.

Walter, Frank Keller. "A Poor but Respectable Relation, the Sunday School Library." *Library Quarterly* 12 (1942): 731—39.

Wardle, Annie Grace. *History of the Sunday School Movement in the Methodist Episcopal Church*. New York: Methodist Book Concern, 1918.

Moral Despair and the Child as Symbol of Hope in Pre-World War II Berlin

J. D. Stahl

Fictional portrayals of children in the Berlin of the 1920s and 1930s suggest that, for fascists and antifascists alike, the child was a symbol of redemption and hope for the future. As moral and social symbol of a possible future, the child could embody contradictory visions; he or she could represent both the hopes of innocent individuals and the collective drives and fears of a desperate society.

During the social upheaval of the Weimar Republic, people looked for the causes of chaos and insecurity in theories of moral decay and social decline. On every side, hopes for a gradual improvement of the human lot were replaced by a sense of apocalyptic urgency. Some foresaw revolution; others, like Spengler, the total collapse of society; some simply retreated into a private world of self-protective resignation. Because the customary patterns of social action seemed threatened or inadequate, literature became important as a means of delineating intolerable conditions and exploring possible changes or avenues of escape. But increasingly those who looked for a fundamental transformation of society began to think of literature as nothing more than potential propaganda to hasten the attainment of that goal.

In this historical context, literature for children took on a particular importance because of its heuristic function. The Hitler Youth novels of Karl Aloys Schenzinger clearly exemplify the messianic purpose of their author; yet even literature that sought to avoid topical issues, such as the children's novels of Schenzinger's contemporary Erich Kästner, provide a reflection of the contemporary situation. I hope to show by my discussion of the works of Kästner and Schenzinger that the idealism evoked by the image of childhood as human potential in German literature of the late 1920s and early 1930s could be used for humane or purely literary ends, but also demagogically, as a constituent of propaganda. I hope to show, more controversially, that literary skill could serve both purposes and that the child-figure portrayed in the novels of these authors became a catalyst of sharply contrasting views of the rapidly approaching fascist state.

Berlin during the late Weimar Republic was the nervecenter and microcosm of the German nation, center stage of its political dramas, harbinger of its future. To many of us, its symbol is a dance on the volcano. Thanks to films such as *Cabaret, The Serpent's Egg,* and, most recently, Fassbinder's epic film version of *Berlin Alexanderplatz,* images of decadence and perversion and a mood of apocalyptic anxiety fill our minds, with an ominous marching of brownshirts in the background. An urbane capital of sparkling if mordant wits, unemployment lines, political chaos and personal resignation, bookburnings, and emigrants packing for every train: this is how many of us think of Berlin in the late Weimar Republic.

But how did Germans of the time see their own city? What moral vision had Berliners of their apocalyptic metropolis? What kind of life did authors envision for the younger generation in the face of the cataclysmic conditions of German society? As we shall see in the following examination of the writings of Kästner and Schenzinger, the child was an attractive symbol of hope in the future and a means of making a moral commentary on the present; but, as a symbol, the child had hidden limitations and dangerous ambiguities.

Erich Kästner, an antifascist, and Karl Aloys Schenzinger, a profascist, each portrayed the roaring, restless city of Berlin in a children's novel as well as a novel for adults. Erich Kästner wrote *Emil und die Detektive* (1928) and *Fabian* (1930); Karl Aloys Schenzinger was the author of *Man will uns kündigen* (1931), translated as *Fired* (1932), and *Hitlerjunge Quex* (1932) or "Hitlerboy Quex."[1] Schenzinger's and Kästner's versions of Berlin during the decline of the Weimar Republic and the rise of National Socialism not only offer vivid insights into the social and political turmoil of Germany's capital; they yield a complex analysis of the moral and philosophical conflicts animating the German people at that time. Both authors achieved major publishing successes with their children's books but not with their novels for adults. But, borne on the political tide, their careers moved in opposite directions. In 1933, Schenzinger's *Hitlerjunge Quex* was filmed from a script he helped to write; on September 11 the film was given an extravagant premiere in Munich, with Hitler and many government officials in attendance; eight days later it opened in Berlin (Arnold et al. 197). Schenzinger's book was distributed in an edition of a quarter of a million, and the film was seen by up to eleven million Germans, mainly members of the Hitler Youth.[2] In contrast, on the 10th of May in the same year, Erich Kästner witnessed the burning of his own books by Goebbels and a mob of SA members, many of them students, at the university in Berlin, an experience he described in his essay "Bei Verbrennung meiner Bücher" ("At the Burning of My Books," 1946: 140−41). After the Nazis took power later that year, Kästner, despite his popularity, was prohibited from writing anything but what he himself called works to entertain readers or "light reading," which he published abroad; and in 1942, he was finally forbidden to write anything at all.

Remarkably, both authors not only survived the war but published widely in postwar Germany. Schenzinger's role as a fascist propagandist was generally quietly ignored in West Germany, where he continued to publish bestselling novelizations of science history. *Anilin* (1936) and *Metall* (1939) were succeeded by *Atom* (1950) and *Schnelldampfer* (1951). Kästner on the other hand vigorously examined his country's disastrous past, becoming actively involved in the writers' organization PEN and founding *Pinguin*, a literary magazine with social criticism for children. In postwar Germany, Kästner has achieved the status and recognition due to a major author.

Contemporaries living in Berlin before Hitler's accession to power, Kästner and Schenzinger in their novels for adults delineated the moral and economic misery of the city. Both presented critical social portraits of life in Berlin, paying particular attention to the insidious effects of unemployment. Both used an understated, dry, reportorial style, with a minimum of authorial comment, eschewing the direct expression of emotions. Here, however, the similarities end.

Kästner's *Fabian*, a novel that has been much misunderstood, particularly by those who fail to see its satiric points, depicts Berlin as a city going irrevocably to hell, ruining the lives of its few decent inhabitants in the process. Fabian, the protagonist, a young man of comparative decency and normality, experiences the corruption of the time firsthand; his friend Stephan is tricked by a cruel practical joke into believing that his dissertation has failed to pass muster, when actually it has passed with distinction. Stephan commits suicide before the truth is revealed. Fabian's own girlfriend marries a wealthy film producer in order to finance her career as a film star. In scenes of scathingly bitter satire, politics, journalism, art, and marriage are shown to be perversions of themselves. The mood of the novel as a whole is one of despair at the moral illness of society, an illness which Kästner presents as repulsive and incurable. Fabian at the end of the novel leaps into a river to save a boy who has fallen in, but Fabian himself drowns, for he has never learned how to swim; the boy swims to shore and saves himself. This ironic disaster symbolizes the utter helplessnes of the individual to rescue himself or those of a younger generation—who may nevertheless survive on their own.

Schenzinger's novel for adults, *Man will uns kündigen*, would produce much the same effect if it were not for the last nine pages. In the bulk of the book Schenzinger presents scenes of demoralization and chaos remarkably like those to be found in *Fabian*—a young woman compelled by economic necessity to marry a wealthy, repellent suitor; the despair caused by unemployment; suicide as a response to financial ruin; and the dull, agonizing life of pretended normalcy and self-respect in Berlin's coffeehouses. Like Kästner, Schenzinger wrote about political clashes between Nazis and Communists, dramatized both in debates and in street battles.

Unlike Kästner, however, who saw these events as pointless absurdities, a useless insistence on personal honor as outdated as the code of the duel, Schenzinger found political violence both fascinating and significant. In fact, he shows his protagonist persuaded to join the Nazis by the stoic devotion his cousin displays after he has been crippled for life in a political brawl. But he gives Communists and National Socialists such equally balanced and portentous attention that one cannot determine with certainty until very near the end of his novel that his sympathies lie ultimately with brown, not red. In fact, Schenzinger described the two movements as the only two vigorous streams in contemporary political life, "nothing but need incarnate."[3] He even speculated that some day the two "streams" might join to become one mighty river. It is necessary to remember that there was a time when many took the "socialism" part of National Socialism seriously, and when more than a few persons envisioned a merging of the political extremes in a wave of national renewal.

Though Schenzinger does not clearly imply a political position except in the final episode of *Man will uns kündigen*, he consistently displays considerable sympathy for political violence itself, no matter what its motive. His voyeuristic, ostensibly dispassionate descriptions of an anti-Semitic outburst at the university and of attacks on a Jewish moneylender betray satisfaction in having found a scapegoat for a vicious, pent-up resentment, the *ressentiment* of the powerless, disenfranchised lower middle class. Near the end of the novel, Schenzinger's hero escapes from corrupt commercial Berlin to the country. Life on the farm, where he fathers a child and gathers resolve to join the Nazis, is primitive, muscular, and impossibly bucolic—a literary analog to the fascist celebration of the peasant *Volk* in the visual arts.

Lionel Trilling, reviewing the English translation of *Man will uns kündigen* (*Fired*, 1932), used the book and another novel about the economic disaster of Germany as examples of novels that "fail esthetically because of their very lack" of doctrine.[4] Trilling accused Schenzinger of irrationality, of propounding "the pseudo-doctrine of Hitlerism, a mere crystallization of irrational hate directed against a false objective" (267). *Man will uns kündigen* is indeed a confused and artistically unsuccessful book, as Trilling charged; however, *Fabian*, which does not fail aesthetically, has no more "doctrine" itself. Trilling argued for the necessity of reason in art:

> Just as, in political life, a class without a centralizing and rational doctrine disintegrates into an eventually weak and unvital factor, so in art the spectacle of mass suffering set down without doctrine of cause or cure, degenerates into hysteria or stupidity. (268).

In art as in politics, however, the centripetal power need not be "rational doctrine." The triumph of fascism in Europe and its glorification in fascist art such as Leni Riefenstahl's films demonstrates the limitations of Trilling's theory. One might of course argue that eventually fascist dictatorships do (and did) disintegrate, and that fascist art is not truly art (most of it is not), but to do so is to underestimate the powerful popular appeal of the irrational, a mistake intellectuals are particularly prone to make. Susan Sontag has penetratingly analyzed the irrational sources of appeal of what she calls "fascist aesthetics," which one might equally well call "fascist ethics": "They flow from (and justify) a preoccupation with situations of control, submissive behavior, extravagant effort, and the endurance of pain."[5] The raw material for these themes was present in *Man will uns kündigen*, but it did not coalesce into fascist symbolism; in *Hitlerjunge Quex* it did.

The nature of the ultimate good for Kästner and for Schenzinger alike was bound up with the potentialities of innocence. Both authors placed their hopes for the future in children, as they revealed in their novels for young readers, *Emil und die Detektive* and *Hitlerjunge Quex*, but the shapes their hopes took were radically different. Kästner sharply divided his moral universe into the realms of child and adult. *Fabian* expresses his despair at moral conditions in the adult world where rationality has become absurd (the subtitle of his satiric adult novel is "The Story of a Moralist"), but *Emil* is a manifesto of confidence in the goodness of the child. Emil Tischbein, the hero, is not an angel—he is affectionately irreverent to his mother and he paints a mustache on a statue in a prank—but Kästner makes a point of emphasizing his virtues. Most important, he is devoted to his mother. Furthermore, he is honest, hardworking, and conscientious. Kästner calls him a model boy ("Musterknabe") but is quick to say that he is not a mama's boy ("Muttersöhnchen").

The plot of *Emil* pits this exemplary but likeable boy against the evil of the adult world, conveniently and stereotypically embodied in the villain who steals Emil's money on the train ride to Berlin from the small town where Emil and his mother live. While Neustadt, Emil's hometown, is a typical provincial town, as even its name suggests, it is not employed as the idyllic side of a contrast with big-city criminality in the shape of Berlin, as one might expect. Instead, Emil's journey to Berlin is a picaresque adventure, a naturalistic fantasy in which Berlin furnishes the cinematic backdrop for a simple *Bildungsroman*. Emil's education by experience combines entertainment and instruction: he learns about evil and has an exciting adventure, making friends in Berlin, tracking the thief, and ultimately bringing him to justice with the help of his newfound friends. Because good and bad characters are so clearly differentiated and so easily distinguishable, Berlin can be seen as a setting essentially uncontaminated by evil, and Kästner's love of the city emerges vividly in his meticulously accurate account of where Emil's pursuit takes him, along the Kaiserallee, through the Motzstrasse, to the Nollendorfplatz. Kästner mentions scores of streets and public places in Berlin, all of which are actual. But the real clue to Kästner's feelings about Berlin in *Emil* is to be found in the scene when Emil and his friends gather outside the hotel where they have trapped the villain, Herr Grundeis.

> By this time it was dark. Electric ads flamed everywhere. The elevated thundered overhead. The subway rumbled beneath. Streetcars and motorbuses, private cars and motorcycles, made a crazy concert. Dance music came from the Woerz Cafe. The movie theater on Nollendorf Place began its last show. And many people crowded in. "Such a big tree as that over by the station looks like a freak here," mused Emil. "It looks as if it had lost its way." The boy was enchanted and thrilled. And he almost forgot why he was there and that he had lost a hundred and forty marks. "Of course, Berlin is wonderful. You'd think you were sitting in a movie." (104–05).

Compare this favorable representation with Kästner's statement about Berlin in *Fabian*:

> Hinsichtlich der Bewohner gleicht [die Stadt] . . . einem Irrenhaus. Im Osten residiert das Verbrechen, im Zentrum die Gaunerei, im Norden das Elend, im Western die Unzucht, und in allen Himmelsrichtungen wohnt der Untergang. (77)

> As far as its inhabitants are concerned, the city is like an insane asylum. In the east resides crime, in the center swindling, in the north misery, in the west immorality, and in all directions lies ruin.

In the children's book, Kästner can indulge his fantasy of a world in which good and evil are neatly separated; Berlin can be an essentially hospitable and exciting place, where the goodhearted hero meets a gang of equally goodhearted Berlin street boys, a colorful backdrop for the children's quest to bring the criminal to justice

virtually without adult assistance. The despair of *Fabian* is consistent
with the idealism of *Emil*; it is merely the reverse side of the coin.
Like the aging Mark Twain, Kästner revealed the intensity of his
idealism about human nature through the intensity of his disappointment at the failure of humanity to achieve his hopes. But in his
children's stories, he allowed his hopes more direct expression. At
the end of *Emil*, Kästner has several characters derive morals from
the story, some serious, others tongue-in-cheek. Emil, for example,
states: "One lesson I've learned from it: never trust anybody" (160).
But Kästner's own lesson is different. At the conclusion of another
of his children's stories, *Pünktchen und Anton*, he states his moral
purpose in both children's books explicitly:

> Ich habe von Anton erzählt, obwohl er dem Emil Tischbein so
> ähnlich ist, weil ich glaube: Von dieser Sorte Jungen kann man
> gar nicht genug erzählen, und Emile und Antone können wir
> gar nicht genug kriegen! Vielleicht entschliesst ihr euch, so wie
> sie zu werden? Vielleicht werdet ihr, wenn ihr sie liebgewonnen
> habt, wie diese Vorbilder, so fleissig, so anständig, so tapfer und
> so ehrlich? Das wäre der schönste Lohn für mich. Denn aus dem
> Emil, dem Anton und allen die den beiden gleichen, werden
> später einmal sehr tüchtige Männer werden. Solche, wie wir sie
> brauchen können. (155).

I've told you about Anton, even though he is so much like Emil
Tischbein, because I believe that one can't talk enough about
this kind of boy, and that we can't get enough Emils and Antons!
Maybe you'll decide to become like them? Maybe if you have
come to like them, you'll become like these model boys, just as
hardworking, as decent, as brave and as honest? That would be
my best reward. Because Emil and Anton and all those who are
like them will later become excellent men, just the kind we
need.

At the conclusion of *Pünktchen und Anton*, Kästner laments the failure of adults to create a better world and expresses his admittedly
utopian but nonetheless fervent hope that the children he addresses
will do better than previous generations have. The dualism of Kästner's portrait of Berlin—glamorous cinematic setting and sordid

have demonstrated the connections between the authoritarian family and the structures of fascism. *Hitlerjunge Quex* supplies ample evidence for the links between oppressive patriarchal families and the personality traits required by National Socialism. Fantasies about escape from authoritarian fathers in particular are certain to have had a powerful effect on many young readers in the early 1930s, when disastrous economic conditions increased the oppressiveness of typical German family patterns of the time. *Hitlerjunge Quex* suggests the attractiveness of escape from the tyranny of the authoritarian father but provides a substitute authority structure in which obedience and loyalty are equally required, though not portrayed as oppressive.

Like Heini's immediate family, the Berlin of *Hitlerjunge Quex* is a prison of social chaos, economic desperation, and political war: an existential condition as much as a place. It is a condition from which Heini seeks escape in three symbolic directions. One is the nearby fairgrounds, a wild, exotic place where carousels and games of change beckon. But Heini, a conscientious boy who like Kästner's Emil is fiercely attached to his mother, goes less to win something for himself than to win something that will make his mother happy. Gregory Bateson, in his analysis of the film version, considers that the fairgrounds are a symbol of the Communists, but in the novel the fair is a symbol of the chaotic allure and danger of night life in the city (Bateson 314). The second direction in which Heini seeks escape from the oppressive circumstances of his life is the country—the woods and the fields beyond Berlin—on his excursion with the Communist Youth to the Bernau forest region. However, this proves to be a disappointment, because of the brutal, boorish behavior of his companions, who steal from one another, engage in fights without rules, and bully weaker boys.

Er hatte sich einen Wochenendausflug mit Kameraden anders gedacht. Was er wollte, war Wasser und Wald und Sonne. Er hatte einen richtigen Hunger nach Freude. (39)

He had imagined a weekend excursion with friends differently. What he wanted was water and woods and sun. He had a real hunger for happiness.

As in *Kuhle Wampe*, Brecht's 1932 film, and in Döblin's *Berlin Alexanderplatz*, the forest around Berlin offers illusory hope of escape from the difficulties of life in the city. But Heini does have a transcendent experience in the forest which points him to the third direction of attempted escape. Stealing through the woods at night, Heini comes upon a scene that bursts over him like an epiphany: a campfire around which the Hitler Youth are singing the *Deutschlandlied*. The experience deeply impresses him and contributes to his later conversion. To him, the massed group fervently singing patriotic songs symbolizes everything he desires: order, meaning, purpose, and a sense of belonging. These are the propagandistic rewards for Heini once he joins the Hitler Youth.[8]

The third avenue of escape, then, is the merging of the self into an authoritarian youth movement, a moral leap of faith in which the bad individual father is replaced by the willed choice of an organizational father—the group and its authoritarian superiors. Schenzinger seeks to glorify total, unquestioning obedience to superiors in the organization, even when their commands contradict Heini's strong desires. The hope Schenzinger posits in his symbolic hero, who is representative of the rising generation, is an irrational, atavistic faith in the force of a blind movement, a stream of followers relentlessly marching to the commands of their Führer. Ultimately, that hope is a form of death-wish. In a curious blend of erotic maturation and regressive self-denial, Heini reaches the brink of physical love but his idealistic devotion to the suprapersonal cause leads instead to his destruction. He is attracted to Ulla Dörries emotionally and physically, but his chivalrous, platonic love requires that he repress his desire for her, which is sublimated into protectiveness and into erotic dream images that connect Ulla with his dead mother, a connection that suggests the morbid character of the oedipal symbolism in this novel.

When Heini is killed, Schenzinger attempts to link the emotion of grief at Heini's martyrdom with the hope and determination of the political movement with which he has become identified. After Heini's funeral, Schenzinger writes:

Wenige Wochen später flattern die Fahnen wieder im Wind, draussen in den Strassen von Potsdam, auf dem Festplatz, im

Stadion, leuchten auf im Schein der Fackeln, im Schein der Sonne. Fünfundsiebzigtausend Jungens ziehen mit den gleichen Fahnen, mit dem gleichen Lied, aber mit strahlend hellen Gesichtern an ihrem Führer vorbei. (264).

A few weeks later the flags wave in the wind again. Out in the streets of Potsdam, on the festival grounds, in the stadium the flags glow in the light of the torches, in the light of the sun. Seventy-five thousand boys march past their Führer with the same flags, the same song, but with glowing, bright faces.

Berlin, the city of despair, had been transformed by Schenzinger from sordid, bleak streets to the prophetic scene of a mass movement marching into a bright future with a ceremonial uniformity that is both pompous and ominous to us now.

Kästner's Emil and Schenzinger's Heini both have remarkably close attachments to their mothers that should not be dismissed as merely coincidental. The sharply differentiated sex roles belonging to family patterns inherited from the Wilhelminian era, in which men were considered authorities and women and children subordinates, are reflected in the boys' preadolescent infatuations with their mothers and even more significantly in the development of those relationships as the boys mature.[9] Emil pursues the thief tenaciously not only to get his money back but also in a sense out of love for his mother. He knows how hard his mother worked to earn the money she entrusted to him and he is determined not to let her efforts be wasted. His sense of responsibility to his mother is fulfilled when he retrieves the stolen bills, and the first thing he thinks of doing with the money he gets for having caught a thief who was on the wanted list is to send for his mother to join him in Berlin. Once she arrives, the first use he thinks of for his money, and the primary use he takes pleasure in imagining, is to buy her "an electric hair-drying machine and . . . a winter coat lined with fur" (154).

Frau Tischbein, Emil's mother, is a widow, a fact that symbolically corresponds to the relative lack of importance Erich Kästner's father appears to have had in the writer's life.[10] In the sequel *Emil und die Drei Zwillinge*, oedipal currents are visible in the reluctance with which Emil and his mother accept police sergeant major Jeschke's courtship of her. Insofar as German society of the twenties and thirties was a man's world, Kästner preferred the world of women and children in an unsentimental though somewhat idealistic way. Emil's reward at the conclusion of his adventure is reunion with his mother, in the company of his cousin Pony Hütchen, his friends the Berlin street children, his aunt, and his grandmother. His uncle is allowed to "take the dog out for an airing"—a euphemism for going out to drink—during the important final reflections on the meaning of what has happened, and in general he is either absent or thickheaded. He insensitively asserts his authority over Emil, saying, "You are only a child," for which Pony, his daughter, soundly scolds him. Emil and his friends are inclined to be sarcastic about the fuss the adult male world of journalism and advertising makes about their adventure, and they undogmatically resolve to reject the offers of suits and footballs made by commercial outfits. Maturity for Emil, within the limits allowed by the novel, is a witty conspiracy between women and children against the mercenary world of men.

Schenzinger, on the other hand, prefigures the fascist concept of the family in his development of the relationship between Heini Völker and his mother. Schenzinger skillfully portrays the dilemmas and inner conflicts of a boy caught between a brutal authoritarian father and a sympathetic, victimized mother, a family pattern all too typical of the era. Because the domineering, hot-tempered father intimidates and physically abuses his wife and son, they create the small measure of freedom that remains possible for them through secrecy and subterfuge. The father does not understand or appear to care what his wife and son think and feel, as long as they do what he tells them to do; in other words, as long as they obey his patriarchal authority. While the boy thus experiences his father as a distant but threatening figure looming over him, his relationship to his mother is inversely close and intense, almost incestuous. He is able and eager to confide all his troubles and hopes to his mother, who is entirely sympathetic, understanding, and protective. For example, after the boy's first, intensely emotional encounter with the Hitler Youth, he comes home to the expected beating from his father, after which he lies in bed a long time waiting for his mother.

Spät erst kam die Mutter und setzte sich an sein Bett. Das Essen, das sie ihm brachte, schob er beiseite. Ganz nahe rückte er an

In the fascist state, the woman's role was to be the bearer of emotions; the man's to be the maker of decisions, the ruthless doer of deeds.

Wir empfinden es nicht als richtig, wenn das Weib in die Welt des Mannes, in sein Hauptgebiet eindringt, sondern wir empfinden es als natürlich, wenn diese beiden Welten geschieden bleiben. In die eine gehörte die Kraft des Gemütes, die Kraft der Seele! Zur anderen gehörte die Kraft des Sehens, die Kraft der Härte, der Entschlüsse und der Einsatzwilligkeit.

We feel that it is wrong when the woman invades the world of the man, his main territory; instead we feel that it is natural that these two worlds remain separate. To the one belongs the power of the emotions, the power of the soul! To the other belongs the power of vision, the power of toughness, of decisions and readiness for action. (Adolf Hitler, September 8, 1934, address to the NS-Frauenschaft, Reichsparteitag, Nürnberg).

These are the two worlds exemplified in the Völker family, and it is precisely because Heini is becoming an adult and a man that he must, in the ideological psychology of National Socialism, cut his ties to the "power of the emotions" which bind him to his mother's world and act decisively, independently of his mother's wishes.

Yet the emotional ties that bound Heini to his mother are transferred to his loyalty to the Hitler Youth and to Ulla Dörries, the girl who represents both the fascist youth organization and the "eternal feminine" that draws Heini onward if not upward. The waking world of the predominantly masculine youth organization requires the suppression and strict channeling of his more intimate emotions; but Heini's mother and Ulla, who represent the world of feeling, are identified with the realms of dreams and death. Heini finds his true freedom in martyrdom, in self-eradication, just as his mother does. Schenzinger first substitutes the masculine-oriented paramilitary youth organization for the authoritarian family, insidiously representing the exchange as a form of liberation. Then he projects the woman's realm into the beyond that is ultimately reachable only through death.

While National Socialist propaganda glorified the family, especially the rural farm family with many sons, in actual fact National Socialism ascribed little significance to the family except as a breedingplace for children, in which a coming generation was to be produced and readied for absorption into the institutions of the totalitarian state. Education and training were transferred largely out of the family into the schools and even more into the Hitler Youth. Schenzinger contributed to the subordination of the family to the purposes of fascism by creating a myth of conversion and liberation from the narrow, oppressive family to the tightly disciplined but companionable Hitler Youth organization, and beyond that, of aspiration to union with the mythical feminine through self-annihilation. A rising generation of young men was to be the bridegroom; war was the bride, a frequent theme of the prewar and war years, suggested through a multiplicity of symbols, including the use of "Mutterland."[12]

But the geography of the battlefield was still largely over the literary horizon. The familiar landscape of the city was in the foreground. The streets and places Schenzinger described in considerable detail, in *Hitlerjunge Quex* are as actual as the setting of Kästner's Wilmersdorf, the section of Berlin where Emil's adventures take place. The Beusselkietz where Heini lived and died is only a few blocks away from the street corners where Emil makes his acquaintance with Gustav and his other detective friends. The streetcar line Number Three, which Heini rides near the beginning of *Hitlerjunge Quex* in order to get out of his squalid neighborhood, passes through Wilmersdorf:

> Die 'Drei' bog jetzt gerade von der Turmstrasse her in die Beussellstrasse ein. Sie hatte nicht umsonst ein grünes Schild über dem Führerstand. Sie fuhr den grünen Ring, fuhr hinüber nach Wilmersdorf, durch Alleen and Parks, bei deren Anblick einem immer so anders wurde, wo die Kinder soviel lärmten und lachten, und die Jungens wie die Teufel rannten. (5–6)

The Number Three was just then turning in to the Beusselstrasse from the Turmstrasse. There was good reason why it had a green sign over the driver's seat. It drove along the green ring, over to Wilmersdorf, through avenues and parks that always made one feel so different, where children laughed and played noisily, and where the boys ran like the devil.

If works of fiction formed a continuous universe, Heini could have stepped off the Number Three and perhaps met Emil and his friends. However, even in that universe a meeting of minds would have been impossible, for their authors' visions are profoundly inimical.

Kästner's Berlin in *Emil und die Detektive* is an ahistorical city, a cinematic dreamworld in which the boy-hero symbolizes his author's idealistic but tough-minded faith in the redemptive goodness of the child. Only in *Fabian*, not in *Emil*, does Kästner reveal his understanding of the historical forces impelling the German nation toward fascism. To Kästner, political forces belonged to the corrupt world of the adult, generally beyond the world of children's stories, or, if the child must deal with those forces, they are to be conquered by an alliance of animals and children through utopian imaginative acts, as in *Die Konferenz der Tiere* (1949). However, Kästner plausibly portrays the conflicts between children who are trying to work together. The "detectives," like the children in many of Kästner's novels for young readers, cooperate, almost democratically, despite tensions: a blending of the ideal and the practicable in the social realm.

Schenzinger, who had a remarkable understanding of what Susan Sontag has called "the vertigo before power," created historical visions of Berlin as a city in which individuals were being crushed by unemployment and hopelessness. But his vision of a redemptive totalitarian future is the counterpoint he imposes on the seemingly objective panorama of a disintegrating society. Most effectively in his novel for children and young people, Schenzinger promoted an apocalyptic faith in the submersion of the individual in the Nazi mass movement—a faith that was eventually to destroy thousands of Heini Völkers and Emil Tischbeins and that left the actual city of Berlin in heaps of rubble, with a deadly wall dividing two new cities. Schenzinger's idealism glorified a dream of solidarity in which personality is annihilated because the pressure of reality has become unbearable. In contrast, Kästner's idealistic didacticism in his children's stories is lightened by a sense of humor and informed by a realistic assessment of the value of individuality. His writing remains popular in fragmented post-World War II Germany. Schenzinger's passionate intensity of illusion and deception has receded into obscurity as the social conditions he was responding to have altered— but it should be understood before it is allowed to be forgotten.

Notes

1. I will not here consider the complex issues of whether and how propaganda can be art. For a discussion of ideology in literature, see Susan Suleiman's *Authoritarian Fictions.* Suleiman analyzes the roman à thèse in twentieth-century French fiction. Translations of quotations from *Fabian* and from Schenzinger's works are my own.

2. Figures about the size of film audiences for *Hitlerjunge Quex* are cited in Arnold et al. 205–06. As they point out, and as I discovered in several conversations, many older Germans still remember details from the film quite vividly (205 n.1).

3. "Beide Parteien sind doch nichts als verkörperte Not" (*Man will uns kündigen* 291).

4. Trilling wrote: "The charge most frequently brought against 'proletarian' fiction is, of course, its inevitable tendency to propaganda. Merely from an aesthetic point of view, hostile critics say, the inclusion of doctrine in emotional literature is disastrous. Sympathetic criticism has had to meet this attack by the difficult task of showing how emotion and doctrine have been combined in classic works, or by declaring moralistically that they must be combined. But these . . . novels give the defenders of indoctrinated fiction an opportunity to make a counter-attack by asserting the esthetic importance of doctrine; for [these novels] fail esthetically because of their very lack of it" (267). Trilling's theory fails to include another, less savory kind of evidence in favor of "indoctrinated fiction"—the aesthetic success of propagandistic works such as the novel and the film *Hitlerjunge Quex.* The aesthetic and the ethical, though linked, do not necessarily validate each other as Trilling wished to believe.

5. Sontag's essay on Leni Riefenstahl, "Fascinating Fascism" (91), is pertinent to a consideration of Schenzinger's writings.

6. See Dagmar Grenz's excellent analysis, "Erich Kästners Kinderbücher in ihrem Verhältnis zu seiner Literatur für Erwachsene." Grenz concentrates on a comparison between *Fabian* and *Pünktchen und Anton.* She writes: "Der Aufklärer Kästner entpuppt sich als ein Nachfahre der Romantik: Er entzieht sich der Aporie seiner eigenen individualistischen Moral, indem er die seit Ende des 19. Jahrhunderts einsetzende und auf das Kindheitsbild der Romantik zurückgehende Ideologie der heilen Kinderwelt übernimmt" (167). (Kästner the enlightener turns out to be a descendant of romanticism: he withdraws from the doubtfulness of his own individualistic morality by adopting the ideology of the idyllic world of the child that gained dominance around the end of the nineteenth century and originated in the romantic image of childhood [my translation]).

7. See Dagmar Grenz, "Entwicklung als Bekehrung und Wandlung, Zu einem Typus der nationalsozialistischen Jugendliteratur." Grenz points out that Heini's development is represented as if it were simply the voluntary change of an individual driven by the universal human need for meaning. She shows how Schenzinger portrays working-class life as a form of miseducation which is supposedly corrected

by the Nazi ideal of a new humanity, deceptively subjectivized and made emotionally appealing.

8. For other discussions of the propaganda context and messages of *Hitlerjunge Quex*, see Peter Aley; Renate Jaroslawski and Rüdiger Steinlein; Christa Kamenetsky (124 and 126); Hansgeorg Meyer (97–98); J. B. Neveux; and Ulrich Schröter. *Hitlerjunge Quex* is narrated in the third person, not in the first person by Heini Völker himself as Kamenetsky states. Kamenetsky's study is a very valuable, wide-ranging analysis of Nazi cultural policies concerning children's and youth literature, particularly of the uses to which folk themes and genres were put in the Third Reich.

9. Cf. Ingeborg Weber-Kellermann, especially chapters 4 and 5.

10. Cf. Kästner's autobiographical *Als ich ein kleiner Junge war.*

11. Max Horkheimer writes: "Der Unterwerfungstrieb ist aber keine ewige Grösse, sondern ein wesentlich in der bürgerlichen Klein-Familie erzeugtes Phänomen. Ob in der Erziehung Zwang oder Milde waltet, ist hierbei nicht entscheidend; denn der kindliche Charakter wird durch die Struktur der Familie selbst weit mehr als durch die bewussten Absichten und Methoden des Vaters gebildet" (61). (The urge to submit is not an unchanging quality, but rather a phenomenon essentially created by the bourgeois nuclear family. Whether force or gentleness is used in the rearing of children is not decisive in this regard, because the character of the child is formed much more by the structure of the family itself than by the conscious intentions and methods of the father [my translation].)

12. "Mutterland" is used in this way in Heinrich Gutberlet's "Grenzlandschwur," for example. Gutberlet's poem suggests war through its imagery of blood, flame, and "Opferstrom" (river of sacrifice). "Wir wollen heim ins Mutterland" (We want to return home to the motherland), the next to last line, while it can be read literally, also carries other, more primal meanings: the yearning to return to the womb, or the longing for a martial union fertilizing the "mother" land. In Günter Grass's *Katz und Maus*, a U-boat commander says, in an address to students in a Gymnasium: "Blendend weiss schäumt auf die Hecksee, folgt, eine kostbar wallende Spitzenschleppe, dem Boot, das gleich einer festlich geschmückten Braut, übersprüht von Gischtschleiern, der totbringenden Hochzeit entgegenzieht" (83). (The stern wave foams blindingly white, following, like a precious billowing lace veil, after the boat that moves like a festively decorated bride, sprayed with veils of froth, towards the death-bringing wedding [my translation].).

Works Cited

Aley, Peter. *Jugendliteratur im Dritten Reich.* Gütersloh: C. Bertelsmann, 1967.

Arnold, Thomas, Jutta Schöning, and Ulrich Schröter. "Inhaltsanalyse und Protokoll des faschistischen Propaganda-filmes 'Hitlerjunge Quex.' " Diplomarbeit Johann-Wolfgang-Goethe U, Frankfurt/Main, 1979.

Bateson, Gregory. "An Analysis of the Nazi Film Hitlerjunge Quex." *The Study of Culture at a Distance.* Ed. Margaret Mead and Rhoda Métraux. Chicago: U of Chicago P, 1953.

Fromm, Erich. *Escape from Freedom.* New York: Rinehart and Co., 1941.

Grass, Günter. *Katz und Maus.* Neuwied am Rhein: Luchterhand, 1961.

Grenz, Dagmar. "Erich Kästners Kinderbücher in ihrem Verhältnis zu seiner Literatur für Erwachsene." Ed. M. Lypp. *Literatur für Kinder. Zeitschrift für Literaturwissenschaft und Linguistik* Beiheft 7 (1977): 155–69.

———. "Entwicklung als Bekehrung und Wandlung, Zu einem Typus der nationalsozialistischen Jugendliteratur." Ed. M. Lypp. *Literatur für Kinder. Zeitschrift für Literaturwissenschaft und Linguistik* Beiheft 7 (1977): 123—54.

Gutberlet, Heinrich. "Grenzlandschwur." *Deutsches Lesebuch für Volksschulen. 5. und 6. Schuljahr.* Giessen: Hessischer Schulbuchverlag Emil Roth, 1935.

Hitler, Adolf. *Reden an die deutsche Frau, Reichsparteitag, Nürnberg, 8. September 1934.* Berlin-Tempelhof: Schadenverhütung Verlagsgesellschaft, 1934.

Horkheimer, Max, ed. *Studien über Autorität und Familie.* Paris: Felix Alcan, 1936.

Jaroslawski, Renate, and Rüdiger Steinlein. "Die 'Politische Jugendschrift.' Zur Theorie und Praxis faschistischer deutscher Jugendliteratur." *Die Deutsche Literatur im Dritten Reich.* Ed. Horst Denkler and Karl Prümm. Stuttgart: Philipp Reclam, 1976. 305—29.

Kästner, Erich. *Als ich ein kleiner Junge war.* Zürich: Atrium, 1957.

————. "Bei Verbrennung meiner Bücher." *Das Erich Kästner Lesebuch.* Zürich: Diogenes, 1978.

————. *Emil and the Detectives.* Trans. May Massee. New York: Scholastic, 1965.

————. *Emil und die Detektive.* Berlin: Williams, 1928.

————. *Emil und die drei Zwillinge.* Zürich: Atrium, 1934.

————. *Fabian.* [1930]. Frankfurt/Main: Ullstein, 1975.

————. *Die Konferenz der Tiere.* Zürich: Europa-Verlag, 1949.

————. *Pünktchen und Anton.* Berlin: Williams, 1931.

Kamenetsky, Christa. *Children's Literature in Hitler's Germany.* Athens: Ohio U P, 1984.

Marcuse, Herbert. "A Study in Authority." *Studies in Critical Philosophy.* Trans. Joris de Bres. Boston: Beacon P, 1973.

Meyer, Hansgeorg. "Die deutsch Kinder- und Jugendliteratur 1933 bis 1945: Ein Versuch über die Entwicklungslinien." *Studien zur Geschichte der deutschen Kinder- und Jugendliteratur* 6/7. Berlin: Der Kinderbuchverlag, 1975.

Neveux, J. B. "La jeunesse et les luttes politiques dans 'Der Hitlerjunge Quex' de K. A. Schenzinger." *Revue d'Allemagne* 8 (1976): 431—48.

Reich, Wilhelm. *The Mass Psychology of Fascism.* Trans. Vincent R. Carfagno. New York: Farrar, Straus & Giroux, 1970.

Schenzinger, Karl Aloys. *Anilin.* Berlin: Zeitgeschichte, 1936.

————. *Atom.* München: Andermann, 1950.

————. *Hitlerjunge Quex.* Berlin: Zeitgeschichte, 1932.

————. *Man will uns kündigen.* Berlin: Dom Verlag, 1931.

————. *Metall.* Berlin: Zeitgeschichte, 1939.

————. *Schnelldampfer.* München, Wien: Andermann, 1951.

Schröter, Ulrich. "Vorbemerkung." *Hitlerjunge Quex: Einstellungsprotokoll.* München: Filmland Presse, 1980.

Sontag, Susan. "Fascinating Fascism." *Under the Sign of Saturn.* New York: Farrar, Straus, Giroux, 1980.

Suleiman, Susan Rubin. *Authoritarian Fictions. The Ideological Novel As a Literary Genre.* New York: Columbia U P, 1983.

Trilling, Lionel. "The Dispossessed." *New Republic* (19 Oct. 1932): 267—68.

Weber-Kellermann, Ingeborg. *Die deutsche Familie.* Frankfurt/Main: Suhrkamp, 1974.

"Playing Puckerage": Alcott's Plot in "Cupid and Chow-chow"

Elizabeth Keyser

Louisa May Alcott, despite the critical attention that she has recently received, remains underrated as a literary artist and misunderstood as a feminist. Eugenia Kaledin, although she puts the case more strongly than most Alcott critics, speaks for many when she deplores the fact that Alcott's "acceptance of the creed of womanly self-denial . . . aborted the promise of her art and led her to betray her most deeply felt values" (251). Like Kaledin, Judith Fetterley believes that Alcott preserved her artistic and moral integrity only in her anonymous and pseudonymous sensational stories. According to Fetterley, "What these stories . . . make clear is the amount of rage and intelligence Alcott had to suppress in order to attain her 'true style' and write *Little Women*" ("War" 370).[1] Unlike Kaledin and Fetterley, Elizabeth Langland reads the adult novel *Work* as a successful "feminist romance" that affirms "the possibility of growth in female community," but just as Fetterley sees Alcott's rage suppressed in *Little Women*, so Langland sees suppressed "the model of female development Alcott wanted to propose" (113, 117).

Those who do find a consistent feminist vision in Alcott's fiction—whether sensational, adult realistic, or children's—see that vision as only moderately progressive. Ruth K. MacDonald and Sarah Elbert, for example, view Alcott as advocating feminism in both her adult and her children's fiction. MacDonald, however, feels Alcott's feminism is compromised by her emphasis on domesticity and the doctrine of feminine influence: "As independent and strong-minded as Alcott would like women to be, she still finds that they are the moral guardians of the world, standing high on the pedestal where Victorian men had placed them, and caring for men who are obviously unable to care for themselves" (55). Elbert, on the other hand, believes that domesticity was a necessary precondition for Alcott's feminism. Thus Alcott's heroine Jo March attains "the final stage of true womanhood" by accepting "maternal responsibility for the whole world" (166). In answer to Elbert, I would argue that Alcott, while apparently portraying a fulfilled woman in Jo March, subtly presents us with the "sorrow of self-denial" that Kaledin attributes to Alcott herself.[2] And in contrast to all of these critics, much as I have learned from them, I would argue that Alcott is consistently subversive of traditional values for women—even in what appear to be the simplest and most sentimental of her children's stories.

Even those critics who praise *Little Women* ignore or, like MacDonald, dismiss the children's stories as mere potboilers.[3] As far as I know Joy A. Marsella is the only critic to have found these stories worth examining, and she admits that in them Alcott was hampered by constricting formulas and a simplistic moral code. Although Marsella is more sympathetic with Alcott as a writer for children than is Kaledin, she ultimately agrees that Alcott "to reach an audience" made "so many concessions that she inhibited her art" (138). These stories, then, present a challenge to those who would defend Alcott's artistic integrity, and a particularly interesting test case is provided by the 1872 story "Cupid and Chow-chow." Kaledin reads it as an "outspokenly hostile argument against the Woman's Suffrage Movement" (256). Marsella reads it as suggesting "cautious approval and acceptance of change; it assumes for women significant roles . . . and yet it affirms the traditional roles and values of 'woman's sphere' " (99). Thus both those who see Alcott as a failed or frustrated feminist and those who see her as a domestic feminist find the story a clear, even outspoken expression of her views.

However, in looking only at the surface of the story, these critics forget that the art of writing for children can—and probably should—involve duplicity. As contemporary children's author Penelope Lively has written: "I am not . . . entirely open with my reader. I am keeping something back, I am trying to construct a story for children like an iceberg. Only the tip is showing—the other seven-eighths is invisible, but without it the whole thing would sink or capsize. Because if the visible tip of it is the story . . . the other seven-eighths is the substance, the product of all that adult experience and preoccupation that I am trying to share with the child without his ever being aware of it" (21). In exposing the invisible seven-eighths of "Cupid and Chow-chow," I hope to show that the substance is Alcott's radical feminism.

The visible tip involves parallels between contrasting pairs: Cupid and Chow-chow; their mothers, Mrs. Ellen and Mrs. Susan; and their mothers' marriages. The story begins with the first meeting of two cousins—a gentle, loving, but rather vain little boy named Cupid and a rough, fiercely independent little girl named Chow-chow.[4] Cupid, with his golden lovelocks and velvet suit, expects Chow-chow to return his cousinly embrace, but Chow-chow, much affronted, wards him off by throwing stones at him. Later her father, Mr. George, apologizes to Cupid's parents by explaining that his wife, Mrs. Susan, has raised her "according to the new lights,—with contempt for dress and all frivolous pursuits; to make her hardy, independent, and quite above caring for such trifles as love, domestic life, or the feminine accomplishments we used to find so charming." To illustrate, he has Chow-chow deliver a tirade he has taught her on "Free speech, free love, free soil, free everything; and Woman's Puckerage for ever!" All laugh, "for it was delivered with such vigor that the speaker would have fallen on her nose if she had not been sustained by a strong arm," but after the laughter subsides, Cupid, puzzled, asks his mother what it all means. When she responds that it is "only fun," Chow-chow's mother upbraids Cupid's mother, Mrs. Ellen, for not preparing him "to take a nobler part in the coming struggle"; Mrs. Ellen answers that, if she raises him to be as good a man as his father, "no woman will suffer wrong at his hands" (693–94). By the end of this first episode the lines between the suffragist, Mrs. Susan, and the "true woman," Mrs. Ellen, are clearly drawn.

The weight of these parallel contrasts seems to favor Cupid, his mother, and her traditional marriage. Mrs. Ellen's reduction of the suffrage movement to childish fun, her refusal to violate the sanctity of childhood happiness with disturbing ideas, and her faith in the power of feminine influence to produce just men—all appeal to sentiment and reinforce conventional views. At the same time, Mr. George's catalogue of all that the suffragists are willing to forgo, including love, together with Chow-chow's unconscious parody of all that they are fighting for, including free love, tends to confirm suspicions of the women's movement. Chow-chow's mispronunciation of the word "suffrage" so that it comes out "puckerage" serves to equate the demand for suffrage with baby talk or babble. Further, Chow-chow's dependence upon the "strong arm" of her father, whom we are told she loves best, implies that the suffrage movement would collapse were it not for the tolerance and good will of men. Finally, the baleful looks exchanged by Mr. George and Mrs. Susan, especially in contrast to the understanding looks exchanged by Cupid's parents, imply that demands for suffrage disrupt family peace and harmony.

Chow-chow's rude, unwomanly behavior, which her father attributes to his wife's involvement in the suffrage movement, continues in the next two episodes. First Chow-chow, by accusing Cupid of being a "dandy-prat," shames him into giving up his velvet suit, cutting off his golden lovelocks, and sticking court-plaster on his attractive dimple. Then, after calling Cupid a "fraid-cat," Chow-chow dares him to place his finger in a "hay-cutting machine," where she accidentally crushes it. In both episodes Cupid is praised by the narrator and adult characters for the courage with which he bears indignity and pain. After the accident to Cupid's finger Chow-chow is chastened, and the narrator comments that, in performing "small labors of love, she learned a little lesson that did her more good than many of mamma's lectures." And her unwonted gentleness prompts her father to remark to Cupid's mother, "I have hopes of her yet, for all the woman is not taken out of her, in spite of the new lights" (696). Although Mrs. Susan stubbornly insists that nursing Cupid is simply preparation for Chow-chow's medical career,[5] Cupid's mother calls it a "good lesson in loving and serving others for love's sake, as all women must learn to do soon or late" (697). Ostensibly, the haircutting and "hay-cutting machine" episodes demonstrate that Cupid is neither a "dandy-prat" nor a "fraid-cat" but a true man and that Chow-chow, were it not for her mother's faulty teaching and bad example, would be a true woman.

Chow-chow's softening during Cupid's convalescence anticipates her own and her mother's change of heart. But first Alcott strengthens the negative parallel between mother and daughter by having Chow-chow agree to "marry" Cupid and then add "certain worldly conditions which she had heard discussed by mamma and her friends" (698). Once again, the narrator, Mr. George, and Mrs. Ellen deplore Chow-chow's unreasonableness. Mr. George, when appealed to, calls her "a little goose" and suggests that such materialism had kept him and his wife from enjoying "love's young dream." Mrs. Ellen tries to help by buying flowers from Cupid's garden and by teaching Chow-chow "sundry feminine arts . . . for Mrs. Susan was so busy hearing lectures, reading reports, and attending to the education of other people's children that her own ran wild" (699). But when she and Cupid finally play house, Chow-chow quickly tires of the domestic role; instead, she insists on attending a "puckerage lecture" and stubbornly refuses to share a pie. Mrs. Susan, who eavesdrops with the other adults, is embarrassed by this parody of her marriage. And when Chow-chow walks out, leaving Cupid to care for their doll family, Mrs. Susan tacitly admits her own fault by acknowledging that Chow-chow is in the wrong (702).

Chow-chow's own conversion is accompanied by a litany of praise for womanly women and of blame for those who make unreasonable demands. Following the breakup of her "marriage," Chow-chow amuses herself by delivering "the droll preachment her father had taught her in ridicule of mamma's hobby." The remorseful Mrs. Susan begs her husband to stop it, calling it "so absurd." Mrs. Ellen, having gained the victory, tries to be conciliatory and consoling: "There is some sense in it, and I have no doubt the real and true will come to pass when we women learn how far to go, and how to fit ourselves for the new duties by doing the old ones well." The narrator adds that Mrs. Ellen "kept herself so womanly sweet and strong that no one could deny her any right she chose to claim."[6] Mr. George, not quite so magnanimous as Mrs. Ellen, cannot resist giving a little lecture of his own: "She is like so many of those who mount your hobby, Susan, and ride away into confusions of all sorts, leaving empty homes behind them. The happy, womanly woman will have the most influence after all, and do the most to help the bitter, sour, discontented ones." As though to demonstrate still further her mother's folly, Chow-chow "burst into a tremendous harangue . . . as if her wrongs had upset her wits" (703). After the secretary on which Chow-chow is standing falls out from under her and Cupid saves her from injury, Mr. George warns against shaky platforms, but by now both Chow-chow and her mother are ready to renounce the "puckerage" cause. The narrator tells us that Chow-

chow "like a true woman, though she demanded impossibilities at first, yet when her heart was won . . . asked nothing but love, and was content with a saucepan" (704). The story ends with both Chow-chow and her mother sealing their surrenders with "a kiss of peace" after vowing never to "play that nasty old puckerage any more" (703–04).

How are we to reconcile such a vow with Alcott's consistent defense of suffragism? In Alcott's *Work*, published a year after "Cupid and Chow-chow," Christie Devon, a widowed mother, finds her calling as a public speaker for women's rights. Characterizing herself as " 'strong-minded,' a radical, and a reformer," Christie feels that "this new task seems to offer me the chance of being among the pioneers, to do the hard work, share the persecution, and help lay the foundation of a new emancipation" (437, 431). In an 1875 letter to the *Woman's Journal* Alcott compared women's protests to the shot "heard round the world"; that same year she attended the Woman's Congress where she approvingly noted young women "getting ready to play their parts on the wider stage" (Stern 441; "My Girls" 26). Alcott actually defended the suffragists against the false stereotype she herself seems to have created in Mrs. Susan, for she wrote to the *Woman's Journal* in 1883 that "the assertion that suffragists do not care for children, and prefer notoriety to the joys of maternity, is so fully contradicted by the lives of the women who are trying to make the world a safer and better place for both sons and daughters, that no defense is needed" (Stern 447). Finally, in 1885, Alcott wrote to the American Woman Suffrage Association that it was impossible for her to "ever 'go back' on woman suffrage." She added that "I should be a traitor to all I most love, honor and desire to imitate if I did not covet a place among those who are giving their lives to the emancipation of the white slaves of America" and professed herself "willing to bear ridicule and reproach for the truth's sake" (Stern 449).

Although Chow-chow and Mrs. Susan betray their cause, Alcott in describing their betrayal does not, for from the beginning of the story she undercuts the sentimental views of both the "true woman," Mrs. Ellen, and the narrator. The story's opening words—"Mamma began it by calling her rosy, dimpled, year-old baby Cupid"—are significantly ambiguous, for to what does the "it" refer? The rest of the paragraph allows us to deduce what the narrator means by "it": Cupid's ability to love everybody and make everybody love him. But the rest of the story reveals what the *author* means by "it": nothing less than the whole trouble between Cupid and Chow-chow, which as we have seen, represents the whole trouble between the sexes.

In the first episode, for example, Cupid's assumption that Chow-chow "*must* love him," an assumption encouraged by Mrs. Ellen, leads to amorous aggression. Slipping up behind Chow-chow, this "contented young peacock" embraces her so that, when she looks up, she sees "two red lips suggestively puckered for a hearty kiss." When the indignant Chow-chow struggles to free herself, Cupid's "velvet arms pressed her firmly," and his kisses "lit upon her nose, chin, top-knot, and ear; for, having begun, Cupid did not know when to leave off" (691). In fact, this attempt to "do the honors of his pleasant home like a gentleman" reads something like a rape. And if read in this way, Cupid's "puckered" lips are indeed "suggestive" —suggestive of a connection between male "puckerage" or sexual aggression and the demand for female "puckerage" or political power. Moreover, the definition of a "pucker" as a "ridge" or "wrinkle," its affinity with such words as "pocket" or "purse," and Chow-chow's innocent association of "free love" with "Woman's Puckerage" all suggest the story's concern with exploring women's sexual nature and men's sexual tyranny.[7]

Alcott underscores the need to restrain male and explore female "puckerage" in the haircutting and "hay-cutting machine" episodes. In the first of these Alcott's allusions to the story of Samson[8] imply that Cupid, rather than establishing his masculine identity, is tricked by Chow-chow into surrendering it. At first glance the gentle Cupid, called an "effeminate boy" by Mrs. Susan, would seem to have little in common with the biblical hero: Samson's masculine strength is in his hair whereas Cupid's lovelocks seem signs of effeminate weakness; Samson betrays his secret in unmanly fashion whereas Cupid consents to cut his hair in an effort to prove his manhood. But in addition to his great physical strength, Samson is remembered for his cupidity—his desire for women—and his violence, the massacres he perpetrates after desire has led him to betray himself. As Phillips P. Elliott has written, Samson "is the incarnation of the kind of power which is out of control" (787). Cupid, in his initial assault on

"Suddenly a pair of velvet arms embraced her." ("Cupid and Chow-chow, etc." *Aunt Jo's Scrap-bag* [1887], 3:4.)

Chow-chow, demonstrates on a diminutive scale the unrestrained desire that, in Samson's case, leads to wanton destruction and eventual self-destruction. And in both cases enslavement to desire leads to more literal enslavement: Samson is taken prisoner by the Philistines, and the shorn Cupid is described as Chow-chow's "slave" (695).

Just as the loss of Samson's hair precedes the loss of his eyes, so the loss of Cupid's hair precedes another symbolic castration—the near-loss of his finger. Chow-chow, challenging Cupid to prove his manliness still further, places his "plump forefinger between two wheels . . . gave a brisk turn to the handle, slipped in doing so, and brought

"The wounded hero, with his arm in a sling, permitted her to minister to him." ("Cupid and Chow-chow, etc." *Aunt Jo's Scrap-bag* [1887], 3:17.)

the whole weight of the cruel cogs on the tender little finger, crushing the top quite flat." According to the narrator's sentimental interpretation, Chow-chow insists, as "penance," on watching the doctor "dress the 'smashed' finger" and flourish "the bright instruments" (696). But what passes for "penance" could very well·be pleasure. Like Jane Eyre after Rochester has been maimed and blinded (and Jane too is eager to cut his hair), Chow-chow now agrees to marriage. None of the adults so absorbed in observing the two children draws quite the right conclusion from these episodes, for rather than teaching manly courage and womanly compassion, they indicate that men's need to prove their masculinity, to meet

social expectations of masculine behavior, actually unmans them—
or prompts women to try to do so.

But Cupid, for all his masculine aggressiveness and desire to
prove his manliness, is closer to the feminine stereotype, and Chow-
chow, despite her feminine wiles in thwarting him, is closer to the
masculine. In the opening paragraphs Cupid is described as if he
were a little girl of the sugar-and-spice variety. In order to gain
and preserve love, he takes great pains with his appearance and frequently consults his mirror. When Chow-chow chides him about his
vanity, he allows her to cut his hair, after which he pleads patheti-
cally, "Do you like me better now?" (695). Thus Cupid's vanity and
its reform derive from a single source: an overwhelming need for
love and approval. And since Cupid's reform is other-directed
rather than inner-directed, he is vulnerable to Chow-chow's capri-
cious charge that he "ain't half so pretty" as he was before. Cupid,
then, is the woman who must somehow cultivate her beauty while
preserving her humility—or at least the appearance of it; Chow-
chow is the man who derides feminine vanity while spurning the
woman not vain enough to attend to her appearance. And once
again Mrs. Ellen, by instilling in Cupid this excessive eagerness to
please, can be said to have begun "it" or to be responsible for Cupid's vulnerability.

However, there is more to Chow-chow's behavior than masculine
contempt for feminine vanity, as is suggested by her calling Cupid's
attractive dimple an "ugly hole" and by her insisting that he refrain
from "fingering it" (694). The covering of the dimple with court-
plaster and in the next episode the crushing and the "dressing" of
the finger indicate men's ambivalence toward women's sexuality or
"puckerage." With Cupid's dimple covered, Chow-chow, like Victorian men, is spared the reminder of women's sexual nature, and
with both dimple and finger covered Cupid, like Victorian women,
is denied the opportunity to explore, develop, and enjoy it. Yet, as
we have seen, Chow-chow on one level represents conventional
feminine thought and behavior, and on this level her fear of and
revulsion at Cupid's dimple express female self-hatred as well as
male misogyny. Just as Cupid sees Chow-chow as his "only mirror,"
so Chow-chow sees in Cupid a mirror of all that her male-dominated
world has taught her to despise in herself.

Alcott's attack on masculine sexual tyranny and feminine emotional dependency is strengthened by parallels between "Cupid and Chow-chow" and two other works that contain haircutting scenes: "The Rape of the Lock" and *The Mill on the Floss*.[9] In the most explicit of these allusions, her use of Pope's phrase "fatal shears," Alcott invites us to see the sexual significance of the children's behavior. For Belinda, who like Cupid is narcissistically vain about her curls, does not willingly sacrifice her hair and indeed regards the theft of a single curl as tantamount to rape. Thus this allusion sheds light on the contradictory situation of women, who are conditioned to excite male interest, as Belinda and Cupid do with their curls, but also to resent the aggressive interest they thereby excite, as Belinda and Chow-chow do their attempted "rapes." The way in which Alcott splits masculine and feminine characteristics between the two children is further suggested by their similarities with Eliot's Maggie Tulliver. Physically the unruly and rebellious Maggie resembles Chow-chow, and her contempt for her dainty cousin Lucy, like Chow-chow's contempt for Cupid, reveals ambivalence toward her own femininity. But though she possesses Chow-chow's wild black hair, Maggie resembles Cupid in her willingness to cut it in a vain attempt to win approval. Like Cupid, Maggie is a slave to those she loves and suffers countless rebuffs and insults from her brother Tom, whom she would do almost anything to please. In any conflict "the need of being loved, the strongest need in poor Maggie's nature, began to wrestle with her pride and soon threw it" (34). Masculine tyranny, like Chow-chow's "love of power," feeds and grows on feminine dependency.

In the marriage sequence, however, Alcott shows that women's economic—as opposed to emotional—dependency enslaves both women and men. When Chow-chow unreasonably demands that Cupid earn the money on which to marry while she waits in idleness, she imitates her mother's pragmatic conservatism, not her radicalism. The insistence of both mother and daughter that their spouses be good providers seems less an expression of their mercenary natures than of their resentment at being excluded from the world of remunerative labor and at being relegated instead to the domestic sphere. And the brief paragraph describing Chow-chow's instruction in housewifely arts, which include hemming a tablecloth, dusting, and concocting "Coopy's favorite pudding," seems subtly designed to justify that resentment. The narrator deplores the fact that these "virtuous efforts soon flagged" and "ended in *ennui*" (699), but the word sums up the effect of such efforts on any lively intelligence. By the standards of Mrs. Ellen and the narrator, Mrs. Susan's bad example has produced an unreasonable, unfeeling, and unfeminine daughter. But Alcott actually points up the absurdity of traditional sex roles: the male works himself to death so that the couple can afford to marry; the female bores herself to death while waiting until they can do so.

Cupid, by working to buy Chow-chow's acceptance, becomes a typical male martyr. But just as he earlier represented women's emotional dependence, here he also represents their economic dependence. Often considered unmarriageable unless able to make a financial contribution to the marriage, women were ill-equipped to do so by means of their own exertions. Cupid must rely on his charm in order to raise money: "Then he went about among his friends, and begged and borrowed small sums . . . pleading for a temporary accommodation so earnestly and prettily that no one could refuse" (698). Even though he works in his garden, the reference to his injured hand suggests how handicapped he is for any economic endeavor, and his mother, by purchasing his nosegays at inflated prices, only fosters an illusion of self-sufficiency. As we have seen, Mrs. Ellen tries to provide Chow-chow with the domestic lessons that Mrs. Susan has neglected, but this episode better supports Mrs. Susan's charge: that Mrs. Ellen has not prepared Cupid "to take a nobler part in the coming struggle" (693).

In the houseplaying scene Alcott continues to undermine what appears to be her antisuffrage statement by having Cupid and Chow-chow literally play the traditional roles. For example, Cupid "put on papa's hat, took a large book under his arm, and went away" to work, while Chow-chow "bestirred herself at home in a most energetic manner" (700). In the evening Cupid wishes to relax after his day's labors, but Chow-chow, who has remained at home, craves the stimulation of her "puckerage" meeting. Even though Cupid objects at first to spending the evening at his club, once there he becomes thoroughly absorbed and does not return home until time for breakfast the next morning. When Chow-chow resents being taken for granted and walks out, Cupid suddenly finds himself helpless: "It was truly pathetic to see poor Mr. Cupid's efforts at housekeeping and baby-tending" (701). Earlier Cupid's blissful "ride on the rocking-horse with his entire family about him" had ended in disaster, suggesting that the traditional marriage, with its sexual division of labor and recreation, is as dangerous a "hobby" as "puckerage."

Alcott further condemns the way in which traditional marriage restricts women to the private sphere by once again inverting sex roles. Although Chow-chow gets the meals and Cupid goes to work, she gives the orders, makes the decisions, and, by refusing Cupid his share of the pie, ends the game. It is she who, in her craving for action and excitement, rocks carelessly, upsetting their doll family, and it is she who walks out, "rejoicing in her freedom," leaving Cupid to experience the trials of a single parent. After the deaths of their children, he tries to amuse himself, but "these wanderings always ended near the ruins of his home." Chow-chow, on the other hand, "bustled up" to give her "puckerage" lecture and so forget her private cares in public activity. One surmises that, were it not for her untimely accident, Chow-chow would have recovered from the loss of domestic happiness, whereas Cupid, who lacks her resources, gives every sign of remaining inconsolable. Although it is Chow-chow who, after her accident, is described as asking "nothing but love," it is Cupid who throughout the story makes one sacrifice after another in order to obtain it and seems utterly dependent upon it. And, as we have seen, his sacrifices earn him a condescending acceptance, not love.

Cupid's injuries, humiliations, and utter helplessness when Chow-chow deserts him should enable us to discern the ironic distance between Alcott and those who have been taken as representing her views: the sentimental narrator, the sardonic Mr. George, and, expecially, the "true woman," Mrs. Ellen. From the story's opening words, Alcott implies that it is Mrs. Ellen who is responsible for Cupid's physical and psychic vulnerability. By naming him "Cupid," after the diminutive version of Eros, she seems determined to infantilize him. As Mrs. Ellen tells Mrs. Susan, she does not "care to disturb his happy childhood with quarrels beyond his comprehension," but she also begrudges him those experiences that would move him beyond childhood. Significantly, when Cupid and Chow-chow quarrel, Mrs. Ellen predicts and even hopes that Cupid will soon give in even though the other three adults believe that Chow-chow is in the wrong. And instead of letting Cupid fight his own battles, Mrs. Ellen wants to intervene and "help the dears bridge over their little trouble" (702). But perhaps most important, Mrs. Ellen, by naming her son Cupid and by prizing the lovelocks that contribute to his sexual ambiguity, seems intent on denying his sexual nature and the nature of Eros, or adult passion, itself. Cupid and Chow-chow achieve a truce when, under Mrs. Ellen's influence, both surrender their "puckerage"—their potential for adult sexual passion and political participation—and instead become little man and little woman. The chaste kiss that Mr. George and Mrs. Susan exchange in imitation of the child couple suggests that Mrs. Susan's unilateral surrender of her "puckerage" has not made their relation-ship more mature but has actually reduced them both to the level of children.[10]

Yet Mrs. Ellen's doctrine of womanly influence seems supported when at the end of the story Cupid divides the pie "with masculine justice" while invoking Mamma's teaching: "The fairest way is to cut it 'zactly in halves, and each have a piece. Mamma says that's the right thing to do always" (704). According to Mrs. Ellen, a woman appeals to masculine justice with her sweetness and insures the efficacy of that appeal by raising her sons to be just men. But Alcott's linking of feminine influence with masculine justice in the division of the pie actually undermines this doctrine, for she suggests that while women like Mrs. Ellen can inculcate and appeal to the principle of justice, they must rely on men to enact it. And by allowing men to determine what constitutes equality, they perpetuate the "separate but equal" spheres that are not really equal at all. Similarly, the narrator's sentimental notion that no one can deny the claims of a "womanly woman" seems at first to be supported, for Cupid gives Chow-chow much more of the pie than she asks for. But Alcott, by having Chow-chow ask for a mere taste when half the pie belongs to her, implies that the "womanly woman" can be depended upon never to claim her rightful share.

Finally, Mrs. Ellen's faith in feminine influence as the means of insuring masculine justice seems undercut by another parallel with

The Mill on the Floss. Tom Tulliver, not content with masculine justice, exercises masculine magnanimity by allowing Maggie the more desirable piece of jam puff. Like the chastened Chow-chow, who wants just a "tiny bit" of the pie, Maggie at first is reluctant to eat her share. But finally at Tom's urging she devours it, only to have him condemn her as greedy and cruelly abandon her. Maggie's lesson, then, is that masculine justice and even magnanimity may exact a heavy toll in female suffering.

Thus the doctrine of Mrs. Ellen, the doctrine that Alcott seems at first to endorse, involves women in a self-defeating circle. Like Cupid, Mrs. Ellen, and the chastened Chow-chow, they rely on sweetness to earn as rewards those rights that should be theirs regardless of their power—or lack of it—to please and inspire love. And because they are dependent upon that power, they must be careful not to offend or alienate men, as Mrs. Susan and the suffragists do, by insisting upon those rights. In short, women, because they are conditioned to believe that their welfare depends upon their power to elicit love, refuse to risk its loss even to gain the political power that would make them independent of it. Alcott, by showing us how Chow-chow and her mother "go back" on suffrage, is not betraying her own feminist values Rather she is demonstrating women's need for political power and, in the story of Cupid's disappointments, exposing the inadequacy of feminine influence.

True, feminine influence does seem to triumph in the sense that Cupid, by patiently enduring his injuries and humiliations, succeeds in transforming the lives of those around him, whereas Mrs. Susan, by railing against her injuries, accomplishes nothing. However, Mrs. Susan's failure is illuminated by her husband's warning against shaky platforms, meaning of course the platforms of the suffragists. At first Alcott seems to imply that only by gaining the support of men can women earn their rights, for Chow-chow when she used "Papa's knee" as a platform was "sustained by a strong arm" and did not fall. Yet perhaps it is the precarious perch on papa's knee that makes the sustaining arm necessary. In fact the platform of Chow-chow and her mother proves treacherous not because they lack masculine support but because they are too dependent, both emotionally and economically, upon it. In another sense, then, it is masculine power that triumphs. Chow-chow's platform collapses in

the final scene only after Mrs. Ellen, her father, and even her
mother have denounced it. As her father predicts that "the happy,
womanly women will have the most influence after all," Chow-chow
"burst into a tremendous harangue . . . as if her wrongs had upset
her wits. All of a sudden the whole secretary lurched forward . . .
and the marble slab came sliding after, as if to silence the irrepress-
ible little orator forever" (703). Betrayed by her mother to the
equivalent of the Philistines, Chow-chow responds, like Samson, by
almost burying herself beneath the ruins of her rage. Thus feminine influence conspires with masculine power to madden those
indignant at their wrongs and silence the demand for their redress.

Unlike Eugenia Kaledin I do not wonder that "Louisa did nothing
to try to keep 'Cupid and Chow-chow' out of the story anthology *Jo's
Scrap Bag*" (257) and that she made it a title story, for rather than
betraying her feminist values it conveys them in a remarkably com-
pressed form. And as though she wanted at least a few of her readers
to discern the shape of her entire fictional iceberg, Alcott included in
the same volume a story entitled "Mamma's Plot."[11] In this story a
little girl named Kitty is disturbed because her boarding school
headmistress insists on reading the girls' letters home and correcting
them as though they were compositions. Kitty's mamma, although
she does not approve of this repressive policy, feels that her daughter should submit to it—or at least appear to do so. However,
mamma enables Kitty to circumvent the policy by providing her with
notepaper of different colors, each of which conveys a covert message. By adopting this strategy Kitty can indicate her desperate lone-
liness while writing that "our meeting will be the more delightful for
this separation" (786). "Mamma's Plot," it seems clear, is a paradigm
for Alcott's "plot" in "Cupid and Chow-chow" and other of her neglected children's stories. Although the action of the story, like
Kitty's words, would seem to indicate submission and conformity, its
ironic reversals, juxtapositions, word play, and allusions conspire,
like the color of Kitty's paper, to tell another story.

Madeleine B. Stern has argued on the basis of Alcott's feminist
letters to the *Woman's Journal* that "her feminism was the feminism
of a human being impatient with indifference, apathy, and intoler-
ance. Neither humorless nor merely aggressive, hers was a firm and
convincing advocacy that advanced a cause while it enriched a life"

(436). In "Cupid and Chow-chow" Alcott does not abandon this advocacy but simply conceals it for what Penelope Lively calls "the best possible motive." Writes Lively, "It is not that I am sugaring the pill or disguising instruction as something else but simply that I am refusing to abandon the things that interest me on the grounds that they may be too complex for someone of ten or twelve" (23). The tip of Alcott's fictional iceberg may present Chow-chow playing and abandoning the game of puckerage, but her concealed seven-eighths is serious—not only about suffrage but about the need for far more radical reform.

Notes

1. See also Fetterley's "Impersonating 'Little Women.'"
2. See my essays "Alcott's Portraits of the Artist" and "Women and Girls in . . . *Jo's Boys*."
3. MacDonald writes in her preface, "Though Alcott was prolific as a short story writer, these stories usually have not endured nor are they an important part of the Alcott canon."
4. "Cupid and Chow-chow" first appeared in *Hearth and Home* 4, nos. 20–21 (18–25 May 1872). It then became the title story of Alcott's *Cupid and Chow-chow, Etc., Aunt Jo's Scrap-Bag*, vol. 3 (Boston: Roberts Bros., 1874). All references will be to the recent reprint of the story in *Works of Louisa May Alcott*, edited by Claire Booss.
5. Chow-chow in many ways resembles "Naughty Nan" in Alcott's *Little Men* (1871). Like Chow-chow, Nan is rough and wild and has no use for dolls. But like Chow-chow, Nan can be gentle with the ill and injured, and in *Jo's Boys* (1885) she fulfills her dream of becoming a doctor.
6. This description of Mrs. Ellen echoes the description of Daisy Brooke in *Little Men*: "Daisy knew nothing about woman's rights; she quietly took all that she wanted, and no-one denied her claim, because she did not undertake what she could not carry out, but unconsciously used the all-powerful right of her own influence to win from others any privilege for which she had proved her fitness" (531). In the same passage Nan, who resembles Chow-chow, is said to possess "the spirit of a rampant reformer."
7. See the *Oxford English Dictionary* for definitions of "puckerage."
8. See Judges 13–16.
9. Still another famous haircutting occurs in Alcott's *Little Women*. Jo's sacrifice of her "one beauty" can be viewed as an act of masculine self-assertion or of feminine self-abnegation.
10. I am indebted to Elaine Showalter for this suggestion.
11. "Mamma's Plot" was first published in *The Youth's Companion* 46, no. 6 (6 February 1873). It was then reprinted in *Cupid and Chow-chow, Etc.*

Works Cited

Alcott, Louisa May. "Cupid and Chow-chow." *Works of Louisa May Alcott*. 1873. Ed. Claire Booss. New York: Avenel, 1982. 690–704.

——. *Little Men. Works.* 393–594.

——. "Mamma's Plot." *Works.* 784–89.

——. "My Girls." *My Girls, Etc., Aunt Jo's Scrap-Bag.* Vol. 4. Boston: Roberts Bros., 1878.

——. *Work: A Story of Experience.* Ed. Sarah Elbert. New York: Shocken, 1977.

Elbert, Sarah. *A Hunger for Home: Louisa May Alcott and Little Women.* Philadelphia: Temple UP, 1984.

Eliot, George. *The Mill on the Floss.* 1860. Boston: Houghton Mifflin, 1961.

Elliott, Phillips P. Exposition to the Book of Judges. *The Interpreter's Bible.* 12 Vols. New York: Abingden-Cokesbury, 1953. 2: 775–98.

Fetterley, Judith. "Impersonating 'Little Women': the Radicalism of Alcott's *Behind a Mask.*" *Women's Studies* 10 (1983): 1–14.

——. "*Little Women*: Alcott's Civil War." *Feminist Studies* 5 (1979): 369–83.

Kaledin, Eugenia. "Louisa May Alcott: Success and the Sorrow of Self-Denial." *Women's Studies* 5 (1978): 251–63.

Keyser, Elizabeth. "Alcott's Portraits of the Artist as Little Woman." *International Journal of Women's Studies* 5 (1982): 445–59.

——. "Women and Girls in Louisa May Alcott's *Jo's Boys.*" *International Journal of Women's Studies* 6 (1983): 457–71.

Langland, Elizabeth. "Female Stories of Experience: Alcott's *Little Women* in Light of *Work.*" *The Voyage In: Fictions of Female Development.* Ed. Elizabeth Abel, Marianne Hirsch, and Elizabeth Langland. Hanover: UP of New England, 1983. 112–27.

Lively, Penelope. "Children and the Art of Memory: Part I." *Horn Book Magazine* 54 (1978): 17–23.

MacDonald, Ruth K. *Louisa May Alcott.* Boston: Twayne, 1983.

Marsella, Joy A. *The Promise of Destiny: Children and Women in the Short Stories of Louisa May Alcott.* Westport: Greenwood, 1983.

Stern, Madeleine B. "Louisa Alcott's Feminist Letters." *Studies in the American Renaissance.* Ed. Joel Myerson. Boston: Twayne, 1978. 429–52.

Bleeding Romans on Leaky Barges: Elijah Fenton's Cleopatra and the Process of Schoolboy Verse

Samuel J. Rogal

Throughout literary history, the poetic productions of the juvenile mind have been viewed from various rhetorical and generic perspectives but with essentially similar purposes and from fairly consistent points of view. We may recall D'Avenant's notion concerning the protection of the young genius, in that "A slender poet must have time to grow, / And spread and burnish as his brothers do" (Lloyd 180), as well as Dr. Johnson's initial, if not erroneous, reaction to Thomas Chatterton as "the most extraordinary young man that has encountered my knowledge. It is wonderful how the whelp has written such things" (Boswell 752). Coleridge, we remember, could admit to the positive reception accorded his 1794 collection only because those juvenile pieces "were considered buds of hope, and promises of better works to come" (Coleridge 110), while Whitwell Elwin writes of Gray's early command of poetical language as being "the chief merits of these fruits of his Eton education, for there is throughout a want of substance in the ideas" (458). Finally, there exists Swinburne's counterattack upon Richard Buchanan; although not totally applicable to the subject at hand, Swinburne's statement can glide easily into this discussion: "The tadpole poet will never grow into anything bigger than a frog; not though in that stage of development he should puff and blow himself till he bursts with windy adulation at the heels of the laurelled ox" (Swinburne 6:425).

In general, the rhymed outpourings of schoolboys hold little to attract the attentions of serious readers. Although, for instance, the seventeen-year-old Milton's Latin elegies and his "Death of a Fair Infant Dying of a Cough" send forth occasional beams of merit, they essentially represent exercises in the self-education of the poet; as such, readers may view them as minor but necessary junctures on the route toward artistic and intellectual maturity. Should a poet, unlike Milton, fail to reach that maturity, or at least fall short of producing a significant body of major poetry, then the juvenilia drops quickly into the chasm of literary obscurity, the reputation of its creator following behind with equal rapidity. To the latter category belongs the focus of this discussion, *Cleopatra. A Poem*, as well as its writer, Elijah Fenton (1683–1730).

A review of the life and work of Fenton requires little time or effort. He preceded Pope into the world by five years and departed fourteen years before him. Aside from his contributions to the translation of Pope's *Odyssey* (1726)—specifically Books 1, 4, 19, and 22—he produced nothing to distinguish him from the legion of intelligent Augustans capable of harnessing occasional thoughts to occasional lauguage, attaching them to occasional couplets, and driving them off to participate in occasional celebrations. Thus, for reasons known principally to himself, Fenton addressed "An Ode to the Sun" at and for the outset of 1707:

> Begin, celestial source of light,
> To gild the new-revolving sphere;
> And from the pregnant womb of night,
> Urge on to birth the infant Year.   (Johnson, *Works* 10:391)

His tributes to Queen Anne, Lord John Gower, Margaret Cavendish Harley, Thomas Lambard, Thomas Southerne, and Pope fare no better; they tend to underscore Johnson's conclusion that "to examine his performances one by one would be tedious" (Johnson, *Lives* 2:279). No less so would be an examination of *Cleopatra*—that is, if such an exercise were to go forth for no other purpose than to pass critical judgment upon the piece. However, if an analysis of the poem led to and produced something of value (or even of interest) relative to the *process* of juvenile verse as practiced in the late seventeenth century, then the tedium might have some merit to it. Let us, therefore, at least indulge in the attempt.

Virtually everything we know about the history of Fenton's *Cleopatra* comes to us by way of an interesting labor of love bearing the anthological/genealogical title *Elijah Fenton: His Poetry and Friends. A Monograph by William Watkiss Lloyd, M.R.S.L., Member of the Dilettanti Society, and Corresponding Member of the Archaeological Society of Rome and Palermo, etc. Edited by The Rev. George Livingstone Fenton, M.A., Late H.E.I.C. Chaplain at Poona. Preceded by a New Life of the Poet, by Robert Fenton, Newcastle-under-Lyme. With a Brief Sketch of the Author*

(W.W.L.) by Sophia Beale. The firm of Albert and Daniel printed 250 copies of this volume in 1894; 195 of those were sent directly to subscribers. Robert Fenton informs us that "at the early age of seventeen years, whilst yet a student at the Grammar School of Newcastle-under-Lyme, Fenton penned the hitherto unpublished poem called 'Cleopatra; in imitation of Chaucer,' which is given to the world—for the first time—at the end of this volume [173–86]; the M.S. bears the autographic signature, in full, of Fenton, and the date 1700" (Lloyd 12–13). In fact, the Lloyd-Fenton-Fenton-Beale effort does not include a photograph (fol. 186) of the last five lines of the manuscript, the autograph, and the date. Apparently, young Fenton left his manuscript at the Staffordshire home of his oldest brother, Thomas, sometime prior to July 1, 1700—the date of the poet's departure for Jesus College, Cambridge. The industrious scholar will come to realize that *Cleopatra* does indeed not appear on the *Miscellaneous Poems* of Fenton published during his lifetime (1712, 1714, 1720, 1722 editions); in or as an appendix to individual poems published between 1707 and 1730; nor in collections of Fenton's poems published with those of other poets and edited by Johnson, Anderson, or Chalmers.

The poem itself comes forward as an example of how well or how poorly—depending upon a reader's particular degree of tolerance—an imaginative schoolboy could follow the advice of his elders. Dryden, in his *Prologue to the University of Oxford* (1674), claimed that "With joy we bring what our dead authors writ, / And beg from you the value of their wit" (Selected Works 202). That couplet forms the motto for *Cleopatra*; what follows serves to measure, with accuracy, the level of young Fenton's poetic abilities. He himself may have undergone periods of utter joy while composing the poem; for the reader, there remains little beyond severe physical and intellectual upheaval, as witnessed by these lines (an obvious allusion to *Aeneid* 8.707–13):

> But harass'd Neptune soon began to frown,
> While bleeding Romans stain'd his naval crown.
> The Queen, o'erpower'd in arms, constrained to yield,
> In shatter'd galleys quits the liquid field'
> And (Phoebus resting in his western dome)
> With leaky barges cleaves the blushing foam.   (Lloyd 183)

While one remains free to admire the young man's ability to treat a significant military engagement with such conciseness, the preceding lines reflect his inability to control his imagination and exuberance—a seemingly natural weakness among young artists of any literary age. He set out to imitate an older form and, at the same time, produce a heroic poem that would meet the critical criteria of his own times; unfortunately, he did not—or could not—take full advantage of all that his sources had to offer him.

The manuscript of *Cleopatra* identifies the piece simply as an imitation of Chaucer, but limiting the model to the work of that poet—particularly his *Legend of Good Women*—perhaps oversimplifies that issue. If Fenton had knowledge of Chaucer (and we can only speculate as to the quality and the substance of his education at the Grammar School at Newcastle-under-Lyme), then he must assuredly have read Shakespeare, and he most certainly had more than a passing glance at Dryden. Those academic contacts would have left the young scholar with three distinct but different variations on the same woman: Chaucer, working principally from Boccaccio, developed the ideal of a medieval woman who faithfully followed the god of Love to the extent that she almost qualified for sainthood; Shakespeare, in *Antony and Cleopatra* (1606), formed the dual image of a fascinating temptress and a tragic heroine; Dryden, in *All for Love* (1677), drew the portrait of a sentimentalized and virtuous mistress striving exceedingly hard to become a loving wife. To see the results of a sixteen-year-old schoolboy's mosaic, we may turn first to the overall structure of Fenton's poem.

Generally, Fenton constructed his four cantos and 172 lines upon the standard frames of historical-biographical information surrounding the relationship between Cleopatra (based on the model of Dido) and Marc Antony: (1) Cleopatra's voyage, presumably to apologize to the Triumviri, but essentially to conquer Antony; (2) the exchange of "entertainments" between Egypt's queen and the Roman general; (3) Cleopatra's eventual conquest of Antony; (4) the battle of Actium, Cleopatra's flight from the engagement, and Antony's self-inflicted death; (5) the Egyptian queen's own death from the bites of the asps that she herself applied to escape the wrath of Augustus Caesar. Thus, the first canto of the poem begins with the death of Ptolemaeus XIII and that monarch's "essay down to th'

Elysian grove" (180) and ends with Antony's invasion of Cleopatra's bed; the second heralds the Egyptian queen's ceremonial march to the local *bagnio*—which in 1699 or 1700 could still be termed a bath house—and ends with her withdrawal from Actium; the third opens with the Roman ships trying to reach their native shores and closes with a description of Antony's embalmed body; the fourth and final canto introduces Cleopatra in a disheveled state and concludes with a triplet noting death's "injurious siege" upon the symbol of her own lifeless form, "Love's citadel, Beauty's victorious shrine" (186). One might also take some note of Fenton's attempt at balance, as his cantos number 45, 44, 42, and 31 lines each; the reasons for the descending order must be left to the imagination.

However, the problems with Fenton's adolescent effort hardly rest within the confines of his organization or symmetry. To the contrary, he evidences the ability to trace a clear narrative pattern. Nevertheless, he underplays the drama of the Cleopatra-Marc Antony relationship and reduces significant historical events to mere couplets. Turning again to the aftermath of Actium, for example, the reader sees only the "chagrin and despairing horror" that palls "the vitals of the vanquish'd admiral" (184). Despite that, Fenton cannot be charged with the responsibilities of a dramatist or a historian—only with those of the poet. Therein lies his immaturity. Simply, he tries terribly hard to imitate—almost simultaneously, it appears—both Virgil and John Dryden; yet he could not, at that stage of his development, control even his own fancy or secure the accuracy of his own poetic language. Notice, for instance, that in translating a line from the *Aeneid* (12.952 = 11.831), Dryden wrote, "And the disdainful soul came rushing through the wound." Fenton, obviously taken with that image, chose to apply it to the suicide of Antony; unfortunately, the reader of his *Cleopatra* must contend, in canto 3, with this uneven couplet: "In shades of death his eyeballs roll around, / Whilst his undaunted soul comes floating through the wound" (184). Was the poet trying to fashion his own Alexandrine form? Was the *floating soul* intended to complement this scene of death on shore with reminiscences of defeat on water? What, if any, is the relationship between the uneven couplet of canto 3 and the one at the end of the initial canto that demonstrates even greater imbalance? "The stars present their golden heads to view, / And

Cynthia (conscious of their bliss) dissolves to silver dew" (182). Are
we to praise young Fenton for attempting to vary the poetic form of
his piece, or do we openly condemn him for not being able to count?

Notice additional examples of the youthful author's struggle to
achieve a reasonable degree of poetic organization. Within the first
twenty lines of the opening canto, he asks the reader to envision
Cleopatra's eyes that "drank in the fever of her soul," while "lambent
fires . . . actuate the whole" of her body (181). A dozen lines later, the
Egyptian queen entices Antony "t'imparadise his soul at large" as
"he sums up the glories of her face" (181); he accomplishes that
summation by means of an interesting triplet:

Her veins meand'ring! and her waving hair
Like gilded clouds, was neither black nor fair,
And ev'ry single tress did prove a snare.   (182)

—after which the Roman commander

Ascends bright Cleopatra's bed of state.
Whilst spheres sing bridal hymns, and orbs express
In dancing sarabands their ecstasies:
The stars present their golden heads to view,
And Cynthia (conscious of their bliss) dissolves to silver dew.   (182)

In defense of Fenton and his attempts to bring Horatian/Homeric/
Virgilian imitation to the sands of Egypt, we may suggest that the
poet appears, at least in the initial section of the piece, headed
toward some definite poetic scheme or design. He paints what he
believes to be a realistic exchange of passion between Antony and
Cleopatra; the reader may observe, immediately and clearly, that at
this point the young poet demonstrates little interest in casting
moral or even historical judgments upon his heroes.

That scheme, however, undergoes obvious alteration at the outset
of canto 2, which begins with an interesting piece of stage machin-
ery: "Night's ebon chariot now had wheel'd away, / And Heaven was
deck'd with universal day" (182). Cleopatra emerges from her bed
and, surrounded by twelve virgins "with nicest art japann'd, / Attired
in white" (182), leads a regal parade to the bath house. Although
Fenton here demonstrates genuine concern for the Egyptian
queen's moral image, the end result seems better suited to the

advancement of Restoration furniture design than to the protection of her virtue. Then, once the scene shifts, within the same canto, to events leading to the naval engagement at Actium, the schoolboy poet sets aside the dual issue of art and morality and takes up the metaphor of pure military and political practicality. When Cleopatra hears of the Romans' intent to punish Antony, "Paleness attacks her cheeks, the blood must guard / The fainting magazine, her heart" (182). At that point, the "mutual flames" (181) of passion fade, to be replaced by the "disorder'd passion" (185) of death and grief.

However, Fenton has not finished with the metaphors of art. The beginning of canto 4 finds his fancy in a disheveled state, almost equal with that of Cleopatra reeling in shock at the news of Antony's death. Thus, he chooses to describe her sad utterances in these terms: "Relenting echo's mirror (dim with sighs) / Can scarce reflect the image of her voice" (185). Hard on the heels of that confusing metaphor, he sends Cleopatra down into a gloomy grotto, there to escape the "mid-day sun, and Syrian dog-star heat" (185) and to calm her unsettled state. Once that has been accomplished, once she has "damp'd her am'rous fires" (186), he proceeds to prepare for her final mortal act and to recast her as an object of art. Naturally but unfortunately, the schoolboy poet has difficulty in rising to that great occasion, as demonstrated by this passage:

> Anon two vipers thro' the grotto rolled
> Twisting their bodies in a poisonous fold;
> Th' audacious fair the deadly snakes caress'd,
> And, fatal frenzy, mov'd them to her breast;
> Their spiry volumes round her body twine,
> Thinking it polish'd ivory had been;
> At last inspir'd with a destructive flame,
> They kissed, and kissing, kill'd the lovely dame.
> While silver streams down her pale cheeks do roll,
> And short breath'd sighs catch at her floating soul,
> Her head reclining upon her snowy breast,
> Like blooming lilies, by a storm opprest,
> Her sprightly eyes are screened with thickest damps,
> Like the faint twilight of sepulchral lamps.   (p. 186)

From there, Fenton requires but three more lines (he seems never to run short of triplets!) to end his poem on a note similar to those sounded by his classical and contemporary models: Chaucer, we recall, concludes his account in *The Legend of Good Women* by pointing out about Cleopatra that "hir deth receyveth with good cheere, / For love of Antony that was hire so dere," while Dryden's *All for Love* closes with the concise but accurate thesis wherein "Fame, to late Posterity shall tell, / No lovers liv'd so great, or dy'd so well" (Chaucer 585; Dryden; *Four Tragedies* 278).

For young Elijah Fenton, the death of his Cleopatra underscored a notion not too far removed from Chaucer or Dryden:

> Thus Cupid's shafts transfix'd the faithful Queen
> And death's injurious siege made her resign
> Love's citadel, Beauty's victorious shrine.   (186)

In his own style, Fenton wove a loose pattern of multi-colored threads that, at the conclusion of four relatively short cantos (*short* in terms of epic poetry), managed to reconstruct the universal but redundant theme of love as a stronger, more permanent entity than superficial beauty. Certainly, major poets of the Restoration, from Rochester to Dryden, found that theme popular, and the versifiers of Anne and the Georges would continue, thoughout the eighteenth century, to belabor it.

However, the sixteen-year-old Fenton did not write *Cleopatra* to seek popularity, gain patronage, or achieve recognition. He simply fashioned the piece for an exercise, and it must be read and considered only on that level. Actually, most of what needs to be said about the poem will be found in Dryden's "Preface" to the *Fables*, published in that same year of 1700. In reference to Abraham Cowley's poetic conceits, Dryden noted, "There was plenty enough, but the dishes were ill sorted; whole pyramids of sweetmeats for boys and women, but little of solid meat for men" (*Selected Works* 494). Fenton either forgot about *Cleopatra* once he left Newcastle, or he chose to ignore its existence, perhaps even hoping that the manuscript would eventually become part of the dust of his native Staffordshire. That it survived to 1894 remains a tribute to the quality of British paper and British ink; that it will endure beyond the present moment depends upon how well time and the antiquarian book trade treat the Lloyd-Fenton-Fenton-Beale volume.

Aside from what *Cleopatra* reveals about the process of poetic composition among adolescents, it serves to foretell accurately the future of Elijah Fenton, adult poet. He had risen from decent Staffordshire stock, in possession of reasonable intellectual capacities; he had formed fairly traditional aesthetic criteria. However, his political and religious principles would force him to sever his ties with Cambridge; he spent his literary life writing essentially average verse and performing as an above-average translator of the classics for those poets endowed with talents far beyond his own. There exists no doubt that his literary reputation will lie forever among the ranks of the undistinguished. However, any poet—young or old— bold enough to give his readers a Marc Antony whose "glowing face / Outvies the blushes of the juice," or a Cleopatra appearing as "Thetis, spooning o'er the tide" (182–83) deserves, as does any other piece of tired equipage, at least one airing every eighty or ninety years.

Works Cited

Boswell, James. *The Life of Samuel Johnson, LL.D.* Ed. R. W. Chapman; rev. J. D. Fleeman. London: Oxford U P, 1970.

Chaucer, Geoffrey. *The Poetical Works.* Ed. F. N. Robinson. Boston: Houghton Mifflin, 1933.

Coleridge, Samuel Taylor. *Selected Poetry and Prose,* ed. Donald A. Stauffer. New York: Random House/Modern Library, 1951.

Dryden, John. *Four Tragedies.* Ed. L. A. Beaurline and Fredson Bowers. Chicago: U Chicago P, 1967.

———. *Selected Works.* Ed. William Frost. 2nd ed. San Francisco: Rinehart P, 1971.

Elwin, Warwick, ed. *Some XVIII Century Men of Letters. Biographical Essays by the Rev. Whitwell Elwin.* 2 vols. 1902 rpt. Port Washington, NY: Kennikat P, 1970.

Fenton, Elijah. "Miscellaneous Poems." In *The Works of the English Poets, from Chaucer to Cowper.* Ed. Samuel Johnson; rev. Alexander Chalmers. 1810; rpt. Hildesheim and New York: George Olms Verlag, 1970.

Johnson, Samuel. *Lives of the Most Eminent English Poets.* Ed. Peter Cunningham. 3 vols. London: John Murray, 1854.

Lloyd, William Watkiss. *Elijah Fenton: His Poetry and Friends.* Ed. George Livingstone Fenton. Hanley: Allbut and Daniel, 1894.

Swinburne, Algernon Charles. *The Complete Works.* Ed. Sir Edmund Gosse and Thomas James Wise. 20 vols. London and New York: Russell and Russell, 1925–28.

Childhood Lost, Childhood Regained: Hartley Coleridge's Fable of Defeat

Judith Plotz

From all accounts "Li'le Hartley," "poor Hartley" Coleridge, eldest son of Samuel Taylor and Sara Coleridge, was the most beguiling child anyone had ever seen.[1] Yet the pathetic story of his life, from precocious infancy to wasted manhood, is a paradigmatic romantic failure, the failure of the supremely gifted child who does not fulfill the enormous promise of his youth. Romanticism taught us, as— more to the point—it taught Hartley, to regard childhood powers of consciousness and temperament as normative. To be a successful Romantic Child, as Hartley so beautifully was, and then go on to be an adult success "carry[ing] the feelings of childhood into the powers of manhood" (S. T. Coleridge, *Biographia* 1:80–81) by accepting the responsibilities of adulthood without letting go of any of the priveleged insights of childhood was a feat not only beyond Hartley's strength, but beyond his real wishes. All Hartley's writings and all Hartley's adult behavior explicitly and implicitly present a child who will not grow up, who refuses adulthood. This pattern is most strikingly manifested in "Adolf and Annette," the fairy story printed below for the first time. In the tale Hartley sets forth with bitter clarity his vision of childhood as paradise, as high success, and of adulthood as hell, as bitterest failure. This essay briefly sketches Hartley's development from boy wonder to ossified boy and then gives a reading of "Adolf and Annette" as a parable of growing up in general and of Hartley's romantic rearing in particular.

The eldest child of Samuel Taylor Coleridge, a doting and observant parent (when he was there), the nephew of Southey (in whose household he was reared), the "darling" of the village (S. T. Coleridge, *Letters* 2:1022), Hartley was celebrated in earliest childhood in major romantic works: he is the babe in Coleridge's "Frost at Midnight" and "The Nightingale" as well as the "fairy thing with red round cheeks" in "Christabel"; he is the recipient of Wordsworth's "To H. C. Six Years Old" as well as the alleged inspiration for the

"best Philosopher . . . Seer blessed" of the Immortality ode (Hartman 35−41 and Newlyn).

From babyhood, the boy seemed a "piscis rarissima," "a thing sui
Generis," "an utter Visionary! like the Moon among thin Clouds . . .
in a circle of light of his own making—he alone, in a Light of his own"
(S. T. Coleridge, *Letters* 2:960, 802, 1014). Two qualities in the boy
struck all observers: his whisking, whirling, almost disembodied joy
in nature and his powers of mind. Unlike his earthy, rosy, cake-
loving baby brother Derwent, Hartley was an ethereal being, so
preoccupied with his thinking that he had to be reminded to eat and
even then "put the food into his mouth by one effort, and made a
second efffort to remember that it was there & to swallow it" (ibid.
2:1022). Most descriptions stress the airy lightness of young Hartley's movements, "like a blossom in a May breeze" (ibid. 2:668), and
stress as well his affinity to the spirit of life in nature, likening him to
those aspects of the natural world that are most ethereal. Wordsworth's tribute emphasizes the boy's powers of spontaneous joy, his
"breeze-like motion and . . . self-born carol" (*Poems* 1:522). Hartley's
other boyhood characteristic, his "prodigious and unnatural intellect," was even more striking and earned him the nicknames of
"young philosopher" from Lamb (*Letters* 1:180) and "Moses" from
Southey (*Letters* 1:241).[2]

Hartley was no knowledge-stuffed homunculus—neither Coleridge nor Southey nor his awe-struck schoolmaster, Mr. Dawes,
made any effort to force advanced studies early—but he exhibited a
preoccupation with what he called *"thinking of my Thoughts"* (S. T.
Coleridge, *Letters* 2:1014), or what his father called *"Thinking* as a
pure act & energy . . . *Thinking* as distinguished from *Thoughts"* (S. T.
Coleridge, *Notebooks* 1:923), to the exclusion of such bodily joys as
eating and playing. Southey reported:

> The boy's great delight is to get his father to talk metaphysics to
> him—few men understand him so perfectly;—and then his own
> incidental sayings are quite wonderful. "The pity is," said he
> one day to his father, who was expressing some wonder that he
> was not so pleased as he expected with riding in a wheelbar-
> row,—"the pity is that I'se always thinking my thoughts."
> (*Letters* 1:241)

At four, Hartley "used to be in an agony of thought, puzzling himself about the reality of existence, as when someone said to him: 'It is not now, but it is to be.' 'But,' said he, 'if it *is* to be, it is' " (Crabb Robinson 1:44). Yet again, Coleridge noted the boy's statement of "some Tale & wild Fancy of his Brain—'It is not yet, but it will be—for it *is*—& it cannot stay always *in* here' (*pressing one hand on his forehead and the other on his occiput*)—'and then *it will be*—because it is not nothing' " (*Notebooks* 3:3547). In boyhood this naive idealist was thus full of high promise. His sayings, his highly elaborated imaginary kingdom (of which a map survives), his nightly episodes of the vast "Tale" which beguiled his schoolfellows, his early powers of reasoning were the wonder of his community. Coleridge reported that Hartley was "considered as a Genius by Wordsworth, & Southey—indeed by everyone who has seen much of him" (*Letters* 2:1022).

Though as he grew up Hartley came to be known as an eccentric boy (a "quizz" he later called himself),[3] dreamily forgetting to eat, wearing peculiar clothes, carelessly picking choice bits of food out of a serving dish, unselfconsciously talking a blue streak to dumbfounded adult visitors, his sweet nature made his parents and his aunt and uncle Southey, all child-lovers, entirely indulgent of his unconventional winning ways. When the nineteen-year-old Hartley went off to Oxford, his mother deemed him so unworldly and impractical that her parting letter contained elaborate instructions on how to pack a trunk and how to address a letter (Stephens 146).

"[It] will be interesting to know what he will be," Coleridge noted of his marvelous boy, "for it is not my opinion, or the opinion of two or three—but all who have been with him, talk of him as of a thing that cannot be forgotten" (*Letters* 1:1014). What he became is soon told. After great success at Mr. Dawes's school in Ambleside, Hartley took a B.A. at Merton College, Oxford, where he dazzled and amused his companions with his Greek, his range of knowledge, and his rambling monologues, unequaled, a contemporary thought, by "any man then living, except his father" (Alexander Dyce, AL, HCP). His election in April 1819 to the coveted Oriel College Fellowship seemed the crown of his brilliant youth. To be a Fellow of Oriel would make Hartley, a man of no private fortune, secure and respectable for life. But the sobersidedness of the Oriel Senior

Common Room (John Keble was a Fellow; so was Thomas Arnold) provoked all of Hartley's willful whimsy. In less than a year, against all precedent, for various unspecified offenses involving "sottishness" and consorting with low company, Hartley was stripped of his Fellowship (John Taylor Coleridge, AL, HCP). Contemporaries at Oxford insisted that Hartley's drinking, later in his life to be a grave problem, was modest by Oxford (if not Oriel) standards. It was as much Hartley's unconventional dress, his cavalier omission of routine duties, and his social simplicity as his poor head for alcohol that lost him the Fellowship. The childlike manners, so long cosseted at home, found no such indulgence at Oriel, where John Keble, for example, initially hoped that the puppyish Hartley might "unlearn some of his manifold tricks" but soon came to regard him as an instance of a good head and heart spoiled by a vagrant temperament.[4]

The Oriel disaster, for so Hartley and his family chose to regard it, marked the end of Hartley's attempt to master the world and the beginning of his lifelong pattern of despondency, wandering, and desultory literary activity. After a spell of literary hackwork in London, Hartley yielded to the pressure of his family and drifted back to the Lake District where he remained for the rest of his life. He spent two brief spells as a schoolmaster. In 1824, immediately after his return to the Lakes, he was an assistant to Mr. Dawes; it was then that Dorothy Wordsworth reported he was "liked by his scholars and . . . the biggest address him 'Hartley'! This will give you an idea of the nature of the discipline exercised by him" (*Letters* 1:162–63). For part of 1837 he taught at the Sedburgh School. He also published a volume of poetry in 1833 and at the same time contracted with his Leeds publisher, Bingley, to write a series of biographies of the great and near-great of Lancashire and Yorkshire. While living in Bingley's house in Leeds Hartley succeeded in completing one volume of the promised series, a volume published in 1833 as *Biographia Borealis*, but he chaffed at the discipline and, disregarding his written agreement, simply walked out on Bingely, leaving "all his clothes & books behind him, but as happy to return as a boy from school" (James Brancher, AL, HCP). From this time he lived without regular employment, earning a pittance from intermittent journalism, but mostly dependent on the bounty of his family and the kindness of friends. He spent the years from 1822 (when he was 25) until his death in 1849 partly in disorganized study and miscellaneous writing and partly in roaming around the countryside, not always sober, in ironic fulfillment of the "Frost at Midnight" prophecy: "But *thou*, my babe! shalt wander like a breeze / By lakes and sandy shores." He wrote obsessively in his notebooks of lost chances: "Alas that I should have made such little opportunity of seeing . . . [the Isle of Wight]" (marginalia in *Atheneum* of March 27, 1847, HCP); "Alas—what I was [at Calne]! What might I have made of myself!" (marginalia in *London Magazine* of October 1822, HCP). He liked to entertain visitors to the Lakes with wry tales of his wasted life or of his previous incarnations as a louse or a wasp or a donkey.[5] By his middle years, Hartley saw his life as void of any meaning save as a negative example:

And now my years are thirty-five,
And every mother hopes her lamb,
And every happy child alive,
May never be what now I am.   ("Written in a Bible," *Complete Poetical Works* 223)

Though many loved him, no one respected him: in the end Hartley achieved neither fortune nor profession, nor reputation, nor wife, nor child, nor self-respect. Without real love or real work, he remained in manhood what he was in childhood, a glorious (if increasingly elderly) boy.

The form of Hartley's failure was a willed choice of perpetual childhood: "I would be treated as a child / And guided where I go."[6] "He lived as a child," Caroline Fox wrote, "and therefore he was loved as only a child is loved" (Griggs 171).

Physically the role was easy: Hartley was a tiny man, barely five feet tall, who sometimes used the pen name of Tom Thumb, who signed a letter to tall Thomas Poole, "your grateful and sincere little friend" (H. Coleridge, *Letters* 18), and who was addicted to self-diminishing anecdotes about his own puniness. He chose a boy's clothes—"a dark blue cloth round jacket, white trousers, black silk handkerchief tied closely round his neck"—and moved with so much lightness of step that even after his dark hair turned white he continued to look like a ghostly boy, "a white-haired apparition wearing in all other respects the semblance of youth with the most delicately grained skin and vividly bright eyes" (de Vere 133). Still more, his behavior was childlike. Children, especially infants, girlish little boys (of big boys he had "an instinctive terror" [H. Coleridge, *Letters* 127]), and prepubescent girls were his favorite companions. In his notebooks (those in the Humanities Research Center collection are mostly schoolchildren's soft-covered composition books with horses and alphabets on their covers) he wrote whimsical poems for his young friends—valentines, riddles, songs, attacks on Latin grammar and on teachers with funny names. He shared the children's delight in local fairs and puppet shows.

Hartley invited characterization as a child since he habitually depicted himself in his poetry and in his conversations as a *son*, "a living spectre of my Father dead" ("Full well I know—my Friends—ye look on me," *New Poems* 69), that "Father and Bard revered! to whom I owe / What'er it be, my little art of numbers" ("Dedicatory Sonnet: To S. T. Coleridge," *Complete Poetic Works* 2). The intimidating father he habitually referred to in his notebooks as a semi-divine "blessed one," *ho makarites*, haunted his consciousness.[7] Hartley's notebooks of the 1840s are full of odd recollections of something his father said in 1807 about volcanoes or Sir Humphrey Davy, recollections of a pun Coleridge made or a literary argument he won against John Pinkerton or a book he recommended, or—more frequent still—recollections of rebukes directed at the boy Hartley thirty or forty years earlier for his bad memory or his lack of pertinacity.

As a poet Hartley's obsession with childhood is obvious. His leading theme is childhood: there are dozens of poems to newborn babies, to two-, three-, or four-year-olds on their birthdays, to his many godchildren, as well as meditations on the mystery of birth and elegiac songs and sonnets about his own infant self and childhood reading. Even his other major subjects, nature and religion, are linked to childhood. The nature poems are all tributes to the greatness of littleness: his theme is the wonder of minimal forms of life such as small animals, birds, fragile flowers, wasps, fleas, microscopic sea creatures:

But who may count with microscopic eye
The multitudes of lives, that gleam and flash

Behind the sounding keel, and multiply
In myriad millions, when the white oars dash,
Through waves electric, or at stillest night
Spread round the bark becalm'd their milky white? ("No doubt
'twere Heresy, or something worse," Notebook C, HCP).

The religious poems almost all use the metaphor of God as father
and man as baby; redemption is depicted as a state of permanently
secure childhood. Hartley is the most absolute romantic eulogist of
childhood, surpassing even Wordsworth (whom he constantly echoes) in his praise of the child as seer, visionary, and minister of grace.
Like Wordsworth and Coleridge, Hartley sees the child's powers of
idealism and joyous oneness with nature (qualities for which Hartley
himself had been praised and hymned by the two older poets) as
essential for all stages of a successful life. Unlike Wordsworth and
Coleridge, however, Hartley attributes to infancy as the "breathing
image of the life of nature" an immutable strength and absoluteness
of Pure Being that makes it utterly distinct from and unassimilable
to adulthood ("The Sabbath-Day's Child," *Complete Poetic Works* 88).
Rather than emphasize the means by which childhood qualities may
be carried into adult life, Hartley enjoins the child, "Stay where
thou art! Thou canst not better be" (Ibid. 351), and depicts adulthood as a state of steady decline best conveyed through metaphors
of impoverishment, death, and even abortion.

Nowhere is Hartley's self-defeating attachment to childhood
more clearly depicted than in "Adolf and Annette," his undated
fairy story here printed for the first time. The story is about growing
up in general and Hartley's coming-of-age in particular.

The story, printed on pages 151–61, follows a familiar fairy-tale
pattern. Infant twins, Adolf and Annette, are carried off to safety in
their cradle-ark by the same icy flood waters that sweep away their
parents' valley cottage. In the safety of the mountains the children
are further recipients of nature's bounty. They become wards of
nature: they are fed by bees and birds and are protected by a
preternaturally beautiful nature spirit, "a lady all of white as if she
had been made of sunbeam." In her voice is nature's peace: "Her
voice was the voice of the wind when it murmurs low and sweet in a
calm cave." She gives them protective parental advice in rhyme and
promises the everlasting protection of their parents' spirits on the

condition of everlasting docility: "If their good wishes you always obey / Their spirits will guard you for ever and aye." As the children grow up the White Lady is less and less frequently seen. At length she announces her departure to her own "far country" just as Adolf and Annette are on the brink of puberty. Her parting instructions enjoin them to remain good and obedient children: they must not be self-assertive, they must not want anything for themselves alone, they must not go beyond bounds into the valley, they must hope for—but not work for—a reunion with their parents. But the children disobey. Like Adam and Eve in Eden, they grow restless, even selfish. Annette longs to possess for herself a strange red-and-white lily, Adolf an opalescent butterfly; but in their eagerness for possession the children crush the very objects they seek. This omen does not stop Adolf and Annette from yearning after the most forbidden object of all. Discontented with the mountain-top, they look down into the valley: "There it lay, far below the mountain hollows, white and glistening, and 'beautiful exceedingly.' "

Resisting no longer, indeed rationalizing their act as bravery and initiative in search of their parents, the children set out for the valley. Persevering through many perils including a vast cataract like a "white abyss," they reach at last the "glittering valley" where everything gleams as in a dream: the flowerspikes here are "encrusted with shining white crystals," the cottages shine, the ground glistens. In this seeming paradise, the children, hungry and thirsty, reach out to pick the gleaming fruit of a glittering tree: "The white balls tasted like their own tears, only ten times bitterer. . . . For the shining vale was encrusted with thick salt and there was no living leaf or bird or creature or blade of grass therein that had not been turned to salt. Everything was white and shining, but everything, except they two, was dead." Instead of men and women, "strange white forms lay huddled together." Doomed to die as well—for no one can reascend the terrible "white abyss"—the children long for the protected childhood they have thrown away. Suddenly they hear the voice of the White Lady, the hidden voice of nature in the hidden stream, directing them up a hillside toward a few "broad rusty streaks" that are a patch of moorland. Disobedience has almost killed them, so the children hasten to obey her. They mount the hill, finally reaching patches of "brown bare earth," then, blessedly, a patch of moss by a cup-shaped pool. There the White Lady greets the children but warns them that they are forever banished from their mountain home:

> Back to the Mountain I may not lead ye,
> Never again may ye wander there,
> They who have passed through the Shining Valley
> Breathe not again that diviner air.

The children must "travel by common pathways" and have "pain for [their] portion" as they seek "the land where all men dwell." Like *Paradise Lost* the tale ends with the protagonists alive, protected, remorseful, and fallen into permanent exile.

The main lines of Hartley's pattern here are plain. "Adolf and Annette" is an autobiographical fairy tale working out the habitual romantic antithesis between innocence and experience, here identified with childhood and adulthood. The mountain is childhood and paradise, the valley independent adulthood and hell, the moorland a state of lifesaving semichildhood, safe indeed but tainted by loss of innocence and loss of hope.

Childhood is located in the "blessed heights," the Edenic mountain realm of "diviner air." The mountain landscape is that of the Lake District where Hartley spent his happy youth and sadder maturity. It features valley, lakes, jutting rocks, "short mountain turf," and "rattling sykes" of cold fresh water. (The *OED* notes a "syke" or "sike" as a Scottish or Northern dialect term for a streamlet. One of the illustrative examples cited comes from a poem by Hartley Coleridge.) The mountain is a place of safety where the children are sheltered in "a little hollow place," are soothed by a sound like the wind murmuring in "a calm cave," and feast on ripe berries in "close nooks." In the womblike serenity of this mountain fastness fear is unknown; so are clothes. The Eden is also the realm of natural poetry. Its presiding spirit, the White Lady, is at once the genius of nature, the spirit of poetry, and the surrogate parent. Wonderfully beautiful, she sings a soothing admonitory music which is nature's very voice.

As the realm of childhood innocence, the mountain psychologically is the realm of unselfconsciousness and socially the realm of communal mutuality. The prepubescent Adolf and Annette together embody the presexual completeness of childhood. Their paradise is lost, however, by their decision to grow up, to grow out of the perpetual nonage enjoined by the White Lady. Growing up separates the children from one another and from the possibility of paradise. Adolf's and Annette's efforts to know themselves, to become more individuated and independent, are represented by their separate pursuits of the butterfly and the lily. The images are suggestive, indicating a mixed judgment on the plight of the children. If the lily is a traditional image of innocence, thus apt for Annette, it is also a rather more negative symbol of vulnerability. A similar ambiguity exists about the butterfly, positively a traditional symbol of the soul, negatively of vanity and transience. The flower and the butterfly further hint at and judge each child's developing selfhood. The lily, "rose colored like the dawn," with a heart "like a white dove," suggests Annette's dawning sexuality; the swiftly iridescent butterfly suggests Adolf's ranging curiosity. In reaching for lily and butterfly each is reaching out to possess and to comprehend herself and himself. As they pursue their separate and, they believe, selfish desires, they lose their oneness with each other and their joy in nature. Their desire for individual distinction and their spirit of aspiration are their fall.

This negative judgment on the impulse toward growth is reinforced by the dire imagery of the "white abyss" with its narrow channel and propulsive forces. Seduced by the mocking voice that lures them on, the children choose to be born into the grownup world. They leap into the dangerous white cataract which churns through the ravine and find that they have made an irrevocable descent. Hartley depicts growing up as a descent from life into death, for when Adolf and Annette go down into their parents' adult world they find themselves in the valley of death. The Fall has long since passed in this valley. The postlapsarian calamities of the flood and of the annihilation of Sodom and Gomorrah have occurred—the salt landscape and the human figures turned to salt give mute testimony to that.

Moreover, even adult virtues appear follies in this dead world. What bring the children to the vale of tears are the adult virtues, are those very qualities normally associated both in traditional and Victorian fairy tales with successful mastery of the world: energy, boldness, initiative, self-confidence, and warily selective use of adult guidance. Just as Hartley had dreamed of the glories and paternal praise that were to be his when he descended to his City of the Plain, his Oxford, so do the children strive for the glittering prizes and the imagined parents they believe to be waiting in their "glittering valley." All this effort is vain, producing only a retrospective yearning articulated in a nursery jingle: "For what we have once thrown away, / To have once more we humbly pray." The fruit of all their efforts, Hartley's and the children's, is not knowledge and companionship, but the Sodom apples of despair, appropriate fare for one who explicitly likened himself to "a Dead Sea below the level not only of the Mediterranean but of the Fleet Ditch" (marginalia in *Atheneum* November 10, 1841, HCP). Hartley's tale thus condemns the very impulse toward growth and achievement as leading to self-destruction.

To save Adolf and Annette from the death-in-life that is adulthood, to give his fable a happy ending, Hartley has them elect to resume their earlier, safer, more obedient state, a state resembling Hartley's own protective detention in Grasmere. Here the White Lady promises them life and, vaguely, a journey into the world "where all men dwell." The tale closes, however, before Adolf and Annette move toward that world or even encounter another human being. It closes instead on a note of exhaustion as the White Lady enjoins the children to "abide" and to "come to me, come to me." The tone suggests that the children's vital life is over and that the rest is mere wearisome anticlimax in a simulacrum of childhood security. Hartley's choice of so sad a return to partial childhood for his twin selves indicates how intense is his commitment to the excellence of childhood and how deep his revulsion from the energetic individuality of adult life.

For all Hartley's commitment to childhood, however, his fable also questions the very ideal it largely glorifies. The White Lady, chief artificer of and presider over childhood beatitude, is as sinister as she is glorious. Her threefold identity—as a figure of whiteness, as a figure of admonition, and as a figure of paternal poetry—suggests Hartley's ambivalence toward the very childhood realm he yearns for. In her whiteness the lady is associated not with what is wholesome and lifegiving like the red berries or the green herbs or even

the "broad rusty streaks" on the moor, nor with what is richly various
like the iridescent butterfly or the rosy lily. She is rather associated
with what is deadly, with the white abyss and the salty "shining valley
of their vain desire." Further, her lapping love is bound up with
things negative—with admonition and with absence. Her addresses
to the children consist principally of restraining warnings: "Hush,"
"Beware," "List to me," "Come to me." Usually present as mere
voice, she not only represents the absent parents but herself aban-
dons the children at their most vulnerable time of life. She is thus the
source of a rather uneasy security. In this as in other ways, the White
Lady seems to be associated with Hartley's father. As a poet who
frequently speaks in tetrameter, as a figure whose words are more in
evidence than her presence, the White Lady recalls Samuel Taylor
Coleridge, who permanently left his family when Hartley was ten.
Further, Hartley uses Samuel Taylor Coleridge's words and themes
throughout "Adolf and Annette," but especially in connection with
the White Lady. Twice the White Lady echoes "Kubla Khan,"
urging the children to "Beware! Beware!" Both times the echoes
occur in lines metrically identical to S. T. Coleridge's "And all should
cry Beware! Beware!" As in "Kubla Khan," rushing waters are
associated with both life and the icy regions of death. Like *The
Ancient Mariner* "Adolf and Annette" depicts want in the midst of
plenty, thirst in the midst of a salt waste. As in *The Ancient Mariner*,
the protagonists endure an experience so horrifying as to make a
return to their earlier serenity unthinkable. Echoes from *Christabel*
are even more marked. The White Lady owes much to Geraldine:
both women are magical, preternaturally bright, white-clad. Both
are temporary guardians for the motherless; both are associated
with a "far countree" (*Christabel* I 225). The quality Coleridge
attributes to Geraldine—that she is "beautiful exceedingly" (*Christabel* I 68)—is by Hartley transferred to the deadly valley which is
"white and glistening, and 'beautiful exceedingly.'" There is an
echo of *Christabel*'s "So free from danger, free from fear" in the
White Lady's parting words to Adolf and Annette: "With much of
love and much of fear." The association of "Adolf and Annette" with
Christabel, particularly the association of the seemingly benevolent
White Lady with the dangerous Geraldine, suggests an even darker
reading for Hartley's tale. Just as his father's *Christabel* can be read

in part as the story of a child seduced, abused, and abandoned by those who should protect her, so can "Adolf and Annette" be seen as a vision of children doubly betrayed, betrayed both by the world of experience and by their guide to the world of innocence. In the figure of the White Lady who is depicted both as the source of a lovely and sustaining vision of human life and as a seductive abandoner, Hartley seems to be setting forth his heartbroken love and resentment of his father.

Certainly the dominant impulses of "Adolf and Annette" are a recoil from adulthood and a desire that childhood last forever. The depiction of the White Lady, however, adds another element. Her equivocal role suggests Hartley's loss of innocence about the very innocence he longs for. Her ominous whiteness suggests Hartley's consciousness that the romantic dream of white innocence may itself be a dangerously self-destructive fantasy. As one who inhabited that dream of perfect childhood, Hartley can write with special authority on themes pervasive in romantic literature. He not only articulates the central romantic assumption of childhood as a state privileged by intuition and imagination,[8] but he criticizes that vision as well. Like Blake in *The Book of Thel* and S. T. Coleridge in *Christabel*, Hartley explores the self-destroying impulse of innocence to shrink back from full knowledge and full experience. A child in so much else, Hartley the artist is mature enough to judge what he loves without ceasing to love it. "Adolf and Annette" can properly be read as a late-romantic postscript to the early romantic poetry of innocence, experience, childhood, imagination, and the loss of vision.

Just as "Adolf and Annette" resembles the great romantic poems that precede it, so does it resemble the Victorian fairy tales that follow it. Like many works of Victorian children's fantasy, "Adolf and Annette" is set in a double universe consisting of one world of childhood and one of maturity. Hartley's childhood realm, as is customary in works of the period, is associated with nature, music, poetry, supernatural beings, helpful animals, and a nonpatriarchal power structure; his child protagonists, like Alice, Mowgli, Jack of *Mopsa the Fairy*, and Diamond of *At the Back of the North Wind*, move through one realm to the other. In their depiction of such a journey, nineteenth-century children's writers tend to adopt one of two attitudes: either a balanced attitude governed, as U. C. Knoepflmacher notes, by "the reality principle" (Knoepflmacher 497)[9] or a regressive attitude governed by nostalgia, loyalty, and imagination. For writers of the first sort—Lewis Carroll, in the Alice books, Molesworth in *Mopsa the Fairy*, Kipling in *The Jungle Books*—the adult world, though certainly more matter-of-fact and constricted than the innocent world, is the destined and largely desirable goal of the child. For such writers the temporary immersion of the reader in fantasy, analogous to the more extended but similarly transient sojourn of the child in childhood, is a refreshing and invigorating respite intended to build strength for the future. For writers of the second kind, however—MacDonald in *At the Back of the North Wind*, Kingsley in *Water Babies*, Barrie in *Peter Pan*—the adult world is a damaging, oppressive place where children do not flourish, at least as children. Only in the realm of imagination, a realm which may look like autism or death to the blurred vision of the adult, can the child thrive.

Hartley Coleridge, whose adult realm is a dead land of salt tears, whose children move from bright mountain to vale of tears only to end as weary, guilty vagrants on the hillside, clearly writes the darker kind of fable of innocence. Moreover, Hartley's fable is further darkened by his children's powerlessness. In most other Victorian fantasies, the magical realm is a realm of at least temporary mastery. In *Phantasmion* (1837), for example, a work by Hartley's sister Sara Coleridge, the hero is a powerful dreamer, whose dreams are a kind of action. In "Adolf and Annette," however, all energy and initiative are depicted as self-destructive or morally wrong. Whether one reads "Adolf and Annette" as a latterday romantic poem, an early Victorian children's fantasy, or an autobiographical experiment, there are few nineteenth-century works which so sadly and clearly illustrate the power of romantic dreams to act upon a life, and to shape not only fantasies, but a sensibility capable of receiving and reflecting back in poetic images the knowledge of its own defeat.

Notes

1. As an adult Hartley Coleridge was commonly referred to as "Li'le Hartley" (Hartman 129, 131, 140) by the local peasants and as "Poor Hartley" (D. Wordsworth, *Letters* 163, 233, 451, 530) by his disappointed friends and family.

2. Southey wrote of the six-year-old Hartley that "Moses grows up as miraculous a boy as ever King Pharaoh's daughter found his namesake to be. I am perfectly astonished at him, and his father has the same fore-feeling that it is a prodigious and unnatural intellect—and that he will not live to be a man" (Southey 1:241). That Hartley was nicknamed "Moses" is an additional reason for regarding "Adolf and Annette" (with its infants rescued from the waters) as autobiographical.

3. "Autobiography of a Quizz," unpublished fragment, Hartley Coleridge Papers, Humanities Research Center, The University of Texas at Austin. All materials from the Hartley Coleridge Papers are printed here with the kind permission of Joan and Priscilla Coleridge for the Coleridge Estate and of the Humanities Research Center, The University of Texas at Austin. I am most grateful to Joan Coleridge and her daughter for their interest and encouragement. I wish to thank as well the kind assistance of the staff at the Humanities Research Center, particularly that of Ellen Dunlap. The Hartley Coleridge Papers will henceforth be cited as HCP.

4. Keble's increasing vexation with Hartley is evinced throughout the six letters he wrote to John Taylor Coleridge between 1818 and 1822 (six extracts/copies [copied by Sir Bernard Coleridge] HCP).

5. In her 1843 notes on Hartley Coleridge, Sarah Fox notes "that Hartley recalled being present at the siege of Troy: 'I was then an insect which in these days is nameless, and having crawled upon [Helen's] bright yellow hair, I was pointed out to her by Paris, and she crushed me with her pearly nail. " On another occasion, Fox notes, Hartley described his earlier incarnation as a clergyman's donkey, a beast so bad-tempered and ungrateful that Hartley was condemned to be reborn as "a man *such as you see me!*" (HCP).

6. The third stanza of "My Times Are in Thy Hands," a manuscript poem (HCP), is a prayer for guidance:

> I would not have the restless will
> That hurries to and fro
> Searching for some great thing to do
> Or secret thing to know
> I would be treated as a child
> And guided where to go.

7. The Greek word *makarites* refers to one who is "blessed," that is, dead. It is cognate with *makar*, "blessed, happy," that is, of the gods as opposed to mortal men. The term, with its association of divinity, imputes an additional grandeur to Samuel Taylor Coleridge. *Ho makarites*, the blessed one, is Hartley's favorite term for his father after Coleridge's death in 1834.

8. For a general account of the high romantic view of childhood privilege, see Judith Plotz, "The Perpetual Messiah: Romanticism, Childhood, and the Paradoxes of Human Development," in *Regulated Children/Liberated Children*, ed. Barbara Finkelstein (New York: Psychohistory Press, 1979), 63–95.

9. Both the article cited and U. C. Knoepflmacher's paper on *Mopsa the Fairy*, "Quest and Loss in the Fantasy World of Victorian Children's Books" (presented at the April 1983 NEVSA Conference), with its illuminating account of Jack's *cheerful* return from fairyland to patriarchy, have been very useful to my thinking about "Adolf and Annette." I am also grateful to Professor Knoepflmacher for his helpful comments on an earlier draft of this paper.

Works Cited

Coleridge, Hartley. *The Complete Poetical Works.* Ed. Ramsay Colles. London: George Routledge and Sons, 1908.

———. *Hartley Coleridge: New Poems.* Ed. Earl Leslie Griggs. 1942; rpt. Westport, Conn.: Greenwood P, 1972.

———. *The Hartley Coleridge Papers.* Austin: U of Texas, Humanities Research Center.

———. *Letters of Hartley Coleridge.* Ed. Grace Evelyn Griggs and Earl Leslie Griggs. London: Oxford U P, 1936.

Coleridge, Samuel Taylor. *Biographia Literaria.* Ed. James Engell and W. Jackson Bate. 2 vols. *The Collected Works of Samuel Taylor Coleridge* 7. Bollingen Series 75. Princeton: Routledge & Kegan Paul and Princeton U P, 1983.

———. *Collected Letters of Samuel Taylor Coleridge.* Ed. Earl Leslie Griggs. Vols. 1–2. Oxford: Clarendon P, 1956.

———. *Complete Poetical Works of Samuel Taylor Coleridge.* Ed. Ernest Hartley Coleridge. 2 vols. 1912; rpt. Oxford: Clarendon P, 1968.

———. *The Notebooks of Samuel Taylor Coleridge.* Ed. Kathleen Coburn. vols. 1 and 3. Bollingen Series 50. New York: Pantheon, 1957 and 1973.

de Vere, Aubrey. *Recollections of Aubrey de Vere.* London: Edward Arnold, 1897.

Griggs, Earl Leslie. *Hartley Coleridge: Life and Work.* London: U of London, 1929.

Hartman, Herbert. *Hartley Coleridge: Poet's Son and Poet.* London: Oxford U P, 1931.

Knoepflmacher, U. C. "The Balancing of Child and Adult: An Approach to Victorian Fantasies for Children." *Nineteenth-Century Fiction* 37 (1983): 497–530.

Lamb, Charles, and Mary Anne Lamb. *The Letters of Charles and Mary Anne Lamb.* Ed. Edwin W. Marrs, Jr. Vol. 1. Ithaca and London: Cornell U P, 1975.

Newlyn, Lucy. "The Little Actor and His Mock Apparel." *Wordsworth Circle* 14 (1983): 30–39.

Robinson, Henry Crabb. *Henry Crabb Robinson on Books and Their Writers.* Ed. Edith J. Morley. 3 vols. 1938; rpt. New York: AMS P, 1967.

Southey, Robert. *Selections from the Letters of Robert Southey.* Ed. John Wood Warter. 4 vols. London: Longmans, Brown, Green, Longmans, 1856.

Stephens, Fran Carlock. *The Hartley Coleridge Letters: A Calendar and Index.* Austin: U of Texas, Humanities Research Center, 1978.

Wordsworth, William. *The Poem.* Ed. John O. Harden. 2 vols. New Haven and London: Yale U P, 1981.

———, and Dorothy Wordsworth. *The Letters of William and Dorothy Wordsworth: The Later Years. 1:1821–1830.* Ed. Ernest de Selincourt. Oxford: Clarendon P, 1939.

Varia

Adolf and Annette

Editor's Note

The text of "Adolf and Annette" below is a transcription of two manuscripts found among the Hartley Coleridge Papers in the Humanities Research Center, The University of Texas at Austin. It is printed with the kind permission of Joan and Priscilla Coleridge for the Coleridge Estate and of the Humanities Research Center, The University of Texas at Austin. The first manuscript, in Hartley Coleridge's hand, is an undated four-page fragment headed "Adolf & Annette"; this text is incomplete and breaks off at the point indicated by asterisks. The second manuscript which supplies the complete tale is an undated seventeen-page manuscript in another hand (probably that of Ernest Hartley Coleridge), labeled "*Adolf and Annette* Fragment from the unpublished mss of Hartley Coleridge." I have been unable to find the full version of the original manuscript from which this copy was made among the Hartley Coleridge Papers at Austin. Although Hartley's fragment is undated, the state of his handwriting and the interest he manifests in the fairy tale form suggest a date of composition sometime between 1835 and 1849. It is possible that the work is a partial response to the publication of his sister's fairy tale *Phantasmion* in 1837. The text here follows Hartley's manuscript to the asterisks and the other manuscript for the rest of the tale. Punctuation has not been regularized. All dashes and discrepancies in names (both "Adolf" and "Adolph," "Annette" and "Janette") are as they appear in manuscript. Manuscript deletions and insertions are furnished in square brackets.

Judith Plotz

Adolf & Annette

It happened once upon a time, there were two children, a brother and a sister. They were both of the same age—for they were both born [together *deleted*] in one hour, and they had the same father

151

and mother and they laid in the same cradle, and their mother
sometimes took them both on her lap. But when their Mama took
Adolph, Janette did not cry. She lay in her cradle and smiled—and
when their Mother took Janette on her knee—Adolph sat up in his
cradle and laugh'd, and clapped his hands, for the Babies loved one
another and their mother loved them both. [and they loved one
another *deleted*]

Now the Cottage wherein their father and mother lived was beside
a very great river, for at the end of the valley many waterfalls fell into
a Lake—that was very black and cold—And the Lake was turned into
thick ice every winter—and when the warm sun melted the snow on
the mountains far away—the ice was broken into pieces with a noise
far louder than thunder. But it came to pass—that many summers
were not like summers—but very cold and long—so the ice gathered
in great heaps at the end of the lake—and there came a great rain
and the waters grew very great, and broke down the wall of ice—and
filled the whole vale—and carried off all the Cottages that were
upon the bank of the River. But the cradle in which the two babies
were, Janette and Adolph, was borne high upon the waves, and they
floated along—along—till they came to a rock that was very high—
and stoop'd over the river. And in the rock was a little hollow place
and thither the cradle with the two babies, Janette and Adolph—
floated of its own accord—and they were still sleeping—But when
they waked, they saw a Lady all in [in *is superimposed on* of] white, as if
she had been made of a sunbeam, slanting from on high into a dark
place. And her voice was the voice of the wind when it murmurs low
and sweetly in a calm cave when the storm is over. And she sang in
the strange tongue—but the words—in English—were these—

> Hush. Babies hush—I pray you hush,
> [The wind that pl *deleted*]
> The hum and the lull of the bending earth,
> When Day departs with a long-drawn sigh—
> Shall be my Babies' lullaby
>
> Hush—Babies hush—I pray you hush—
> The night is old—and the maiden blush—
> [That the waters *deleted*]
> The innocent blush of the smiling Lake
> Shall tell my babes, that tis time to wake.

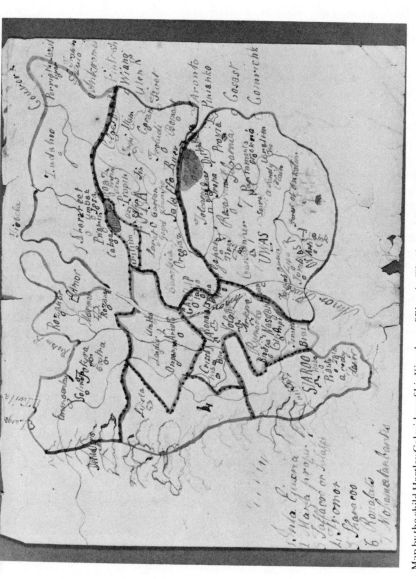

Map by the child Hartley Coleridge of his Kingdom of Ejuxria. The date of the map is uncertain but probably between 1804 and 1810. Some scholars speculate that Hartley and his map are the "six year's Darling" and his "little plan or chart" in Wordsworth's "Ode: Intimations of Immortality." (From the Hartley Coleridge Papers, reproduced with the permission of Joan and Priscilla Coleridge and of the Humanities Research Center, University of Texas at Austin.)

Your father and mother [are far away *deleted*] I cannot say—
How far they are gone since yesterday—
But if their good wishes you always obey
Their spirits will guard you for ever and aye—

Now the two children did not at first understand the words of this
song. They only heard the music that it was very sweet, and they
loved to hear it. But in after time, they came to understand it—but
then they never could hear it when they were awake—only when
they were asleep, they sometimes heard it in their dreams.

And while they were Babies—the bees came and brought them
honey—and little birds, as soon as they could walk, came singing and
fluttering before them—and led them to close nooks among the
rocks—where there were ripe berries and green herbs—and cool
water. And their long hair was unto them instead of clothes. And
they were very happy—for they loved one another exceedingly. But
still the older they grew, the White Lady came to them seldomer and
seldomer—and at last she told them—that she was going away into a
far country—and that they must learn to find out the berries for
themselves—and to plant them where they would grow. But if they
loved one another still, and never quarrelled—or said this is mine—
or this is not yours—they should never want, and she would come to
them again—after a long time—and carry them to the place where
their father and mother were gone—And then she sang—

I leave you now, my children dear
With much of love and much of fear.
My love—ye know—that it is true—
Fear is a thing ye never knew—
But it will come, if eer ye go
To see the vale that lies below—
As many living souls as ever
Were swept along the ravening river
When rushing o'er—the icy mound
It left behind the hamlets drownd
So many now are dwelling there
But yet I say—Beware—Beware—

And so she departed in the mist, and Adolph and Janette were alone on the mountain.

* * * * * * * * * * * * * * * * * *

For a while the children gave heed to the White Lady's parting words and lived together as though they had one heart and one will. Whatever they found they shared in common, and what was out of the reach of one the other did not long possess. But one day when Janette had run on a little way ahead of Adolph she caught sight of a tall lily which grew by itself in a cleft of a rock—The stem bore a single flower rose coloured like the dawn, and when Janette standing on tiptoe with eager fingers pushed aside the petals she saw that the heart of the lily was shaped like a white dove. Her heart began to beat with joy and her first thought was to run back and call Adolph, but the next moment she had [reached *deleted*] resolved to say nothing about it, but to come again when Adolph was asleep and look at it once more all by herself. Perhaps she would tell him the secret tomorrow and they would go together and look for another lily which of course would be Adolph's very own. But no sooner had she made up her mind to do this than she fancied she heard a voice which she had heard before, but she could only catch a few notes and perhaps it was only her fancy—And this is what she thought she heard.

> If that be sweet, and this be fair,
> But this nor that ye may not share,
> Ye must not covet it, nor take
> One thought thereof for dear love's sake.
> If this be sweet, if that be fair,
> Regard it not. Beware! beware!

But her head was full of the beautiful lily and the warning voice fell on unheeding ears. Slowly she retraced her steps in search of Adolph, but when she met him she did not look up into his face or throw her arm around his neck, but walked beside him in silence. Adolph did not ask her where she had been or notice her changed demeanour, but he thought for the first time that the mountain was a dull place

and wished that something amusing would happen. The children
had gone but a few steps when both uttered a cry of delight and
astonishment. For just beyond their reach a radiant butterfly of
unwonted size and brilliance wheeled and fluttered in the sunlit air.
All the colours of the opal flashed from its wings, and now green,
now fiery red and now a lustrous blue the enchanting creature
tempted and eluded their pursuit. Janette had already overtaxed
her strength and Adolph without a word or a backward glance sped
gaily on never doubting that he would gain the prize. At last the
butterfly seemed to tire of the chase and of a sudden settled, so
Adolph thought, on a tall flower spike that was well within his grasp,
and at once weary and eager he pounced upon his prey stumbling
crushing both the butterfly and the flowerstalk in his fall. Alas! it was
Janette's lily, and when Adolph rose to his feet and perceived what
mischief he had done he knew what his sister had found and why she
had been silent. This time no warning voice was heard, and sorrow-
ful and alarmed the boy returned to his sister and told her what had
befallen him. And the two children lifted up their voices and wept.
[But child *deleted*]
   But childish troubles are soon forgotten and the next day and the
day after Adolph and Janette were sharing the same innocent pleasures and delighting in each other's presence as if they had never
dreamt of keeping a secret treasure to themselves—Only they were
no longer content with the mountain's height but kept wondering
and talking about the vale which the White Lady had forbidden
them to enter. There it lay far below in the mountain's bottom white
and glistening, and 'beautiful exceedingly'—Perhaps one might find
there beds of lilies like the solitary one in the mountain cleft! Perhaps it was the haunt of many coloured butterflies! Perhaps, ah!
what had the White Lady meant when she went away? Perhaps their
father and mother were living there still. Surely [they <re *deleted*>
reasoned *inserted above line*] it would not be wrong to seek them out,
and though at first the descent seemed rocky and precipitous so
soon as they reached the bottom of [the *deleted*] younder [*inserted
above line*] ravine the lower spurs of the mountain were smooth and
grassy, and the vale the shining vale would speedily be won. Twas
long since they had seen the White Lady and perhaps if she knew
what strong brave children they were she would not be angry at their

making the attempt. And so one morning when the sun rose and coloured all the mountain peaks with the hues of the rainbow the boy and the girl started on their perilous enterprise.

> For [th *deleted*] what we long for, that we will,
> And now we fancy, then fulfill.

The children soon scrambled down the steep side of the ravine which cut into the forepart of the mountain like a deep wound which had been scored by some monstrous enemy in times gone by, but when they reached the bed of the torrent they found that it taxed all their skill and strength to leap from one boulder to [boulder *deleted*] the next. At length they reached a spot beyond which it seemed impossible to proceed. The sides of the ravine had gradually become more and more precipitous, and were now sheer walls of rock wet and polished with perpetual spray, while the bed of the stream had narrowed into one vast scoop over which the smooth coil of water descended for a few yards like a skein of brown silk and then with a dull roar broke into a cloud of white foam. Adolph and Janette were at their wits' end and Janette began to sob and cry and to reproach Adolph for bringing her into this terrible place. But the boy was not so easily daunted and kept searching for some side ledge of rock by the help of which he might at least descend a few more steps and then perhaps slide down to another ledge and so get to the bottom. But all in vain.

For a long time the baffled children peered with fascinated gaze into the white abyss, when lo! of a sudden a puff of wind for a moment dispersed the cloud of spray, and close at their feet lay a broad sunny river which flowed right into the shining vale, and whether from above or from below they could not tell, but sweet and clear a voice they had never heard before sounded in their ears. And this was the burden of the song.

> Saw ye ever sight like this?
> Yonder is a land of bliss.
> Where the broad bright waters flow
> To the shining vale below.
> There are butterflies and lilies,

And a thousand daffodillies
Velvet turf beneath your feet
Berries juicy, ripe and sweet!
There are joys beyond all measure,
Mirth, and fun, and sport and pleasure;
Plunge into the white abyss
Ye shall win that land of bliss.

Then the children leapt over the torrent's brink, and as they leapt a silvery mocking laughter rang in their ears.

For the first few moments Adolph and Janette were stunned with the swiftness of their fall and the roar of waters, but when they came to themselves they found that they were swimming with an easy and pleasant motion in a wide shallow river. The water was so bright and clear that they could see the pebbles and waterweed over which they were swimming and the banks were so low that the flowery meadows on either side were full in view. It was a peaceful flood, but ever and ever bubbling fountains welled up to the surface of the stream and broke in eddying circles, and so buoyant was the water that the children floated along without any effort of their own. Now, thought they, we shall soon reach the shining vale. But, all too soon, the flowery meadows gave place to muddy shoals strewn with [dead *inserted above line but deleted*] yellow reeds and dead boughs of trees bleached with the incrustations of byegone floods, and the stream itself grew dull and discoloured, and at length appeared to lose itself in a vast reedy swamp [on which there was no foothold, but *deleted*] through which it was almost impossible to swim. By dint however of pushing and wriggling between the stems of the tall grey reeds, the children made their way a little farther, and after a while they found that the ground was like hard mud beneath their feet, [and *deleted*] then that it [grew *deleted*] was [*inserted above line*] dry and crumbling and that the reeds were growing thinner. Their hearts beat fast for now they must be close to one of the shores of the lake which lay in the [centre *deleted*] midst [*inserted above line*] of the shining vale. And they were not mistaken, for in another moment they were scrambling up a sparkling white slope and full before their eyes was the longed for vale, its lake, its shores, and the hills which encircled it on every side save that towards the mountain from which they had come. At first they almost screamed with delight and amazement, for the vale and everything therein, the lake, the fields, the trees, the hillsides all but their farthest summit were white and glistening and flashed in the sunlight with a dazzling brilliancy. A pathway led along the shores of the lake, and here and there half-sheltered by white trees in the midst of white gardens were white cottages. The flower spikes were encrusted with shining white crystals on which here and there huge butterflies poised motionless. The air was neither hot nor cold, but there was no breeze and the children walked and breathed with difficulty. Living creatures, men and women or children like themselves Adolph and Janette had never seen and were not expecting to see, but [more than *inserted above line*] once they noticed [that *inserted above line*] beside the cottage doors strange white forms lay huddled together, but these, they knew not why, they feared to approach. It was now two hours past midday and the children, their wonder and excitement being over, began to search for the ripe and juicy berries which the spirit of the waterfall had promised them. All the berries they had ever seen grew on little bushes not a foot above the ground, and of these there were none to be found, but on some of the trees, which hung over the low walls of the cottage gardens, there was an abundance of sparkling white balls which the chldren thought they would pick and eat for their meal. And now for the first time they were seized with doubt and fear, for the white balls tasted like their own tears, only ten times bitterer, and before they could swallow a single one they were forced to spit it out. For the shining vale was encrusted with thick salt and there was no living leaf or bird or creature or blade of grass therein that had not been turned to salt. Everything was white and shining, but everything, except they two, was dead. And once again the children wept. "Hungry & thirsty their soul fainted within them", and they longed, alas it was too late, for the short mountain turf, and the red & purple berries and the [mountain's herb *deleted*] rattling sykes which sprang bubbling out of beds of green moss.

> For what we once have thrown away,
> To have once more we humbly pray.

Adolph and Janette were, indeed, in a sore plight. They could not retrace their steps, for not only had they already travelled a long

day's journey, but they knew that they could neither swim against the current of the broad flood, or reascend the precipitous ravine. The blessed mountain heights which they had been so eager to quit were shut off from them for ever, and in the shining valley of their vain desire there was no abiding place for the living. Their poor little feet weary and wayward smarted with the crackling salt-crystals, and their eyes were dazed with the intolerable sheen of unbroken whiteness. But they must go forward, [and *inserted above line*] hand in hand they plodded silent and heart-broken. They did not dare to console one another, or to confess the horrible dread which had come over them, but they walked on and on hoping against hope that the White lady would once more appear if only to upbraid them and to pronounce their doom. And now they were nearing the farther end of the valley. The hills which shut in the foot of the Lake were shaped like a horseshoe, and the declivity from the rim of the horseshoe down to the Lake was smooth but exceedingly steep. Just where the rim met the horizon and for a few hundred feet downward the white mountain side was scored with broad rusty streaks, and when they had first caught sight of these, the children had almost hoped that, if they could reach these, they might win their way to some brown moorland where they would find wholesome berries and [pur *deleted*] pure spring water. But the evening shadows were now lengthening, and a dreary stretch of white hillside rose up between. In another moment Adolph and Janette would have laid themselves down to [die *deleted*] sleep and to die, when beneath their feet they heard the sound of running waters, and the clear tinkle of the hidden stream was was [*sic*] as it were the voice of the White Lady—
And thus she sang—

> List to me, list to me, children dear!
> Under your feet I am near, I am near—
>   A rivulet clear—
> Follow me upward, follow me still,
> Follow the sound of the hidden rill
>   Up the Hill—
> Till ye come to the spring on the bare hillside
> To the living well where the moor spreads wide—
>   There abide—

And it was even so. For a few hundred feet the children climbed in the track of the hidden streamlet and as they climbed the glittering steep began to be interspersed with patches of brown bare earth, until at length their tired feet once more trod the soft green [earth *deleted*] moss which seemed to grow brighter and brighter as they neared the cup-shaped pool of water which lay at the upper end of the moss. [And *deleted*] There with arms outstretched to receive them stood the White Lady—

And this was how she greeted the forlorn children—

> Come to me, come to me, all is over,
>   Never a journey but hath an end;
> Sweet to the thirsty the cool spring-water
>   Sweet to the lonely the voice of a friend.
>
> Back to the Mountain I may not lead ye,
>   Never again may ye wander there,
> They who have passed through the Shining Valley
>   Breathe not again that diviner air.
>
> But ye must travel by common pathways
>   Seeking the land where all men dwell,
> Pain for your portion, and life and laughter
>   Land that is halfway 'twixt Heaven and Hell.
>
> Come to me, come to me, just for a moment,
>   Cool is the moss to your weary feet—
> Sweet to the thirsty the cool spring water—
>   And a friend to the lowly is passing sweet—

Ideology, Form, and "Allerleirauh": Reflections on Reading for the Plot

Marianne Hirsch

Since Bruno Bettelheim reminded us in 1976 that "fairy tales depict in imaginary and symbolic form the essential steps in growing up and achieving an independent existence" (73), feminists have turned to myths, fairy tales, and children's stories to discover the gender-related developmental paradigms that Bettelheim leaves out of his analysis. When we do so, we find emblematic representations of gender stereotypes; as Ellen Rose puts it: "In fairy tales, boys are clever, resourceful and brave. They leave home and slay giants, outwit ogres, solve riddles, find fortunes. Girls, on the other hand, stay home and sweep hearths, are patient, enduring, self-sacrificing. . . . They marry and live happily ever after" (209, 210). The tales' economical form and clearcut message has tremendous usefulness for the feminist critic. Sandra Gilbert and Susan Gubar, for example, begin their analysis of a "feminist poetics" with a reading of "Snow White," stating that "myths and fairy tales often both state and enforce culture's sentences with greater accuracy than more sophisticated literary texts" (36). As we search for an understanding of female oppression in the familial and social structures that define our culture, as we consider models of female responses to social and psychological constraints, we have a great deal to learn by reading fairy tales.

Theorists of narrative also traditionally turn to fairy tales to illustrate, by means of these paradigmatic and economical texts, how the structures of narrative function. Thus, in his recent book *Reading for the Plot: Design and Intention in Narrative*, Peter Brooks offers a new psychoanalytically based theory of narrative. In this model, plot is the "logic and dynamic of narrative" and its primary attribute is its inherent temporality. Brooks turns to a Grimms' fairy tale, "Allerleirauh" or "All-Kinds-of-Fur," in order to illustrate how temporal unfolding operates to reinforce narrative's function of understanding and explanation. His discussion, a purely formal, narratological analysis of the tale, is very instructive for the feminist critic for,

163

through Brooks's reading, we can discover not how fairy tales represent women, but how analyses of narrative form can contribute to "culture's sentences."

Brooks summarizes the story of a queen who, before her death, extracts the king's promise that he will not remarry a woman who does not equal her in beauty, a king who can find no one but his own daughter to fit this description, and a princess who, to avoid marrying her father, makes several demands she hopes he cannot meet and, when he does, resorts to fleeing, disguised in a coat made of the furs of a thousand animals. After she serves as a kitchen maid in another kingdom, her beauty is discovered by its young king, who marries her.

For Brooks, the tale offers a perfect example of narrative functioning. Typically, the story "takes on the central issues of culture—incest, the need for exogamy—without commentary" (9). In its progression through several triply repetitive actions (she asks for three dresses, one like the sun, one like the moon, one like the stars; she appears at the king's ball three times; and she cooks into the king's soup three objects brought from home), the story, according to Brooks's reading, "works through the problem of desire gone wrong and brings it to its cure" (9). Temporal progression and generational transmission are both worked out not discursively but in the indirect form of "thinking" that narrative, especially in its emblematic fairy-tale form, exemplifies. "Like a number of Grimms' tales," Brooks asserts, "it seems to ask the question, 'Why do girls grow up, leave their homes and their fathers, and marry other men?'" (9).

In Brooks's reading of this tale, a tale he takes to be an example of narrative functioning in a much broader sense, the subject of desire, therefore the protagonist, is the father. It is *his* desire that has gone wrong and must be cured; it is *he* who must hand on his knowledge and possession to another, and presumably younger, king. The narrative model developed here is oedipal and the daughter, "Allerleirauh," for whom the story is named, is an "overly eroticized object" who "loses all erotic and feminine attributes, becomes unavailable to desire, then slowly, through repetition by three, . . . reveals her nature as erotic object again but now in a situation where the erotic is permitted and fitting" (9). Brooks relegates his explanation of the story's "female plot" to a footnote, defining female plot as "a resistance and what we might call an 'endurance': a waiting (and suffering) until the woman's desire can be a permitted response to the expression of a man's desire" (330).

Clearly, from Brooks's perspective (and the rest of his book bears this out) woman's role in narrative is to be the object who waits to be exchanged and passed on at the right moment. As he sees it, the experience of learning and development is not hers but the father/ subject's: *he* must learn about giving her up to another man. It is clear that such a reading ignores the girl's central and active role in this tale: after all, the father disappears after the first scene and the other king's part is minor. Yet for Brooks the story's unfolding in time, its plot, depends on the female character's collusion and partic- ipation in a process motivated by a male dynamic, on her willingness to wait and endure until it is appropriate for her to respond to male desire. In order to develop his narrative theory, Brooks depends on such female compliance. What he deemphasizes is that Allerleirauh *is* the protagonist. Although her name demonstrates that she de- pends for her identity on her disguises, her animal skins do not conceal her role as agent in the tale.

Interestingly, another recent book also uses "Allerleirauh" as an initial illustrative example. Judith Lewis Herman's *Father-Daughter Incest* suggests a very different reading of the Grimms' tale, a read- ing centered on the daughter and on the story's theme rather than its form. Here Allerleirauh and one of her literary ancestresses, Saint Dympna, are seen as versions of Cinderella, heroines who "warn young girls that it is dangerous to be left alone with a widowed father, for a widowed father must remarry, and the daughter's fate depends upon his choice of a wife. In some variants of the tale, the daughter suffers because the father replaces her mother with a cruel stepmother. In others, the daughter suffers because the father wishes to marry her himself" (1).

This shift of emphasis from the father to the daughter, from paternal desire to daughterly resistance, allows us to look at the details of the story and to see them not merely for their formal configuration, but also as factors and stages in a tale relating a young girl's development in a patriarchal world. It is possible, in fact, to read the tale as an emblematic dramatization of female development in the realm of infinite paternal power, a realm where the father's privilege extends even to include the body of his daughter. In such a reading, Allerleirauh emerges as a particularly female hero. Brooks's description of female endurance and waiting fails to do justice to her ingenious understanding and successful manipulation of the world into which she has been born powerless.

Motherless, Allerleirauh must protect herself. In asking for the three dresses, she not only knows how to enhance her own physical beauty (a supreme value for women in fairy tales), but also enlists the protection of sun, moon, and stars. In asking for the animal skins, moreover, she enlists the protection of the animal realm and also reveals her understanding of the need to hide her beauty, to become sexually unattractive and unavailable until the right mate appears. By disguising herself repeatedly, she manages to overcome the terrible confinement of women in fairy tales, to explore the world, and to try out different identities, even while pretending to hide in a womblike closet under the stairs. In revealing herself to the other king, she again uses her feminine attributes—her beauty, her cooking skills, and her patience. She knows about the economic and political reality of marriage and reveals to her king that she is rich by leaving different gold objects in his soup. She exemplifies not passivity and endurance, but an active and imaginative response to a situation in which she has no power at all, where she is, as she herself repeats three times, "good for nothing but to have boots thrown at my head."

Her rebellion against incest is not by any means a rebellion against patriarchal power. By manipulating the other king into marrying her, she could, in fact, be said to commit a kind of incest: in the terms of Phyllis Chesler, "Women are encouraged to commit incest as a way of life. . . . As opposed to marrying our fathers, we marry men like our fathers . . . men who are older than us, have more money than us, more power than us, are taller than us . . . our fathers" (cited in Herman 57, 58). The road from incest to exogamy leaves unchallenged the assumption of male privilege.

This still leaves the question of the mother in the tale. Why does she extract from the king the promise that he will not marry someone who does not equal her in beauty? How must *her* gesture be interpreted? Does the mother create the problem by insisting on the resemblance of the new queen to herself? As Judith Herman documents, psychiatric literature most frequently holds the mother responsible for the development of an incestuous relationship between father and daughter. While Herman insists that this judgment must be reinterpreted in light of the powerless position mothers occupy in families, she concedes that "maternal absence, literal or psychological, does seem to be a reality in many families where incest develops" (49).

Rather than seeing the mother's ambiguous request as her collusion in the father's scheme or as a mere assertion that she is of unequalled beauty and thus irreplaceable, it is possible to interpret it more positively, as an enabling gesture for her daughter. In "Peau d'âne," the Perrault tale that is one of the sources for this story, the dead mother is replaced by a fairy godmother who tells the princess how to outwit the father and when to run away. This figure has only limited power; her function is not to offer the princess absolute protection, but to initiate her into her dangerous and subordinate position. By eliminating this figure, the Grimms have not increased the story's psychological complexity, as is commonly argued, but have robbed the growing heroine of any adult guidance, of any female companionship. One could argue that the roles of mother and fairy godmother are conflated. By making sure that the king will not replace her with an evil stepmother but will focus all of his love and attention on the daughter, the mother extends her protection to the years following her death. Beyond that, she leaves the girl to her own ingenuity, to cope in a world where all women are, in a sense, motherless and powerless. The lack of guidance forces Allerleirauh to develop the resources she will need to succeed as a woman in an androcentric world.

Such a feminist reading shifts the emphasis quite considerably away from Brooks's classically psychoanalytic and formalist interpretation. While Brooks's vision of narrative accepts as its foundation woman's position as object of exchange, a feminist reading calls attention to this fundamental power structure and reveals possible responses to it. In so doing, we are enabled to see the ways in which the heroine can nevertheless assume an active, however limited, role—how, beyond total and obedient consent, she can manipulate her fate to achieve at least what her mother had.

In the terms of narratologists like Peter Brooks, repetition is an essential feature of plot, necessary to bind its elements together so that they make sense. Temporal unfolding proceeds through repetition to the conventional culmination, in this case marriage, which guarantees not only the closure of plot but the stability of culture. In feminist terms, this form of repetition and progression signals woman's continued subordination and confinement. Repetition images reproduction, the mirroring of mother and daughter, the impossibility of escaping the mother's early sacrificial death. It is not coincidental that Brooks's literary reading of "Allerleirauh" should focus on formal features, while Herman's feminist reading highlights the story's theme. Not until we bring these two approaches together, revealing the ideological implications of formal structures we tend to take for granted, can we read this tale and others in ways that transcend repetition and lead to transformation and perhaps to innovation.

Works Cited

Bettelheim, Bruno. *The Uses of Enchantment.* New York: Alfred A. Knopf, 1976.
Brooks, Peter. *Reading for the Plot: Design and Intention in Narrative.* New York: Alfred A. Knopf, 1984.
Gilbert, Sandra, and Gubar, Susan. *The Madwoman in the Attic: The Woman Writer and the Nineteenth-Century Literary Imagination.* New Haven: Yale U P, 1979.
Grimm's Fairy Tales. New York: Pantheon Books, 1944.
Herman, Judith Lewis. *Father-Daughter Incest.* Cambridge: Harvard U P, 1981.
Rose, Ellen Cronan. "Through the Looking Glass: When Women Tell Fairy Tales." In *The Voyage In: Fictions of Female Development.* Ed. Elizabeth Abel, Marianne Hirsch, and Elizabeth Langland. Hanover and London: U P of New England, 1983.

Reviews

Censorship and Mythmaking in Nazi Germany

Hamida Bosmajian

Children's Literature in Hitler's Germany: The Cultural Policy of National Socialism, by Christa Kamenetsky. Athens: Ohio State University Press, 1984.

In the language of Nazism, *Gleichschaltung* meant the complete ideological coordination of all political, social, and cultural activities, so that every element of German life would become part of the National Socialist machine under Hitler's dictatorship. Literature, including children's literature, was either banned, censored, "adjusted" to Nazi mythology, or produced specifically to propagandize for that mythology. As Christa Kamenetsky repeatedly demonstrates in her comprehensive and carefully researched study, all children's literature published under Nazism was aimed to further single-minded and politically empowered indoctrination.

Professor Kamenetsky's book affects the reader beyond its declared intention of demonstrating how the Nazis used censorship and "völkisch ideology" to teach children to "internalize National Socialist ideology and defend it enthusiastically" (xii). Her study overwhelms the reader with the picture of what must surely have been a censor's utopia, for she reveals the two-fold dream of censors in operation: aggression against everything that does not fit the censor's view and imposition of a predetermined value system by the censor whose aggression has been successful. The personal and developmental needs of the child and young adult were, of course, totally disregarded under ideological *Gleichschaltung*. Kamenetsky covers all aspects of her subject, from origin to publishing trends, but all her discussions are variables of those key terms—censorship and mythmaking.

In Part One of her four-part study, Kamenetsky finds the origin of Nazi "Literary Theory and Cultural Policy" in nineteenth-century German romanticism which, along with an emphasis on the free play of the imagination and a revival of folklore and mythology, reflected a developing German nationalism and built up the complex meanings of the words *Volk* and *völkisch* with their concomitant anti-Semitic connotations. Concerted efforts were made to bring art and folklore into the educational system. Heinrich Wolgast, who supported this movement and wanted to bring its principles to children's literature, argued for quality control in *The Troubled State of Our Children's Literature* (1896). Because Wolgast argued that children's literature should never be used as a means to an end, his work was criticized for its "art-for-art's-sake" stance (11). The great variety of German children's literature guaranteed indeed that it would not be used as a means to an end.

All this changed when the Nazis came to power and made their intentions clear with the book burnings beginning May 10, 1933. This "cleansing action" destroyed one third of all library holdings in Germany; in Berlin alone 70,000 tons of books were removed from the libraries. "In contrast to the Romantic concept, the Nazis' concept no longer stood for diversity in unity" but aimed for a society "totally committed to the *Führer* and the National Socialist ideology" (37). Kamenetsky cites the new goals of children's literature as they were outlined for the Hitler Youth and the Reich Youth Library in Berlin:

We Expect of Good Books That They Will:
1. Arouse among children an enthusiasm for the heroes of sagas, legends and history, for the soldiers of the great wars, the *Führer* and the New Germany, so as to strengthen their love of the fatherland and give them new ideals to live by.
2. Show the beauty of the German landscape.
3. Focus on the fate of children of German ethnic groups living abroad and emphasize their yearning for the Reich.
4. Deal with the love of nature and promote nature crafts.
5. Relate old German myths, folktales and legends, in a language reflecting the original folk tradition as closely as possible.
6. Give practical advice and help to the Hitler Youth, both in relation to recreational programs and camp activities.   (55–56)

In Part Two, "The Interpretation of Children's Literature," Kamenetsky shows how the genres of folktales, sagas, and picture books were adjusted to Nazi ideology while books with religious themes, nonsense verse, books about urban life, and books about friendships between children across ethnic and national boundaries were omitted from lists of recommended readings. Where necessary, folktales, Norse mythology, and sagas were retold and reinterpreted so as to be acceptable to "mold the character" of the child. Cleansed of "alien influences," German folktales projected the "Nordic Germanic world view" through a masculine drive for action while women, destined to give birth to the heroic male, were shown as "the needed complementary force for the fighting man" (79). Sagas were thought to be especially important in the education of boys since they furthered ideas of service and sacrifice as well as faith and loyalty to the leader. Kamenetsky rightly distinguishes between voluntary deviation from a mythological source for the expression of one's own creative imagination and deviation prescribed by censors. She observes how ethnocentric Nazi interpretation deprived folktales of their universal human meanings: "Essentially, the mythos of Nazism was not a myth of the people but only an ideology that simulated an organic connection with the genuine folk tradition" (97).

In Part Three, "The Uses and Adaptations of Children's Literature," we see how *Gleichschaltung* was extended to "Primers: The ABC of Folk Education" and to the anthologies, particularly the influential *Deutsches Reichslesebuch* (German Reich Reader, 1935) with its conformity to the following ideological principles: "1. Blood and Soil. 2. Leadership and Followership. 3. Honor and Loyalty. 4. Service and Sacrifice. 5. Struggle and Work" (187). Puppet plays and children's theater were also very popular means of indoctrination, as were the *völkisch* rituals, such as solstice ceremonies, intended to replace religious rites, especially those associated with Christmas. Kamenetsky points out that the Nazis emphasized "constructive propaganda" in their indoctrination of children and avoided, with few exceptions, virulent anti-Semitism.

Kamenetsky begins her last section, "Methods and Limitations of Control," by outlining the vast network and enforcement methods of Nazi censorship. The great number of censors needed for children's literature came first of all from the teachers themselves, who had to join the National Socialist Teachers' Organization and take a loyalty oath to Hitler if they wished to teach (242). By 1937 teachers had endorsed the censorship decrees and accepted the *Reichslesebuch* and its ideology.

In order to reach more young people, the Nazis greatly increased the number of community and school libraries. Their obsession with recordkeeping has left us a survey of children's reading preferences in Leipzig between 1935 and 1937 which indicates that 24.5 percent preferred picture books, 18.1 percent folklore, and only 7.4 percent war stories, 3.7 percent sagas, and a mere 2.6 percent National Socialist children's literature! Throughout the Nazi era, boys stubbornly persisted in reading Karl May's adventure stories about American Indians while girls continued to enjoy oldfashioned stories such as the *Little Nest Hook* series by Else Ury, even though the author had been condemned as a Jewish writer (291). Though the Hitler Youth magazine *Hilf Mit* went so far as to encourage youths to purge their parents' libraries of undesirable books, it seems that "children managed to use books as an escape into their private dream worlds" throughout the early forties (294). Lest we have too much trust in youthful common sense, however, we must keep in mind that only the end of the era prevented the Nazis from achieving their goals. Kamenetsky concludes that the ultimate aim of Nazi children's literature was not to benefit the child but only "the folk community and the state. Outside this goal, neither children nor books were thought to have a purpose and justification for existence" (311).

Censorship and mythmaking were in reciprocal relation because the Nazis could not tolerate any other gods besides those they had created. Theirs was not a politics of reason and discussion but one of effective dramatic gestures, myths, and symbols enveloped with religious connotations. In the story "The Search for Balder," for example, the Norse sun god whose birthday was the winter solstice was made to symbolize the "good news" that Adolf Hitler, the "redeemer," had been sent by God to save Germany from darkness and utter destruction (92–93). Kamenetsky argues that "in the Nazi approach to myths and folktales the sun never set" and that doomsday and death, except the individualized heroic death, were played down (310). In this we find the ultimate subversiveness of Nazi children's literature: the child was given "positive" and "healthy" fictions and symbols that ultimately would make him willing to accept obedience unto death if the *Führer* demanded it. Nazi character building was an education for death.

Kamenetsky's inclusive descriptions and analyses, her thoughtful notes, and extensive bibliography should stimulate further research on specific texts in children's literature of the Third Reich as well as in other totalitarian societies. Finally, her greatest contribution is that she begins to uncover the dread of the politically empowered censors who define all creative work as dangerous and "other" if they see it as contradicting their impoverished and closed perceptions of a sealed world.

Mixed Signals: Three British Books

Peter Hunt

The Case of Peter Pan or The Impossibility of Children's Fiction, by Jacqueline Rose. London: The Macmillan Press, 1984.

In Defense of Fantasy. A Study of the Genre in English and American Literature since 1945, by Ann Swinfen. London: Routledge and Kegan Paul, 1984.

Developing Response to Fiction, by Robert Protherough. Milton Keynes: The Open University Press, 1983.

Jacqueline Rose sums up *The Case of Peter Pan* thus: "Instead of asking what children want, or need, from literature, this book [asks] what it is that adults, through literature, want of the child." Using *Peter Pan* as a central example on which to base her critical paradoxes, Rose explores some of the ill-considered or unconsidered attitudes surrounding children's literature. Her approach may seem to be on occasion willfully obscurantist, and the organization of her book a trifle esoteric, but as she is a more-or-less poststructuralist critic making an excursion into the world of children's literature, her book should be welcomed, rhetorical affectations and all.

From the subtitle onward, she challenges the status quo. The first assumption about children's books, she thinks, is that "there is a child who is simply there to be addressed, and that speaking to it might be simple." It is always possible that some of Rose's first assumptions might bear reexamination, but there is a lot of truth in this one. For attitudes to children, and books, and language (in relation to children and books) have changed very little, she feels, since Rousseau, and to think that communication with the child is simple is to be naive. Adults control literature as "author, giver, maker" and the child therefore "comes after [as] reader, product, receiver." "Children's fiction sets up the child as an outsider in its own process, and then aims, unashamedly, to take the child *in*."

Much the same might be said of the relationship between Rose and *her* audience: but her point is salutary. Children's books rarely address the gap implicit in the relationship between writer and word, and word and reader. "Control" is more subtle and pervasive than mere didacticism; it runs through our very concepts of signification. By setting up the child as a symbol of purity (linguistically and culturally, as well as physically) we at once sublimate, impose, and distance our more ambivalent motives—sexual as well as linguistic.

Peter Pan, Rose thinks, has just the kind of association with purity which is at the heart of the "mystique" of children's literature; it is an institutionalized "classic"; and it "claims" (or as we might say, "is assumed") to speak to, and through, and for the child. But it does none of those things—indeed, its rather curious history is presented as a metaphor of the work's recoil from the "impossible" ideal of writing for children.

Peter Pan became a classic before it became a written text. It was first an episode in an adult piece, *The Little White Bird* (1902), a story about the controlling, and ambiguous, relationship between adult and child. It was not *for* children in any sense. Barrie's unsuccessful attempts to rewrite it (as a story in 1911, and as a play as late as 1928), simply emphasize this: the shifts of narrative stance and tone, among other things, run counter to any convention of children's writing because they continually break the narrative contract. Arthur Applebee sees the learning of a concept of authorship as a crucial stage in the child's acquisition of narrative, and Barrie's uncertainty directly militates against this. Further, the fact that *Peter and Wendy* was rewritten in 1915 (as *Peter Pan and Wendy*—even this title is unstable!) in accordance with contemporary educatonal linguistic policy is adduced as evidence that, if anything, the work is *anti*-child. All adjustments are adult-based—indeed, the inherent attitudes of the whole work tend to the repression and subjugation of the child's spirit, rather than to the encouragement of freedom and the imagination.

As can be seen from the issues raised, *Peter Pan* is really peripheral to Rose's main arguments: its "illegibility" is only one indication that the history of children's fiction might be rewritten in different terms. The "placing" and "possession" of the child through fiction and language is seen to reflect basic structural oppositions of "child—oral culture—innocence," and "adult—written culture—decay" (oppositions which are questionable in poststructuralist terms); by extension, this "possession" relates to colonialism and the infantilization of the older cultures enshrined in the child (as Tolkien remarked, the fairy tale has been "relegated to the nursery").

Rose's fashionably metaphorical and associative discourse tends to disguise the fact that this is not all new. Nevertheless her observation that critics of children's literature seem to hold up the "classic realist" text as the approved norm, and that as a result the child is forced to accept (or is seduced into accepting) the story without questioning situation or language, is worth pondering. By what reasoning is the child deprived of just the linguistic and intellectual questing that marks the contemporary "adult" novel? Even—perhaps especially—fantasy has been domesticated as part of an inevitable narrative pattern (if you don't believe in the unconscious) or as part of a fixed allegorical pattern (if you do). Consequently, Rose questions the innocence of Piaget's and Applebee's taxonomies of development (in "competence" and "narrative" respectively). She even challenges the validity of attempting to create "a poetics for children's literature" (the "ultimate fantasy")—and it may be that as long as critics remain in the prisonhouse of covert prescription, she is right.

However, if we apply her technique of exploring what texts suppress, or cannot express, to *The Case of Peter Pan*, some of her stances are undermined. (One might, of course, do the same to this review.) I found—another unconsidered trifle, perhaps—that the sexist bibliography in which male authors are given initials and female authors Christian names (for example, "Bettelheim, B., and Zelan, Karen. *On Learning to Read*") oddly symptomatic. Rose's book has many refreshing insights, and the breadth of her associations can be highly suggestive (as in the link she sees between *Peter Pan* as purity symbol and the preoccupation with money that she perceives as surrounding it); but it can also be merely silly. Discussing the difference between children's play (*Peter Pan*) and pantomime, she notes "the connection is there, latent to the title itself" (*pan*tomime). (Or, one is tempted to say, the connection is also there to gold prospecting, cooking, piping, and Pan-Am Airways).

There is a danger, then (and I speak as an apologist for critical theory), that Rose may seem, to many readers, to be merely pretentious. For example:

> In this context another separation is worth noting in commentaries on children's books which seem to divide up and redistribute the different components of this emphasis, between a new attention to language (the "poetics" of children's writing) which does not speak of psychic and sexual conflict, and an attention to psychic and sexual conflict in, for example, the fairy tale (Bettelheim) which does not speak of the divisions of language itself.

Or, "Some people write about form, others about content." And if I am accused of being reductive, I would argue that clarity and simplicity are no more inevitably linked than obscurity and complexity.

After the rhetoric has faded, one is sometimes left wondering quite what the fuss was about. Much energy is spent on exposing the immanence of sexuality in the children's book situation, with what one can only assume (otherwise why mention it?) to be an implication that this is somehow sinister. Yet, is it important? Is it worth asserting? Is it worth challenging a denial of it? But this may well indicate the extent to which I have been convinced of its presence.

Or to take another example, Rose speculates on what is happening when we put a child on the stage (psychologically and ideologically). Who is watching whom? Is *Peter Pan* a "spectacle of childhood for us, or a play for children?" Perhaps what I find least convincing about *The Case of Peter Pan* is that it ignores the strength of the sub- or anticulture of childhood to be aware of, and to resist, adult manipulation—and thus Rose reveals herself as subscribing to the very point of view that she purports to question. Robert Robertson, the British writer and raconteur, describes a performance of *Peter Pan* in which, when Peter turned to the audience to say that Tinkerbell would die unless they all said they believed in fairies, the child audience (this being the way of the modern world) stoically refused to do so. The actors were forced to negotiate, and at length one small boy was bullied into saying he did, and the show went on. A little later, the small boy, on his way to the lavatory, stopped in the aisle, and, in a lull in the proceedings, shouted, "I don't really!" By what complicity, I wonder, did the show continue?

If it is curious that Jacqueline Rose only mentions that most influential disseminator of *Peter Pan*, Walt Disney, in a footnote (about royalties), it is even more curious that Anne Swinfen only mentions Freud in passing in *In Defense of Fantasy*. But from a book that is full of stances, we move to one which scarcely has a stance at all.

Jack Zipes has observed that fantasy—as a study—scarcely needs any defense, and Swinfen, *pace* her title, does not offer one. Hers is an academic overview, rarely making a judgment, which paraphrases and describes books in order to show the modes, structures, and historical roots of fantasy about animals, parallel worlds, secondary worlds, types of symbolism in fantasy, and so on. In comparison with Rose's book, it is calm, well-ordered, and lacking in passion—or indeed, in much sense that the books have struck any chord with the writer.

But if it is not a "defence," neither is it "a study of the genre" of fantasy. Unlike Rosemary Jackson in *Fantasy: The Literature of Subversion* (Methuen, 1981), Swinfen deals primarily with books that are "clearly" either "children's books" (the Narnia, Prydian, and Borrowers series, *Mrs. Frisby and the Rats of NIMH, Tom's Midnight Garden*) or in the borderland between the adults' and the children's lists (the Earthsea trilogy, *The Lord of the Rings*, *The Mouse and His Child*, and Cooper's "The Dark Is Rising" series). With the best will in the world, I would think that this *part* of the genre of fantasy is precisely one which does need defense, and it is not satisfactorily defended by ignoring distinctions (however nebulous or complicated). Swinfen's book begins (as Rose might put it) with an evasion:

> It is clear from any prolonged study of what might be termed "high fantasies" that to label them as children's books is grossly misleading. They operate on an adult level of meaning, and the issue of deciding the dividing line, if such could ever exist between worthwhile literature for children and for adults, seems to be a futile exercise.

A whole book could, and probably should, be written about that paragraph alone. To talk about an "adult level of meaning" implies a nonadult level; to talk about "worthwhile" literature is to make several simultaneous assumptions about definitions. Distinctions *must* be made, and to call, for example, Susan Cooper's *Over Sea, Under Stone* (which is most obviously bound by children's book conventions and most obviously intended for the child reader) a "lightweight novel" is to move perilously close to the identification of secondrate and "for children." To ignore the implied reader, and the modifications to authorial stance (let alone "levels of meaning") which are inherent in any book which approaches the category of children's book, is to imply that all the books studied in *In Defence of Fantasy* are equally acceptable and equally amenable to the same type of "abstract" criticism. This is simply not so. The books *are* of a different kind, even if their fantasy elements are shared with another genre. There is never a hint by Swinfen that Lewis's Narnia books are different from Le Guin's Earthsea novels not only in kind but (I would argue) in quality—or that the kinds of critical approach she applies might not be quite appropriate to what many would see as minor art (such as the early Cooper novels, which just happen to be children's books). Neil Philip, in his excellent and pioneering study of Alan Garner, *A Fine Anger* (Collins, 1981), adopted a similar stance, and he was only successful as far as his material allowed him to be. The result of this lack of discrimination is the occasional lapse into A. C. Bradleyesque speculation: where, in the view of the agrarian background implied in *The Lion, the Witch, and the Wardrobe*, does Mrs. Beaver get her sewing machine?

In short, Swinfen's book is "traditional" in just the sense that Rose finds so questionable. Phrases such as "the reader is forced to realize" or "the underlying . . . theme . . . *is*" or "the reader has already begun to wonder" imply an acceptance of just those critical attitudes that Rose (and many others) have found to be eminently challengeable. *In Defence of Fantasy* may well be "accessible," and it is certainly quotable (in the way of undergraduate quotations), but I am not sure that its empiricism does much service to the texts it treats of.

To counterbalance the differing extremes of Rose and Swinfen (and, perhaps, as some indication of the range of approaches brought to children's literature) I must include, and praise highly, Robert Protherough's *Developing Response to Fiction*. Its purpose is to "relate classroom practice directly to a clearer awareness of what children are actually doing as they engage with stories" and, by extension, to consider what we are all doing when we read. The snobberies of the academic world being what they are, it might be that an "education-based" text may be less highly regarded than a "criticism-based" text—but Protherough's account of reader-response criticism is probably the clearest I have come across and his insistence that theory should and can be applied the most clear-headed.

He examines the work of critics, psychologists, and educationalists (notably some inservice reading workshops at the University of Hull) and puts this together with case studies—"some of the approaches that capable and experienced English teachers use when teaching fiction." From this he derives some possible strategies for teaching. Although he takes the point of view of the classroom teacher, the person in the middle, "a sort of literary Pandar," his account should be required reading for anyone concerned with children and fiction, as well as for undergraduates (and graduates) grappling with criticism and critical theory.

Protherough is aware that reading a children's book (for an adult) is more difficult than reading any other kind of book. "The critical judgments have to be more complex, because they draw not only on literary experience and critical ability, but on knowledge of children, their tastes and responses." It is odd that although reader-response seems to be so obviously applicable to the interaction of children and books, a synthesis is so rarely attempted.

One reason may be what Protherough identifies as "the broken-backed curriculum." Using surveys, he points out that there is considerable discontinuity in the teaching of literature (in Britain, at least): "there is an apparent gulf between the responses teachers say they value and wish to encourage and those which much of their work and most of their examining processes actually elicit." There is a tension between the children's personal responses to texts and the assessable "right" answers required by the system (quite apart from the inadvertent distortion of response through group or teacher influence). This not only affects readers: it unmakes them. With all respect to Rose, it is not so much the texts that are hostile to the child, but the way they are treated, the way they are *used*.

It may seem to be trivial or naive in a literary-critical context to trouble about such things, but they are, ultimately, the result of a Leavisite elitism which excludes a vast number of readers not only from the interactive creation of the literary experience, but from the book itself. When we are dealing with *developing* readers, this exclusion is only the more obvious. Nor has Leavis been discredited: his spirit lives on, implicitly, in books like Swinfen's and is only side-stepped by books like Rose's. The "right answer," held mysteriously by those with "superior sensibility," is the way to the good grade and it is difficult for teachers to break away from this.

The second reason why theory rarely meets practice is that so many awkward questions have to be answered. Robert Protherough faces them: What is fiction? Why teach it? How do you judge if a book is worth reading—and what does that mean, anyway? What degrees of "misreading" are possible? What do you mean by popular, or useful? And, practically, how can a teacher (or a critic, or a theorist) cope with the multiplicity of readings?

The case studies show attempts of teachers to elicit responses without directing or forming the responses, and Protherough uses the cases to demonstrate the difficulties involved. There is not, he observes rather scathingly, much empirical evidence to work on; research on response "has tended to concentrate more on what can be measured than on what teachers need to know." His tentative developmental model, based on this cleareyed view of the problems, may, of course, ultimately be serving the same ideology as the one it sets out to question, and for some readers it may be of little comfort that he offers arguments and tactics rather than the vague generalizations, endless booklists, and rigid sets of exercises which customarily grace (or disgrace) books on the teaching of children's literature.

But, in its way, *Developing Response to Fiction* is a subversive text. It works through the rhetoric of "common-sense"—but not, I think, that "common-sense" so derided by some poststructuralists as being a disguise for ideological blindness (or, more sinister, for maintenance of the status quo). The implications of the changes he argues for go far beyond teaching methodology; they suggest the need for a "poetics" of children's fiction which is child-based. As Rose also points out (although in the rather regrettable process of establishing her own intellectual superiority), the application of critical techniques (and critical values) rooted in the study of the "ordinary" or "adult" texts has only a limited relevance to children's literature. Confronting us with the realities of book and child, Protherough, with his virtues of accessibility and clarity, may be more successful in undermining the entrenched attitudes to children's books than the more aggressive and fashionably obscure Rose.

Casting Nets for Children's Literature

Irving P. Cummings

Children's Books in England: Five Centuries of Social Life, by F. J. Harvey Darton. Third edition, revised by Brian Alderson. Cambridge: Cambridge University Press, 1982.

Fifteen Centuries of Children's Literature: An Annotated Chronology of British and American Works in Historical Context, by Jane Bingham and Grayce Scholt. Westport, CT: Greenwood Press, 1980.

The Oxford Companion to Children's Literature, by Humphrey Carpenter and Mari Prichard. Oxford: Oxford University Press, 1984.

A new edition of a standard history and two new reference works join the rapidly expanding materials for students, teachers, and scholars of children's literature in England and America. The new edition of the history makes that book even more valuable, but the two reference works are not entirely successful in realizing their aims.

F. J. Harvey Darton's *Children's Books in England* has been meticulously and tactfully edited by Brian Alderson, bringing this classic history up to date. Darton's text has been clarified, corrected, and amended where information not available or not known in 1932 has emerged in the last fifty years. Sometimes silent corrections have been made, sometimes paragraphs have been recast, and sometimes editor's notes, at the back of the book, have extended or commented on Darton's text. The net effect of these editorial amendments has been to leave Darton's narrative relatively untouched but at the same time to make the facts as dependable and as accurate as current scholarship can make them and to keep the paraphernalia of footnoting to a minimum.

If there is—as there might well be—an uncomfortable feeling about this kind of tinkering with the text, a reading of that text makes clear why the revision was done that way. For Darton's book is an engaging narrative, with the impress of a relaxed, informed, and discriminating mind. If one wonders how the "good godly books" of the Puritans, with their narratives of the edifying deaths of children, could have been called "pleasurable," Darton's page or so in chapter 4 effectively explains it. We may not accept those books on our own terms. There is a largeness of mind here that avoids temporal provinciality and yet can articulate judgments that are not trapped in mere historical relativism. The several pages on Martha Mary Sherwood's once famous (notorious?) *The Fairchild Family* or those on J. M. Barrie's still famous (notorious?) *Peter Pan* are only two instances of Darton's large mind, acute judgment, and elegant prose.

This is still the best history of children's books in England: its opening sentence clearly and accurately announces its focus. "By 'children's books' I mean printed works produced ostensibly to give children spontaneous pleasure, and not primarily to teach them, nor solely to make them good, nor to keep them *profitably* quiet." It is a deceptively simple sentence whose crucially discriminating adverbs make clear that Darton knows how difficult it is to chart this terrain. Newbery is the one pole of Darton's history; in six brief chapters he tells how Newbery used the six kinds of children's tales that preceded him. In his middle chapter Darton narrates the Newbery story, and then, in seven chapters, sweeps from Day and Edgeworth to his other pole, Lewis Carroll, then on to the age of Kipling, Barrie, Grahame, Nesbit, and Stevenson.

Throughout Darton does more than survey books. He indicates the context in which the books appear, a context that reviews the shifting ideas of what spontaneous pleasure might and ought to be, and a context that depends upon the changing technology of printing, the creation of audiences, and the financial concerns of publishers. Darton's narrative laid out the mainlines of the history; most of the works since then have been expansions of his work, rarely matching his in elegance, easy clarity, and narrative power.

Alderson's edition is a remarkably handsome book. There are more illustrations than in the earlier editions, most of them the actual size of the originals, and all carefully captioned so that they do more than illustrate the text—they extend it. Alderson has updated Darton's bibliographies, and he has provided four appendixes: a chapter which reappraises the last chapter on late Victorian and Edwardian times from a late twentieth-century perspective; an outline history of the Newbery and the Darton publishing companies; a bibliography of Darton's extensive work as editor and writer; and a reprint of an amusing essay Darton wrote about editing a notable children's magazine, *Chatterbox*. One can easily see why the authors of the *Oxford Companion to Children's Literature* list Darton's history as one of their six "indispensable guides for . . . large sections" of their work, "more useful than ever in its third edition, thoroughly revised and annotated by Brian Alderson."

The other two works reviewed here cast their nets wider than Darton. Not only do they seek to give equal attention to English and American works, but they take the phrase "children's literature" in wider senses than he does. Jane Bingham and Grayce Scholt, in *Fifteen Centuries of Children's Literature*, aim at recording 750 "significant or representative books *written for* or *used with* or *appropriated by* British and American children from the sixth century to 1945" (italics added). But each of their 750 chronological entries is for a different author or illustrator, and all the entries include, where relevant, a list of the author's or illustrator's other works; thus Bingham and Scholt list nearly 9,000 titles. Humphrey Carpenter and Mari Prichard cast even wider nets, beyond English and American literature to sweeps of the world, and beyond books and magazines to lore, popular culture, games, and the various media. Both books are valuable, but each has problems: in one the nets get tangled, and in the other things slip through.

Fifteen Centuries is awkward to use. Fortunately the two indexes, one to authors and illustrators, one to titles, seem admirably complete. If one, for example, wants to consult the entry for E. Nesbit and *The Railway Children*, either index will lead to pages 255–56 where one of the entries for 1899 is Nesbit's *The Story of the Treasure Seekers*. Following some succinct comments on the content and publication of that book, seventeen other works by the author (one of which is *The Railway Children*) are listed along with dates and publishers. But, because Bingham and Scholt announce in their introduction that they do not claim their lists of authors' other works to be complete, one does not know whether or not these eighteen works

by Nesbit comprise a complete list—one would have to look elsewhere to find out. There seems to be no sign in an entry whether the
list is complete or not.

The authors' lack of clearly articulated principles for listing other
works by writers of books for children not only leaves one uncertain;
in many instances it proves frustrating. Their longest entry, for
example, makes the point most dramatically. That entry is for Edward Stratemeyer, 1895, *Reuben Stone's Discovery*, a book notable only
because it was the first produced by the founder of the Stratemeyer
Syndicate. Under many pseudonyms, for nearly a century, Stratemeyer and his daughter and their employees have produced hundreds of books, known less for their individual titles than for their
series names: the Bobbsey Twins, the Rover Boys, Nancy Drew, the
Hardy Boys, Tom Swift, and on and on. Bingham and Scholt
handle this entry clumsily. After some concise annotation about
Stratemeyer and his syndicate, they present fourteen densely
packed pages of hundreds of titles. It is a jungle through which it is
difficult to move, but since the list is not complete (not that one
would want it to be), one wonders why the authors did not in some
way make their list more analytical and more selective. As it is, a
reader faces a forbidding expanse of unconsidered titles, wondering
why there is neither completeness nor a thoughtful partial listing
based on some clear principles and distinctions between complete
and representative lists.

The entries for authors whose works have, in Bingham and
Scholt's phrase, been *appropriated by* children tend to reveal another
kind of editorial carelessness. There seems to be little consistency
and often misleading implications in their listing of "other works" by
authors such as Charles Dickens, H. G. Wells, Herman Melville, and
James Fenimore Cooper. Dickens's titles are rigorously selective—
although *Little Dorrit* seems out of place as a book *appropriated by*
children and his posthumous *Life of Our Lord*, certainly written for
children, might have been included. But this selectivity about Dickens is inconsistent with the inclusion in the Wells entry of books such
as *Ann Veronica, Tono-Bungay, The New Macchiavelli*. No selection
seems to have operated in the cases of Melville and Cooper, almost
all of whose works are listed. In addition the Cooper entry includes
two glaring errors: *The Spy* is listed as the first of the Leatherstocking

Tales, and *The Last of the Mohicans*, although listed, is not included among the Leatherstocking Tales. Is this a lapse of editorial attention or a lack of information?

There are other regrettable errors. Lewis Carroll's name is given as Charles Ludwig Dodgson. While it may be debatable whether Michael Wigglesworth's *Day of Doom* should have been listed for the year 1662 as a work certainly *used with* if not *written for* children, the only mention of either the work or the author (according to the indexes) appears in the entry for Wanda Gág's *Millions of Cats*, 1928. There we read that among Gág's other works is a 1929 illustrated edition of *The Day of Doom* "first published by American News Company in 1858." What is going on here?

Bingham and Scholt's book includes more than the chronology I have been examining. There are chronological listings of American and British periodicals for children, a coded list of libraries and collections holding copies of the works indexed, a list of facsimiles and reprints, a twelve-page unannotated bibliography of secondary sources, and a set of three essays for each of the six periods into which they divide their chronology. These eighteen essays, on historical backgrounds, development of books, and attitudes toward and treatment of children, are well written but inevitably superficial and derivative. It is an ambitious work but needs much more rigorous editing and clearer principles for inclusion, clearly spelled out.

The Oxford Companion to Children's Literature, first proposed by Iona and the late Peter Opie to a "comparatively cool" Oxford Press in 1958, was undertaken in the late 1970s. Its appearance announces that children's literature has arrived, in case anyone is uncertain. The authors, Humphrey Carpenter and Mari Prichard, note in their introduction that they modified the Opies' plan in several ways, but the interests and the works of the Opies permeate this most attractive and brilliantly written treasure house of information. Thoroughly crossreferenced—and therefore seductive—and richly illustrated, the *Companion* defies comprehensive description of the kinds of entries it includes and the pleasures it affords the student and the browser: Superman; *Sesame Street*; *Swallows and Amazons*; Science fiction; and Sunday schools . . . "Beauty and the Beast"; Bevis of Hampton; Barrie; *The Borrowers*; and Billie Bunter . . . Hamilton, Charles; *Heidi*; *The Hobbit*; Historical novels; Henty, G. A.; *The Heir of Redclyffe*; and "Hop o' my Thumb" ... Puppets; *Peter Pan*; Problem fiction; Potter, Beatrix; *Pinocchio*; Perrault; and Picture books ...

Geographically the range is also wide. Although the emphasis of the book is on English and American children's literature, with a large number of Australian books and authors, there are more than thirty entries surveying children's literature from Africa and Argentina to Turkey, Wales, and Yugoslavia, "from China to Peru."

Probably everyone who reads through this book sooner or later finds admiration for all the authors have so finely done qualified by awareness of entries that seem inadequate or of entries that are not there. It is notoriously easy for a reviewer to complain and cavil, especially when, as in this case, the book casts so wide a net with its sense of the phrase *children's literature*. Yet realizing that space is limited and that judgments vary, I do want to discuss one area where I think Carpenter and Prichard do not succeed as well as they should. The central professed purpose of the *Companion* was to deal "equally with both English and American children's books and authors." The phrase is from the Opies' proposal but is not denied by Carpenter and Prichard. I do not, of course, take this statement to mean that American and English materials are given the same space, but that the two areas will be evenly proportioned and representative. In some areas, especially those of the media and popular books—the kind of books our teachers and librarians were distressed at our wasting time with—the authors (and perhaps their American informants) are weak. Some examples follow: Dan Dare (see entry for *Eagle*) is discussed and illustrated, but neither Buck Rogers nor Flash Gordon is mentioned. "Westerns" is the subject of one entry, but neither the Lone Ranger nor Tom Mix nor Zane Grey is mentioned, though Karl May is. The entry for Indians of North and South America doesn't note the steadily increasing amount of lore, poetry, and folktales of those peoples available to children. American radio and television provide several entries, but compared with the English representation in these areas, the American is weak; one misses such radio programs as *Let's Pretend* and *The Singing Lady*, or such television programs as *Captain Kangaroo*, *Mister Rogers*, and Shirley Temple's Fairy Tale series of the 1950s. And where are Frank and Dick Merriwell and their chronicler "Burt L. Standish"? And where is Uncle Wiggily?

Finally, Carpenter and Prichard seem unacquainted with Edward Stratemeyer and the works of the Stratemeyer Syndicate, works that American children have devoured for nearly a century and continue to do. Bingham and Scholt may be faulted for not presenting their information as usably as they might, but they get the basic facts of the story. Carpenter and Prichard come close to the Stratemeyer story several times but seem unaware of its presence. There are entries for Nancy Drew, the Hardy Boys, and the Bobbsey Twins, and authorship for these three series of books is attributed, respectively, to Carolyn Keene, Franklin Dixon, and Laura Lee Hope. All three of these authors are fictitious creaitons of the Stratemeyer factory. The Bobbsey Twins series did begin in 1904, as Carpenter and Prichard have it, and many of the books were revised and reissued in the 1950s. But the entries for Nancy Drew and the Hardy Boys erroneously assert that they were published in the 1970s. The dozens of Nancy Drew books began to appear in 1930, and the Hardy Boys books in 1934; in the 1970s many were revised and new adventures were written, and both series are on sale in most bookstores around the country. The Stratemeyer products are as important for the study of American popular children's literature as are the works of Charles Hamilton and Enid Blyton for studying English popular children's literature.

One might raise other questions about the inclusion of portraits of some of the authors and illustrators, about the uneven treatment of books not written for but read by children, as well as of the authors of those books (a subject that perhaps merits its own entry). But when so much is attempted, dissatisfactions must surely follow. If the authors do not "cover" all they survey, they are most satisfying in their discussions of the books, authors, and illustrators that are the heart of British and American children's literature. On the whole, *The Oxford Companion to Children's Literature* is an impressive pioneering work, elegantly and pungently written, richly informative, provocative, and never dull.

Classic Illustrators

Joyce Thomas

A Treasury of the Great Children's Book Illustrators, by Susan E. Meyer. New York: Harry N. Abrams, Inc. 1983.

Ever since those first tantalizing chapbooks were peddled for pennies on the streets of London, the letter "a" has been coupled with the rotund image of an apple and the story of Jack the Giant-Killer linked to its pictorial counterparts of cloud-capped beanstalk, thieving lad, and pursuing Brobdingnagian crashing to earth. Just as children claimed for themselves works such as *Robinson Crusoe* that were originally written for an adult audience, so did they take over the province of illustrated literature. Somewhere along the line, children's literature became synonymous with illustrated stories, and adult literature retreated to solid print. We may well lament that loss, but one has merely to pick up a book such as *The Wind in the Willows*, illustrated either by Ernest Shepard or by Arthur Rackham, to experience again the magic and power of words wedded to images.

The complementary union of print and picture has become a main criterion by which children's literature is evaluated. Even a weak story if skillfully illustrated seems to metamorphose into a different, stronger work, as shown by Beatrix Potter's less imaginative tales presented alongside those superb watercolor miniatures. And when a good story is well illustrated, the result is a doubly satisfactory experience for the child (or adult). At no other time in history have artists been vouchsafed such technological freedom as they have today in illustrating children's books; given this century's advances in printing and the reproduction of pictures, there seems to be virtually nothing an illustrator cannot technically do. If the latter twentieth century represents the Golden Age of children's book illustration, it does so precisely because the nineteenth century raised the illustration of children's literature to the level of true art. Today's illustrators are the descendants and heirs of individuals such as Walter Crane, Randolph Caldecott, Beatrix Potter, and Kate

Greenaway, who sketched and printed and painted during that other Golden Age of children's literature.

In *A Treasury of the Great Children's Book Illustrators*, Susan E. Meyer reacquaints us with thirteen of those artistic predecessors. The chronological spectrum runs from Edward Lear, born in 1812, to Kay Nielsen, born in 1886. In between come the familiar illustrators John Tenniel, Edmund Dulac, Howard Pyle, Walter Crane, Kate Greenaway, Randolph Caldecott, Beatrix Potter, Ernest Shepard, Arthur Rackham, W. W. Denslow, and N. C. Wyeth. As Meyer notes, this baker's dozen represents the classic illustrators who had the most influence on the later illustration of children's books. While most of these artists are associated in some way with the Victorian era, many continued to work until World War I, and several of them witnessed the resurgence of children's literature and its illustration that followed World War II. Decidedly individual in their respective styles, media, and artistic interpretations, they nonetheless share an appreciation of words, a concern with printing techniques, and "the triumph of the imagination, the blend of reality and magic that transforms the written word into something seen and experienced" (8).

That transformative gift is clearly—sumptuously—evidenced here in the wealth of illustrations that have been expertly reproduced. The book is a treasure chest of full- and half-page spreads, colored and black-and-white pictures. The selection seems representative of each artist's body of work within the sphere of children's literature. For example, there are twelve full-page color reproductions of Kay Nielsen's stylized, evocative paintings—five from *In Powder and Crinoline*, five from *East of the Sun and West of the Moon*, two from the unpublished *A Thousand and One Nights*—as well as three reduced black-and-white pictures. Arthur Rackham's versatile, fantastic art is reproduced in ten full-page color and eight black-and-white pictures. All his major works are represented: *Aesop's Fables, Mother Goose, Grimm's Fairy Tales, Peter Pan in Kensington Gardens, Cinderella, The Arthur Rackham Fairy Book, Alice's Adventures in Wonderland, The Wind in the Willows.*

Overall, each illustrator's work is suitably reproduced, whether it is Wyeth's rich and realistic oil paintings, Greenaway's pastel pastorals, Crane's bold and meticulously designed murals, or Lear's stark pen-and-ink drawings (surely striped, cavorting Foss is the grandparent of Garfield as well as Kliban's feline menagerie). However, a few illustrators would have appeared to better advantage had certain of their works been reproduced in the original size. Regrettably, Beatrix Potter's work is inappropriately presented: several of her watercolors have been enlarged, and there is even a blown-up, full-page reproduction taken from *The Tailor of Gloucester*. Unfortunately, such enlargements do not and cannot reproduce the desired effect of the originals' precise proportions and deliberately circumscribed images—that "peephole" perspective Potter provided into the animals' world. Bigger is not always better; here, bigger results in a splashy, almost garish rendering that is the exact opposite of what Potter intended.

Despite this oversight, *A Treasury* is a rich and rewarding book. Nor is it just another expensive coffee-table book. While undoubtedly the superb illustrations more than justify the book's cost, Meyer supplies an informative biography and knowledgeable, at times illuminating, commentary upon each artist and his or her work. Her introduction offers a brief overview of the historical periods in which these classic illustrators worked, the changing attitudes toward children and their literature, and the ensuing changes in the publishing and printing of children's books. We find information about the state of American publishing and picture books during the nineteenth century and the influence of the pre-Raphaelites and other reformist groups upon book illustration. Though she neglects to examine the influence of forerunners such as Gustave Doré and George Cruikshank, whose illustrations of fairy tales must have exerted an influence upon later artists, Meyer does provide a good general introduction to her subjects and their times. Noting that the nineteenth century institutionalized the awareness of childhood as distinct from adulthood, she explores some of the causes and consequences of that awareness. Though actually the Puritan age began such a recognition of childhood, it was a decidedly bleak one; with the Victorians the view became, if not entirely joyous, multifarious in its manifestations, as evidenced in the array of children's books that cluttered the publishing market: "picture books containing nursery rhymes or fairy tales, alphabet books and poetry, nonsense limericks, adventure stories and fables, all designed to make children laugh or cry, tremble or dance for joy" (14).

Especially informative is Meyer's commentary upon each artist's major contribution to children's book illustration. Appropriately, she tends to stress the individual's history as an illustrator, so that we get a dual "biography" of artist and work. Particular emphasis is laid upon the individual's relationship with publishers and collaborators and his or her personal relationship with the public work; in a sense, the artist comes into being and ceases to be within the context of his or her work.

There is much of interest and value in the biographies presented; where additional, more detailed information or further illustrations are sought, one can turn to the book's bibliography for other sources. Most welcome is the frequent use of the artist's and his associates' own words via excerpts from diaries, letters, and interviews. One can just imagine Lear grumbling that "every human capable of writing ever since the invention of letters must have written to me, with a few exceptions perhaps, such as the prophet Ezekiel, Mary Queen of Scots, and the Venerable Bede" (59). We can accept or reject Crane's pronouncement, "Children, like the ancient Egyptians, appear to see most things in profile, and like definite statements in design. They prefer well-defined forms and bright, frank color" (88). One appreciates Rackham's insight that "children will make no mistakes in the way of confusing the imaginative and symbolic with the actual. Nor are they at all blind to decorative or arbitrarily designed treatment in art, any more than they are to poetic or rhythmic form in literature" (169). And surely Wyeth gives us a wise summation of one universal quality animating all good art when he states "The elemental feelings of long ago are identical with our own. The costumes and accessories of the twelfth century may be different, but the sunlight on a bronzed face, the winds that blow across the marshlands . . . are strictly contemporaneous in feeling" (235).

Meyer does full justice to the long and prosperous careers of Sir John Tenniel, Rackham, and Shepard, each the lifelong beneficiary of his popular success. It is interesting to note that both Shepard and Rackham received a commission to illustrate *The Wind in the Willows* with an emotionalism appropriate to one who has glimpsed the Holy Grail (indeed, references to Grahame's classic pop up in several of the biographies). Though both Shepard and Tenniel continued to stay in the public eye and to work into their nineties, others were less fortunate. Despite the phenomenal popularity of *The Wonderful Wizard of Oz*, W. W. Denslow parted company with Frank Baum in 1903, having experienced a difficult collaboration—though far less trying than that Tenniel suffered working with Lewis Carroll. While Baum went on churning out yearly sequels to *Oz* and thus continued to reap royalties, Denslow passed his last days working for an art agency at $25 per week. When he died in 1915, not even the newspapers he had once worked for printed his obituary. Similarly, Kay Nielsen, once acclaimed as one of the three great children's book illustrators—after Rackham and Dulac—died in 1957 impoverished and unmourned by both the press and the public. Not until twenty years later, when his work was republished, did he receive his fitting if belated recognition.

While all the biographies are informative and serve to yield insight into the artists' work, that work ultimately exists independent of the life. Occasionally Meyer departs from her usual intelligent, factual presentation in order to hazard a rather facile psychological interpretation. This is unfortunate, for it encourages a simplistic perspective on scarcely simplistic matters. The machinations of creativity are far too complex for reductive equations between an allegedly "deprived" life and artistic productivity; and such equations always fail to account for all those "undeprived" artists who also produced. Art as compensation is a tenuous proposition at best. At worst, it reduces the work to the product of neurosis.

One might also detect in such psychologizing a touch of bias that, in some of the biographies, emphasizes the artist's physical appearance and marital status. It seems quite beside the point and hardly instructive to hear Kate Greenaway repeatedly described as dowdy, as a "plain—even frumpy—spinster" in contrast to her beautifully drawn children. Oddly, very little attention is given to Edward Lear's physical appearance and its far more obvious translation to his limericks and drawings. Elsewhere Meyer writes, "Late in life Beatrix Potter was lucky enough to marry, fulfilling her deepest yearnings, and she ultimately abandoned her writing and illustration altogether, no longer seeming to require a creative outlet for her frustrations" (49). "Lucky," indeed. Potter, in fact, did not abandon her work entirely, though she did put it second to the demands of her life in Sawrey. Still it is a risky intimation that *The Tale of Peter Rabbit* was only an outlet for a spinster's frustrations.

Several of the illustrators presented here suffered from the vicissitudes of the book publishing market after World War I and again during the Depression. The horrors of those global nightmares perhaps eclipsed the public's taste for certain styles of book illustration and writing. Ironically, it has been after the incredibly worse nightmare of World War II and during the contemporary mushroom-specter of nuclear holocaust that the fantastic, so well rendered by these classic illustrators, has had its greatest popularity, resulting in the publication of works such as this.

A Treasury of the Great Children's Book Illustrators is an informative and stimulating book. Despite occasional flaws, it offers something of everything, from illustrations and biographies to discussions of the artists' works. In itself it is visually pleasing, with close attention obviously given to the book's design and layout. Each large page, printed on sturdy white stock, is framed with a fine black-lined border, to convey a sense of image and symmetry. Pictures and text are well-balanced, well-integrated, and harmoniously arranged. As with the best of picture storybooks, nothing intrudes between the printed text and accompanying illustrations; one experiences the successful, complementary union of word and image. This is a work that anyone interested in children's literature or in illustration and art would find of value. If, as Picasso once said, "Art is a lie that lets us see the truth," then *A Treasury* provides a welcome introduction to some of the best liars in all children's literature.

Illustrated Words

Martha Carothers

*Image and Maker: An Annual Dedicated to the Considera-
tion of Book Illustration*, edited by Harold Darling and
Peter Neumeyer. La Jolla, California: Green Tiger Press,
1984.

Image and Maker, edited by Harold Darling and Peter Neumeyer,
was recently stacked next to an annual of American illustrations in a
New York City bookstore. Many styles, artists, and subjects from
editorial and advertising illustration were packed into the annual,
itself only one of a jostling crowd of such overviews. *Image and Maker*,
by contrast, made its point by selectivity. Describing itself on the
flyleaf as an annual "that dedicates itself to an eclectic consideration
of the fine art of book illustration," it fulfilled this aim with a diverse
and thoughtful collection of five articles that discussed children's
book illustration and reproduced selected illustrations, tipped in.

The articles are simply written, with the most theoretical at the
beginning. The first article, "How Picture Books Work" by Perry
Nodelman, discusses what an effective illustrated book is and should
be. Nodelman presents his opinion by comparing two versions of
the fairy tale *Snow White*, one illustrated by Nancy Ekholm Burkert
and the other by Trina Shart Hyman. Nodelman contends that the
two books actually present quite different stories because of the illustrative style and the text/illustration relationship. His reference to
Maurice Sendak's *Where the Wild Things Are* points out that this
text/illustration relationship, or symbolic transformation, works well
there since Sendak is both the author and the illustrator; he con-
ceives and produces the book as a whole, not as a separate story and
illustrations joined together.

The next article, "What Manner of Beast?" by Stephen Canham,
essentially agrees with Nodelman's premise that different illustrative styles can determine the tone and believability of a fairy tale.
Canham deals with the specific character representation of the Beast
in *Beauty and the Beast*. Fourteen versions of the Beast are shown in

illustrations depicting various scenes of the fairy tale, and Canham is comprehensive in comparing varying aspects of the Beast's character in different versions. He feels that the more explicit the text description is of the Beast's characteristics, the less powerful is any visual depiction. There is less for the reader/viewer to imagine and less for the illustrator to envision.

"Luther Daniels Bradley: Guide to the Great Somewhere-or-Other," by Helen Borgens, is appropriately placed third as it addresses some of the questions raised by the first two articles. Bradley, an editorial cartoonist for the *Chicago Daily News* in the early 1900s, also illustrated and wrote two children's picture books which are discussed here. Borgens's article presents a biographical framework which helps to explain the context of Bradley's only two children's books. Like Sendak's, Bradley's books show a unique blend between words and pictures. The verbal descriptions are not overdone; they are enhanced by visually detailed pictures which fill in the gaps, so that there is a give-and-take between these two elements. Bradley has furthered this working relationship by lettering the text in his own refined calligraphic style.

There are no other illustrated versions of Bradley's books for comparison, for his books are not old familiar fairy tales but new stories dealing with real-life characters. These characters were his niece and nephews, and Bradley made up the stories from their dreams and imaginings, thus establishing a working literary relationship between real life and fantasy. The characters and animals are believable, but, as in a fairy tale, the situations playfully combine usually unrelated phenomena that make sense in a dream context.

Borgens feels that Bradley's books, as well as the individual illustrations, are well-conceived and composed. The dreamlike pictures are "matted" by transitional pictures both before and after. The transitional pictures are further "framed" by pictures of reality. These sequential images, reality-to-fantasy-to-reality, give the books a beginning, middle, and end. This is evident in the three pages of tipped-in color plates of Bradley's book, *Our Indians*. According to Borgens, each of Bradley's books is "essentially a 'picture' book in that one can glean the basic plot of the story merely by looking at the illustrations." Like the comic book style, this does not seem such a bad solution to children's book entertainment. It is unfortunate that such an entertaining illustrator/author as Luther Daniels Bradley produced only two books.

Carolyn Haywood provides a biographical article, "Jessie Willcox Smith." This article is a brief reporting of the illustrator's career written from Haywood's personal insight and friendship with Smith. No questions of verbal/visual relationship are raised here. For the most part, it appears that Smith was quite successful because of her style of illustrating charming, endearing, and ideal children. Like Bradley, she illustrated children from life with adult as well as child models, but Borgens' article uses Bradley's biographical information to reveal that his child models also provided the context for his stories and illustrations. Perhaps Haywood's article is intentionally placed as a happily-ever-after conclusion to the first four. After the lively articles that precede it, Haywood fails to provide an analytical discussion.

A concluding observation by Kenneth E. Luther in "The Great Catalogs: An Alternate Way to Study Early Children's Book Illustration" is "that the past fifty years have been most significant for the documentation of juvenile illustration; that the last ten seem to have been the most fruitful of all . . . and that the next ten years may see the work continuing with considerable momentum." In light of this observation and the fact that collections are generally not easily accessible for review, Luther has made a great contribution in suggesting an alternate way to study early children's book illustration. This last article gives an annotated inventory of catalogs of children's picture books in various collections. The five included are the Osborne catalog (Toronto), the *Gumuchian* (Paris), Dr. Rosenbach's catalog (Philadephia), the Morgan Library's catalog (New York City), and Old German Children's Books (Berlin). Luther has briefly introduced each catalog with bibliographic details, a general description, and pertinent illustrations from each catalog. The descriptions include the origins of each collection and its subsequent catalog. A sampling of catalog entries highlights Luther's text, and Luther quite effectively sums up each catalog's importance to the study of children's book illustration. All catalogs included are still available, and Luther has been diligent in listing where they may be obtained either in original form or as reprints.

Image and Maker makes an admirable and lively first attempt at the

study and discussion of children's book illustration. It prints an
appropriate number of thoughtful articles which complement each
other without diluting their premises. The tipped-in illustrations
support the text and remind the reader of the illustrative purpose of
the annual. *Image and Maker's* design, format, and intent are as
pleasurable and engaging as a child's one-sitting book; as the study
of picture books gains momentum its importance as a forum for
discussion of such books can only increase.

Wizards of Oz

Jerome Griswold

The Wizard of Oz, by L. Frank Baum, pictures by W. W. Denslow, edited by Michael Patrick Hearn. New York: Critical Heritage Series (Schocken Books), 1983.

The Wizard of Oz, by L. Frank Baum, pictures by Michael Hague. New York: Holt, Rinehart and Winston, 1982.

Others might say what I say: Michael Hearn taught me how to read *The Wizard of Oz*. After the book, the place to turn was Hearn's *The Annotated Wizard of Oz* (Clarkson Potter). Until now the next step was to find the works listed in that volume's bibliography.

Schocken's new critical edition of *The Wizard* makes this last step obsolete. In place of my sheaf of photocopies, I can now substitute this single volume which collects in one place all the criticism I had to acquire through hours of labor in the library. Here are most of the works listed in the earlier bibliography together with some new additions (for example, Brian Attebery's section on Oz in his *Fantasy Tradition in American Literature*).

Those familiar with Oz criticism will find many standard works here: the anecdotal and personal essays (usually of first encounters with Oz) by James Thurber, Gore Vidal, Ray Bradbury, and Russel Nye; the treatises by Wagenknecht, Bewley, Sackett, and Littlefield which argue (much too seriously, in my opinion) that Oz is a utopia. There are two sections containing material fresh to me: one prints four essays that chronicle the petulant rejection of Oz books by librarians; the other section contains both an important essay by Baum ("Modern Fairy Tales") and Hearn's own intelligent gloss on it ("L. Frank Baum and the Modernized Fairy Tale"). Finally, there is one thing I missed: for nearly everyone (except, perhaps, subscribers to *The Baum Bugle*) the book and the MGM movie are so inextricably entwined in memory that they seem like, say, two versions of "Little Red Riding Hood"; I would have been pleased to have found an essay or two about them.

Schocken's *Wizard* is the first volume of their new Critical Heritage Series which, apparently, will follow the pattern of Riverside's Critical Editions—it will print the text followed by a collection of commentaries. Without the text and the pictures, the volume would make a handy casebook; as it is, the book belongs on the scholar's and enthusiast's bookshelf. Its price ($19.95) will probably prevent its adoption in the classroom, unless an inexpensive paper edition is made available; even then, teachers may prefer Dover's edition of *The Wizard* which has color plates of Denslow's pictures instead of the black-and-white reproductions that appear here.

My opinions are less decided in the case of the new *Wizard of Oz* illustrated by Michael Hague. So, let me simply chronicle my reactions to it as an individual still in the process of making up his mind.

First, there was resistance. My images of the book's characters and landscapes are enduring ones that have been given me by the MGM movie and Denslow's pictures, and who was Hague to upset this? Wasn't he the presumptuous fellow who wandered into the domain of Arthur Rackham and Ernest Shepard to give us "new and improved" illustrations for *The Wind in the Willows*?

But then an urge for fairmindedness set in. Honestly, didn't I find many of the pictures lovely and interesting? Was I resisting the charm of the book like an old fogey with *idées fixes*? Isn't it easy to snigger at the new and dismiss the work as a Golden Book writ large?

Then a compromise suggested itself. Perhaps Hague was someone like Mercer Mayer when the latter did a "Beauty and the Beast." Both were yeomen with considerable gifts, still learning, but doing far too much in the business of illustrating to acquire depth.

After patronizing, it occurred to me that what I actually felt was that something was missing. Whimsy had always been a part of Denslow's pictures (and an even greater part of the work of John R. Neill in the subsequent Oz books), but it was absent here. And—except for a picture where Dorothy and her companions jump a ditch and the ditch is the spine of the book—there did not seem to be an imaginative use of design.

But this seemed wrongheaded, like looking at the landscape of southern California and seeing the absence of elm trees instead of the presence of eucalyptus. Hague is less whimsical and more serious; but, after all, consider how the book ends with its answer to

Aunt Em's question about where her niece has been: " 'The Land of Oz,' said Dorothy *gravely*." And in place of daring in design, Hague is more concerned with portraiture and landscape; imagine, if you will, a *Wizard of Oz* illustrated by Kay Nielsen or Maxfield Parrish and you will begin to understand what Hague has done with this book.

It is this last observation that led me to a conclusion. Every generation, Borges argues in his story, "Pierre Menard," has its own *Don Quixote*; though the words remain the same, subsequent events lead us to reread the text as different "versions." Hague made me, unwillingly, read another version; and that is what is wonderful about his own *Wizard*.

Dissertations of Note

Compiled by Rachel Fordyce

Billica, Anne Heasley. "Readers' Choices versus Critics' Choices in Children's Literature." Ph.D. diss. Arizona State University, 1983. 166 pp. DAI 44:3308A.

The twofold purpose of this dissertation is to examine the critical response of children and critics to popular children's books and ultimately to examine their response to books critically acclaimed as exemplary. "The investigation revealed 125 intermediate-grade-level fiction titles that were critically acclaimed by adults and 40 titles that were extremely popular with young readers in grades three through six." Interestingly, only three titles were common to each list. Young readers, in their evaluation, seemed concerned only with content and action. Critics were more concerned with style, interpretation, and "transcendent-residual levels of comprehension." Billica concludes that because librarians rely on critics' judgments to buy books, they may be stifling a child's desire to read and his or her enjoyment of books.

Brown, Carolyn Schmidt. "Petrified Truth: The Tall Tale in American Folklore and Literature." Ph.D. diss. The University of Virginia, 1983. 223 pp. DAI 45:1398A.

While Brown focuses primarily on nineteenth-century works such as Augustus Baldwin Longstreet's *Georgia Scenes*, George Washington Harris's *Sut Lovingood*, and Mark Twain's *Roughing It* and his *Autobiography*, she is really concerned with the way oral and written tales intertwine. She asserts that "Folklore has inspired subliterature; folklore and subliterature have inspired literature; and subliterature and literature have in turn re-inspired folklore. Because of these complex interactions, the oral and written tall tales can best be studied together, with the skills and techniques of two disciplines—folklore study and literary criticism—brought to bear on each."

Christian, Linda Kathryn. "Becoming a Woman through Romance: Adolescent Novels and the Ideology of Femininity." Ph.D. diss. University of Wisconsin-Madison, 1984. 512 pp. DAI 45:1282A.

Christian examines thirty-four adolescent romance novels written in America between 1942 and 1982 "to determine how ideologies of adolescent femininity were constructed through the interplay of form and content. Using models from semiotics and reproduction theory," she studies the relationships between romance, femininity, power, and control. Although it is difficult to generalize about works spanning forty years, for the most part these romance novels portray a stereotyped female who is taught by family, boyfriends, and society in general to grow up to be a good little girl. She is viewed as a passive consumer of goods (those guaranteed to beautify rather than edify), as a potential homemaker rather than a member of the mainstream workforce, and as someone to be esteemed only if she adheres to traditional romantic conduct and filial obedience. While conflict occurs "in the novels of 1960–1970 as heroines were caught between adherence to traditional sexual codes, boyfriends' pressures toward genital relationships and heroines' demands for increased autonomy," in fact the romances reinforce intense social, economic, and ethnic controls over women.

Deubner, V. "Das Bild der männlichen und weiblichen Helden in Bestsellern der Kinderliteratur" (The Image of Male and Female Heroes in Best-Selling Chil-

dren's Literature). Dr. Phil. diss. Universität Salzburg, 1979. 383 pp. DAI Section
C: European Abstracts 7/5122c.

Deubner surveys twenty-one popular (over half a million German-language
copies) children's books to determine what role-typical images these "bestsellers"
exhibit. Because the heroes and heroines of the novels seem likely to be models for
identification and imitation, and because of their high level of popularity, they
may be viewed as an important aspect of the socialization of the children who read
about them. Deubner analyzes the novels to determine how male and female
characters differ in their response to conflict. The thesis of the dissertation is that
there are certain fixed male and female sex roles in these novels. Male characters
must rise above adversity in highly adventurous circumstances. They fight for
individual freedom despite society's attempt to make them conform. Female
characters, on the other hand, must prove themselves within the constraints of
society; they are frequently confronted with sickness, physical weakness, and
helplessness. Society wishes to view them as hallmarks of stability, harmony, and
conservativeness.

Haupt, Carol Magdalene. "The Image of the American Indian Female in the Biographical Literature and Social Studies Textbooks of Elementary Schools." Ed.D.
diss. Rutgers University, the State University of New Jersey (New Brunswick),
1984. 246 pp. DAI 45:408A.

Haupt examines twelve social studies textbooks and biographical literature
about American Indian women, all written between 1972 and 1982. She analyzes
six descriptive textual categories of Indian women: active, passive, traditional
roles, nontraditional roles, evaluative terms, and nonevaluative terms. Illustrations are evaluated in terms of background, foreground, traditional and nontraditional roles, as well as evaluative and nonevaluative terms. She concludes that the
majority of Indian women were portrayed as active, although traditionally so, that
"Indian females in children's biographical literature published after 1970 have
been portrayed accurately and objectively," and that the stereotypes of the "Indian
Princess" and the "White Man's Helper" have largely disappeared.

Hauser, Paul Dale. "A Study of Male and Female Protagonists in Selected Novels for
Adolescents Published in 1982." Ph.D. diss. University of Iowa, 1983. 160 pp. DAI
44:2393–94A.

Hauser looks at twenty American novels with teenagers as protagonists: ten
female and ten male. "The approach used in examining the characters [is] a
phenomenological one; the actual portrayals determine what traits would be used
for discussion." He concludes that traditional stereotypes abound, "particularly
regarding the passive/aggressive dichotomy that has prevailed in fiction of the
past." Males are dominant and self-directed, they control situations aggressively,
are not particularly affectionate or emotional, and adhere to middle-class, urban
standards. Females, on the other hand, tend to come from small towns and wealthy
families; they show their emotions readily and have a tendency to fall apart when
confronted. Their friends are predominantly female, they usually date only one
person regularly, but they are "more sexually active" than their male counterparts.
While they are as ambitious as males, they are not as self-directed.

Hines, Bonnie Mathews. "A Study of the Effect of Children's Literature with Nonstereotyped Black Characters on the Racial Attitudes of Sixth-Grade Children." Ed.D.
diss. Northwestern State University of Louisiana, 1984. 57 pp. DAI 45:1295A.

Hines's main purpose is to determine what effect nonstereotypical black characters might have on racial attitudes of typical sixth-grade students of average

reading ability. She concludes that reading about nonstereotyped black characters does not change racial attitudes and that "children's literature alone does not appear to affect the racial attitudes of children as claimed by censors, promoters of bibliotherapy, didactic authors, and publishers who have revised classics to delete racial stereotypes."

Horn, Ila Dean Grey. "A Content Analysis of Selected Books of Realistic Fiction Written for and about Children as They Relate to Selected Characteristics of Gifted Children." Ed.D. diss. University of Nebraska-Lincoln, 1983. 155 pp. DAI 44:3309–10A.

The purpose of Horn's dissertation is to identify those traits that distinguish fictional gifted children. She assesses sixty works "to determine whether the gifted main characters reflect reality or [are] stereotyped in behaviors, characteristics, and relations with others." She concludes that there is a sizeable amount of contemporary children's literature that treats giftedness and that the number of such works is increasing appreciably. "Intellectual ability and creativity" are the most often identified attributes of gifted characters, "but creativity as a factor increased greatly" in recent literature. Leadership, in realistic novels, was another major ingredient of giftedness, and the representation of strong female characters has increased significantly in contemporary literature. Horn suggests that there is "no support for the hypothesis that gifted main characters [are] stereotyped" in children's fiction and that the books she studied reflect a changing society "in plot, setting, theme, and especially in characterization."

Kwon, Kyoon. "A Study of Values and Children's Biographies." Ph.D. diss. University of Tennessee, 1984. 187 pp. DAI 45:1578A.

Kwon studied the frequency with which certain biographies were read by Knoxville, Tennessee, elementary students to determine what values were cited in those works, to what extent those values might differ from those recommended by adults, and what degrees of difference might exist. Kwon examined thirty-six biographies and concludes that the most frequent value characteristics that biographical characters exhibit are capability, ambitiousness, helpfulness, courage, cheerfulness, "self-control, a sense of accomplishment, social recognition, a comfortable life, family security, an exciting life, and happiness." While the subjects of the biographies represented a wide range of both racial and professional backgrounds, there appears to be no significant difference between children's and critic's preferences.

Lomax, Earl Dean. "After *The Outsiders*: The Literary Characteristics of Contemporary American Young Adult Fiction, 1968–1979." Ph.D. diss. University of Missouri-Columbia, 1983. 360 pp. DAI 45:401.

Lomax solicited lists of significant fiction for young adults from thirty-nine authorities across the country and from their recommendations compiled a list of thirty books, each of which had appeared on at least six of the initial lists. By analyzing subject matter, characterization, structure, selected archetypes, moral vision (based on the criticism of John Gardner) and mode (based on the critical theories of Northrop Frye), Lomax concludes that the contemporary novel for young adults is preeminently a problem novel. It "is concerned with a fourteen-to-seventeen-year-old protagonist's problems with his/her family or inner circle of friends." It often treats previously taboo material and is shorter and less complex than most adult novels. Moreover, it is romantic, nondidactic, and "concerned with developing a theme dealing with the difficulty of growing up."

MacCurdy, Bruce Alan. "The Child Hero in Walt Disney's *Snow White, Pinocchio,* and

The Sorcerer's Apprentice sequence of *Fantasia*." Ph.D. diss. Syracuse University, 1983. 376 pp. DAI 44:2019–20A.

Noting that Disney has his critical detractors, MacCurdy admits that he is not one of them because of the numerous mythic themes, particularly associated with the young hero, that the works exhibit. Because Disney "has seldom been seriously discussed in light of psychology (other than Freudian) and mythology," MacCurdy applies the work of Adler, Freud, Fromm, Bettelheim, Jung, Campbell, Jaynes, and Janov to the films. Among other things, MacCurdy observes the "chronological change and growth of the main characters, along classical patterns of hero development" and postulates "that the development of the characters [is] directly related to the growth and changes in the personality of Walt Disney—that the characters were, in a sense, personal projections of him." He further suggests how the study of mythology in popular art forms can be beneficial to the fields of education, psychology, sociobiology, biography, and criticism if the "balance and integration of seeming opposites" is kept in mind.

Marks, Constance L. "An Exploratory Study to Determine Procedures for Revealing Children's Aesthetic Responses to a Select Sampling of Children's Literature." Ph.D. diss. Michigan State University, 1983. 329 pp. DAI 44:2394.

Using fifth-grade students, Marks tries to develop a method "for revealing children's aesthetic responses to contemporary picture books approached as an art form." She concludes that children in this age group can verbally express "the nature of their feelings, thoughts, and images involved in an aesthetic response" but that there is no identifiable pattern to the responses.

Marshall, Barbara Marie. "Assessing the Authenticity of the African American Experience in Children's Fiction Books." Ed.D. diss. University of Massachusetts, 1984. 274 pp. DAI 45:105A.

Working with twenty illustrated works of fiction for ten-to-fifteen-year-olds, Marshall tried to determine if these works "functioned as an agent of socialization which introduced children to their cultural heritage and oriented them to the world in terms of values, goals and sensibilities." Ten of the works she studied were by Euro-American authors, ten by Afro-American. In the latter she emphasizes the degree "to which books affirmed salient aspects of shared African American experience." In the former she is concerned with "the extent to which the phenomena of racism, oppression and caste influenced the presentation" of the books. About these works, published between 1967 and 1982, she is convinced that they differ substantially in terms of "black identity development," a "view of Africa," a "view of oppression," and a "view of the status of African American people in the United States." Marshall finds those books by Euro-American authors particularly guilty of racism, prejudice, and oppression.

Mauro, Linda Hanrahan. "Personal Constructs and Response to Literature: Case Studies of Adolescents Reading about Death." Ed. D. diss. Rutgers University, State University of New Jersey (New Brunswick), 1983. 266 pp. DAI 44:2073A.

Working with fifteen-, sixteen-, and seventeen-year-old students, Mauro notes their "highly complex and highly personal" responses to literature and concludes that literature on death and dying is appropriate in the classroom.

McGowan, Maureen Ann. "An Analysis of the Fantasy Plays of James M. Barrie Utilizing Vladimir Propp's Structural Model of the Fairy Tale." Ph.D. diss. New York University, 1984. 362 pp. DAI 45:347.

This dissertation in theatre, directed by Lowell Swortzell, deals specifically with Barrie's five fantasy plays: *Peter Pan, A Kiss for Cinderella, Dear Brutus, Mary Rose,* and *The Boy David* in an attempt "to yield a clearer interpretation of his dramatic technique." Using Propp's model, McGowan concludes that "the fairy tale is both the foundation (theme) and frame (structure) upon which Barrie constructs his dramatic fantasies." She also analyzes the plays in terms of Barrie's own stated philosophy about man's constant struggle with illusion and reality.

Nixon, Julia Hubbard. "Christianity in American Adolescent Realistic Fiction from 1945 to 1981." Ed.D. diss. Virginia Polytechnic Institute and State University, 1983. 403 pp. DAI 45:184A.

The purposes of this study are to identify works of realistic fiction for adolescents that refer to the Christian religion and to determine the significance of these references as well as the depth of the treatment of the subject. She notes that "most of the references to Christianity in the books relate more to cultural issues or to traditional ritual rather than to theological issues such as the nature of God," and she suggests that this sort of treatment does not really answer the questions about religion that most children have. Over the thirty-five-year period that the dissertation covers the subject of Christianity appears with diminished frequency although, in the last decade, Christianity has been treated more seriously and emphatically and with a greater emphasis on difficult theological issues. Nixon observes that "the renewed interest in Christianity in the late 1970's has not yet been reflected in novels for adolescents."

Poston-Anderson, Barbara Joy. "Australian Aboriginal Folktales: An Analysis of English Language Versions Published or Reprinted Between 1970–80 and Recommended for Children and English Language Versions Available to the Public prior to 1910." Ph.D.diss. University of Iowa, 278 pp. DAI 44:2038A.

Although aboriginal tales of Australia have gained considerable recognition in recent years, Poston-Anderson contends that contemporary retellings have been "diluted" when compared with the original tellings. She finds that the stories available before 1910 were considerably more readable and lively than recent publications and that most works between 1970 and 1980 "differed significantly" from the pre–1910 tales.

Poucher, Judith G. "Marjorie Kinnan Rawlings: A Study in Romantic Realism." Ph.D. diss. Florida State University, 1984. 249 pp. DAI 45:1754A.

Using the extensive Rawlings Collection at the University of Florida, Poucher applies the author's "own romantic-realistic approach to her work as a critical framework." Emphasizing "an affinity with nature," which is an essential ingredient of Rawlings's work, Poucher shows how Rawlings delineates the Florida Cracker—much in the tradition of Natty Bumppo. In *The Yearling*, Rawlings reveals her romantic love of the past through the use of old hunting tales. Her realism is demonstrated through the use of detailed personal experience. Poucher believes that Rawlings "shows a realistic viewpoint toward nature" in *The Yearling*. "Although she saw it poetically and responded to its beauty, she also recognized the malevolent side of nature and its ability to harm man." *Golden Apples, The Sojourner, South Moon Under,* and *Cross Creek* are also discussed.

Safford, Barbara Ripp. "High Fantasy: An Archetypal Analysis of Children's Literature." D.L.S. diss. Columbia University, 1983. 298 pp. DAI 44:2280–81A.

Safford is concerned with works of high fantasy written since the end of World War II. Using the literary theories of Northrop Frye, she analyzes the works for "the pattern of the plot, the nature of the hero, dialectic symbolism, cyclic symbolism, and the resolution of the plot and quest" within a structure that illustrates that a quest can be both physical and spiritual: a journey as well as a quest for identity.

She observes that "it is consistently apparent that the hero is displaced from myth to romance" and that "this is marked by his stage in the identity quest and by archetypical characteristics in related categories." Noting the frequent use of nature as both symbol and motif, and the constant struggle between good and evil in children's high fantasy, Safford concludes that "the cyclic symbols such as the seasons of the year and the stages of human life further structure the high fantasy plot as does the resolution of the quest."

Salazar, Laura Gardner. "The Emergence of Children's Theatre and Drama, 1900 to 1910." Ph.D. diss. University of Michigan, 1984. 266 pp. DAI 45:348A.

While "early in American history, puritanism, romanticism, and male dominance of the audience kept children out of theatres," by the beginning of the twentieth century children had become a fairly well-established part of the audience for family-directed plays. Significantly, Broadway averaged at least three plays a year which children attended with regularity. "Despite this, when melodrama faded and realism took its place, adult theatres became less appropriate for family audiences. At the same time . . . growing interest in amateur theatricals and art theatres encouraged experimentation with special audiences, including children." In this atmosphere a real children's theatre emerged, often with the intention of educating—if not delighting. Salazar discusses the appeal of such works as Frances Hodgson Burnett's *The Little Princess*, Austin Strong's and R. H. Burnside's *The Pied Piper*, Baum's *The Wizard of Oz* and, in seven appendices, she chronicles the pioneers of Broadway children's theatre.

Spaulding, Amy Elizabeth. "Closet Drama for Children: A Study of the Picture Book as Storyboard." D.L.S. diss. Columbia University, 1983. 501 pp. DAI 44:2281A.

While students of interregnum drama may be taken aback by this use of the term "closet drama," Spaulding means by it "a form of picture book rather than a hardcover comic book" which is displayed on storyboards and employs the technique of comic books, comic strips, and comic papers. Applying Aristotelian principles to the works, she studies the visual effect of these story boards in terms of style, dialog, color, line, and page layout. She contends that "the use of the present tense within the narrative and the fact that much of the action is portrayed in picture rather than word combine to produce an effect that is as much that of drama as of illustrated fiction."

Tyson, Eleanore Ely Smith. "Texas Writers of Children's Literature: A Collection of Interviews and a Critical Examination of Their Works." Ed.D. diss. University of Houston, 1983. 352 pp. DAI 44:3618A.

Tyson hypothesizes that a child's reading of a book is enhanced by knowing something about its author and for that reason she interviewed the twelve children's literature authors then residing in Texas, analyzed their works critically, and examined the development of the career of each. She demonstrates that the majority of the authors can be considered "Texan" writers because most treated the history, folklore, legend, and humor of the region.

Vanlandingham, Michael A. "Winning is Everything: Myths and Realities in Selected Contemporary Adolescent Novels of Sport." Ed.D. diss. University of Tennessee, 1983. 218 pp. DAI 45:105−06A.

Vanlandingham is concerned with contemporary novels dealing with both individual and team sports. At the beginning of his dissertation he poses three questions: "To what extent is the 'winning is everything' ethic present in the novels?" "What effect does competition have on the protagonist's character?" and "What effect does the role of the coach have on the protagonist?" Among the sixteen novels analyzed he observes that most exhibit some form of the "winning is all" ethic, that the protagonist is usually affected directly and positively as a result of participating in sports, and that coaches are generally quite influential "by encouraging the individual to do his best job and bring victory to the team." In the final analysis, Vanlandingham believes that these novels might encourage reluctant readers and promote critical reading and class discussion of the sport ethic.

Walen-Levitt, Peggy. "The Critical Theory of Children's Literature: A Conceptual Analysis." Ph.D. diss. University of Pennsylvania, 1983. 251 pp. DAI 44:3618–19A.

This dissertation, directed by Gordon Kelly, is "designed as a systematic analysis . . . to take account of significant efforts within the Anglo-American tradition to raise theoretical issues relevant to the criticism of children's literature." Walen-Levitt is concerned primarily with the distinctions between fiction and reality and how these relate to a child audience, with the "evaluative and descriptive" meanings of the term *literature* when applied to children's literature, with the fundamental critical characteristics of criticism of literature for children, and ultimately with the distinctions between the child and the adult audience and between child and adult critics. She concludes that a viable feature of criticism is "to make a contribution to the process by which children enter the institutions of literary art within their cultures."

Also of Note

Bird, Jan J. "Effects of Fifth Graders' Attitudes and Critical Thinking/Reading Skills Resulting from a Junior Great Books Program." Ed.D. diss. Rutgers University. State University of New Jersey (New Brunswick), 1984. 133 pp. DAI 45:407–08A.

Caron, James Edward. "Mark Twain and the Tall Tale Imagination in Nineteenth-Century America." Ph.D. diss. University of Oregon, 1983. 358 pp. DAI 44: 3383A.

Daigle, Marsha Ann. "Dante's *Divine Comedy* and the Fiction of C. S. Lewis." Ph.D. diss. University of Michigan, 1984. 234 pp. DAI 45:513A.

Driessen, Diane Zlatec. "A Description of a Select Group of Six Fifth-Grade Students' Responses to Picture Books." Ph.D. diss. Ohio State University, 1984. 314 pp. DAI 45:1668A.

Hawk, Jane Ward. "The Development and Validation of the Hawk Adolescent Literature Attitude Scale: Assessment of Attitudes that Educators, Students, and Parents Have toward Certain Potentially Censorable Topics Found in Literature Read by Adolescents." Ed.D. diss. Auburn University, 1983. 244 pp. DAI 44: 3337A.

Konrad, Zinta. "Aspects of Trickster: Form, Style, and Meaning in Ewe Oral Narrative Performance." (Volumes I and II) Ph.D. diss. University of Wisconsin-Madison, 1983. 256 pp. DAI 44:2471A.

Lain, Laurence B. "Life Situations, Exposures to News Media in Childhood, and Gratification: An Exploration of Three Routes to Newspaper Subscribership." Ph.D. diss. Ohio State University, 1984. 195 pp. DAI 45:1563A.

Newman, Sharon K. "Children's Programming in Commercial Television: The Effect of the Implicit Curriculum on Producers' Intentions." Ph.D. diss. Michigan State University, 1983. 175 pp. DAI 44:3533A.

Stoll, Joyce Phyllis. "The Effects of Imagery Training and Listening to Fairy Tales on Reading Comprehension and Creativity of Third Graders." Ed.D. diss. Rutgers University, State University of New Jersey (New Brunswick), 1983. 145 pp. DAI 44:2039A.

Tanner, Fran Averett. "Readers' Theatre": A Cumulative Approach to Theory and Creative Activities for Use in Secondary Schools." Ph.D. diss. Brigham Young University, 1984. n.p. DAI 45:348A.

Warburton, Terrence L. "Toward a Theory of Humor: An Analysis of the Verbal and Nonverbal Codes in *Pogo*." Ph.D. diss. University of Denver, 1984. 245 pp. DAI 45:1573A.

Warren, Daniel Yeomans. "Dickens's Christmas Books." Ph.D. diss. Cornell University, 1984. 200 pp. DAI 45:1411–12A.

West, Mark Irwin. "Defenders of Childhood Innocence: Reformer Responses to Children's Culture in America, 1878–1954." Ph.D. diss. Bowling Green State University, 1983. 131 pp. DAI 45:1503A.

Yasin, Jon Abdullah. "Bibliotherapy, The Use of the Decision Tree Model and the Teacher of English." Ph.D. diss. Indiana University of Pennsylvania, 1983. 189 pp. DAI 44:2075A.

Ziemke, Dean Allen. "Adolescent Television Viewing and Family Communication Patterns as Facilitators of Role-Taking Development." Ph.D. diss. University of Wisconsin-Madison, 1983. 210 pp. DAI 44:1965A.

Contributors and Editors

GILLIAN ADAMS, who teaches children's literature, fairy tales, and fantasy at the University of Texas, is currently completing a translation of *Ysengrimus*, a twelfth-century Latin beast-epic.

HAMIDA BOSMAJIAN teaches English at Seattle University. She has published works on children's literature and is the author of *Metaphors of Evil: Contemporary German Literature and the Shadow of Nazism* (1979).

FRANCELIA BUTLER, founder of *Children's Literature*, teaches children's literature at the University of Connecticut. She has published widely in criticism, has published an adult novel on child abuse, *The Lucky Piece* (1984), and has a book for teenagers, *Madame Ghandi*, forthcoming.

MARTHA CAROTHERS teaches art and graphic design at the University of Delaware and is a letter press book artist and a researcher of children's novelty and pop-up books.

JOHN CECH recently served as president to the Children's Literature Association. *From Inside a Swan's Egg*, his play based on the life and works of Hans Christian Andersen, was performed at the 1984 World Festival and Symposium of Theater for Young Audiences at the World's Fair in New Orleans.

IRVING P. CUMMINGS teaches English at the University of Connecticut and has a special interest in novels of the nineteenth century. He has taught classes in children's literature, in popular genres, and in the drama of Shaw.

RACHEL FORDYCE is an associate dean of the College of Arts and Sciences at Virginia Polytechnic Institute and State University and Fellow of the American Council on Education.

JOANNA GILLESPIE has published work on eighteenth- and nineteenth-century Sunday school fiction and will be working on nineteenth-century women and their religious autobiographies as a senior fellow at the Institute for Early American History and Culture, William and Mary College.

JEROME GRISWOLD teaches literature at San Diego State University and is the author of a forthcoming study of Randall Jarrell. He reviews books regularly for the *Los Angeles Times*; his essays and interviews appear in *Paris Review*, *New Republic*, *The Nation*, the *New York Times Book Review*, and other publications.

MARGARET HIGONNET teaches English and comparative literature at the University of Connecticut. She has edited two volumes of feminist essays, written on literary theory, and is writing a book about suicide.

MARIANNE HIRSCH teaches French and comparative literature at Dartmouth College. Her publications include *Beyond the Single Vision: Henry James, Michel Butor, Uwe Johnson* and a coedited anthology, *The Voyage In: Fictions of Female Development* (1983). She is currently at work on a book about mother-daughter relationships in women's novels.

PETER HUNT teaches English, and is Director of Communication Studies, at the University of Wales in Cardiff. He has written thirty articles on children's literature, lectured on it world-wide, and produced two novels for children, *The Maps of Time* (1983) and *A Step Off the Path* (1985).

ELIZABETH LENNOX KEYSER teaches English at the University of California at Santa Barbara. She has published essays on Hawthorne, Melville, James, Burnett, and Gilman and is completing a book on Louisa May Alcott.

MITZI MYERS teaches at the University of California at Los Angeles, Scripps College, and California State Polytechnic. She has published numerous essays on Mary Wollstonecraft and other eighteenth- and nineteenth-century women writers. Her book in progress, *Rational Dames and Moral Mothers: British Women Writers and Juvenile Literature, 1780–1850*, is supported by two grants and a fellowship.

JUDITH PLOTZ teaches English at George Washington University. She has published on romanticism and child development, Thomas Day, nineteenth-century experimental child-rearing, and the Wordsworthian child in the twentieth-century novel. She is currently writing a book on romanticism and childhood.

SAMUEL ROGAL is chairman of the Division of Humanities and Fine Arts at Illinois Valley Community College. He has written on Izaak Watts, James Boswell, Johnson, Addison, Steele, and published *John and Charles Wesley* (1984) in the Twayne Series.

BARBARA ROSEN teaches English at the University of Connecticut. She has edited Shakespeare, a book of reports of Elizabethan witch-trials, and *Children's Literature*.

J. D. STAHL teaches English at Virginia Polytechnic Institute and State University and is working on a study of Mark Twain and the genteel tradition in nineteenth century American writings for children.

JOYCE THOMAS teaches English at Castleton State University, Vermont, where her particular interests are children's literature, folktales, and women's literature.